CALIFORNIA'S PRODIGAL SONS

# CALIFORNIA'S

UNIVERSITY OF CALIFORNIA PRESS
Berkeley and Los Angeles 1968

*Hiram Johnson and the Progressives*
*1911–1917*

# PRODIGAL SONS

### By SPENCER C. OLIN, Jr.

UNIVERSITY OF CALIFORNIA PRESS
BERKELEY AND LOS ANGELES, CALIFORNIA
CAMBRIDGE UNIVERSITY PRESS
LONDON, ENGLAND

COPYRIGHT © 1968 BY THE REGENTS OF THE
UNIVERSITY OF CALIFORNIA
LIBRARY OF CONGRESS CATALOG CARD NUMBER: 68-11968
DESIGNED BY BETSY DAVIS

*To My Mother and Father*

# PREFACE

It has been seventeen years since the publication of George Mowry's pioneer study *The California Progressives*. In that excellent work Mowry was primarily concerned with the California Progressive movement as a social phenomenon, asking such questions as: Who were the Progressives? What motivated them? What were they trying to accomplish? He also hoped to cast light upon the nature of national progressivism and recent American "liberalism."

Similar questions are asked in this study, but the approach is somewhat different. Here primary concern is with practice rather than ideology. The major focus is on the impressive gubernatorial administration of Hiram W. Johnson, and on Johnson's role as a popular and extremely effective reform governor. This study is not a comprehensive personal biography of Hiram Johnson, for the available source materials preclude such an effort. Nor is it a total reevaluation of Mowry's book, although it utilizes manuscript collections unavailable seventeen years ago (including the Hiram Johnson Papers), incorporates material published since 1950, and at certain points reaches conclusions contrary to Mowry's.

The organization is chronological rather than topical. Except for the first chapter, which provides background information, the emphasis is on the means by which Johnson sought and won through politics not only personal power, but also reform and good government. Johnson's goal in California was to develop an efficient public service that reflected the public good, not the good of special interests. Two major themes of the study, therefore, deal with efficient and rational approaches to social and economic problems—with what might be called "scientific management" of state affairs—and with efforts to use the immense resources of California "rationally and equitably" on behalf of all rather than ruthlessly exploiting them for private gain.

A subsidiary theme is the intense battle between conservatives and progressives in California, a battle that culminated in the fateful Hughes campaign of 1916. An important aspect of that campaign was the challenge it presented to Hiram Johnson's continued control of state politics. It was a challenge not only to a powerful political boss but to a passionate, zealous, narrow, crusading individual.

The legislative sessions of 1911, 1913, and 1915 were extraordinarily creative and productive attempts to solve the acute problems of railroad control, corruption in government, labor conditions, immigrant housing and education, and agricultural production and distribution, to mention just a few. Yet it is clear that after 1911, any setback to Hiram Johnson in politics or in the reform program meant great damage to his personality and to his image of himself. To Johnson, therefore, state politics, and national politics to a lesser extent, became his means of personal projection, the defense of all that went on before, the raison d'etre of his existence as both man and leader.

I am particularly indebted to Professor W. John Niven of the Claremont Graduate School and University Center. As my dissertation adviser he patiently corrected the stylistic imperfections of the original draft. His perceptive comments and imaginative suggestions improved the final manuscript beyond measure. In addition, I am very grateful to Professor John H. Kemble of Pomona College, who first suggested Hiram Johnson as a promising research topic and who carefully read the manuscript in dissertation form. My colleague R. Alan Lawson read the final draft and provided valuable stylistic and contextual criticism. Several people read parts of the manuscript and I thank them for their helpful suggestions: Professors John W. Caughey, Douglass Adair, Charles S. Campbell, Jr., Roger Daniels, and Miles Everett.

The entire staff of the Bancroft Library deserves my gratitude for the many courtesies extended during the past six years. I express special appreciation to Dr. John Barr Tompkins, Mrs. Helen Bretnor, Miss Estelle Rebec, and J. R. K. Kantor, university archivist. I am also grateful to the Special Collections librarians at Stanford University, the University of California, Los Angeles, the Huntington Library, and the Library of Congress.

A summer grant in 1966 from former President Clark Kerr's Humanities Institute enabled me to complete the research and writing of the manuscript. I appreciate the support of Professor Henry Cord Meyer, who as chairman of the Department of History, University of California, Irvine, made funds available to defray last-minute typing and travel expenses. Miss Cathy Smith, who meticulously typed the final draft, deserves both my thanks and my praise. I am also grateful to Mrs. Kathleen Jasonides of the University of California Press for her careful editing.

And finally, to my wife Ann, who worked so that I might write, my enduring affection and appreciation.

# CONTENTS

1. THE GENESIS OF REFORM — 1
2. "A FIGHT AGAINST THE INTERESTS" — 20
3. ONWARD CHRISTIAN CAPITALISTS — 34
4. THE "BULL MOOSE" CAMPAIGN — 57
5. ACCEPTANCE AND REJECTION IN 1913 — 70
6. MUTINY AND PARTY DISCORD — 92
7. THE DECLINING YEARS — 104
8. DISINTEGRATION AND DEADLOCK — 117
9. BLUNDER BEGETS BLUNDER — 128
10. THE INITIAL RESPONSE — 145
11. THE FINAL RESPONSE — 156
12. AN APPRAISAL — 169

APPENDIXES — 183
NOTES — 190
BIBLIOGRAPHY — 228
INDEX — 243

# 1

## THE GENESIS OF REFORM

"It all amounts to this," declared Annixter, the proprietor of the Quien Sabe Rancho in Frank Norris' *The Octopus*, "You can't buck against the railroad. We've tried it and tried it, and we are stuck every time. . . ." The railroad, he explained, had "the whole thing organized like an army corps."[1] This was not merely a fictional exaggeration. For in addition to the political corruption that existed in many parts of the nation at the turn of the century, California had a special problem: domination by one large corporation—the Southern Pacific Railroad, Frank Norris' "Octopus."

Organized in 1865 by the Big Four—Huntington, Crocker, Stanford, and Hopkins—the Southern Pacific had established a complete monopoly of rails in California by the 1870's. Then that corporation entered politics to preserve its monopoly and to extend its influence throughout the state. While it is impossible to gauge precisely the extent of the railroad's political power, it is clear that until the adoption of a new state constitution in 1879 it wielded enormous influence in the state Senate. Thereafter, the Southern Pacific concentrated its manipulative efforts on the members of the newly created Railroad Commission and thereby successfully prevented rate reductions. So pervasive did its power become that within a few years it was attempting to name and control virtually every candidate for every political office from governor on down. Powerful, well-financed, and superbly organized, the railroad machine worked confidently toward its goals: continued prosperity and freedom from effective state regulation.[2]

The Southern Pacific Railroad Company was thus the greatest single influence operating in California politics from 1880 until it was "kicked out of politics" by Hiram Johnson and the California progressives in 1911. It was also a very constructive force contributing to the state's economic and social growth, employing more labor and owning more land than any other individual or business organization, and operating the longest transportation system in the United States. When Collis P. Huntington, last of the Big Four, died in 1901, control of the Southern Pacific passed to Edward Harriman, owner of the Union Pacific Railroad.

Several factors accounted for the absence of effective opposition to railroad influence up to 1900.[3] First, California's still relatively sparse population consisted for the most part of newly arrived residents who lacked interest and influence in local and state politics.[4] Second, the railroad, by virtue of its transportation monopoly, had such power to gain and withhold benefits that it could always isolate and fractionate opposition. A noted historian of California, John W. Caughey, writes that "by arbitrary manipulation of freight rates it could make or break almost any merchant, industrialist, or agriculturist in the state."[5] Third, partisan election laws required that each candidate's party be stated, and all candidates for public office were nominated by partisan conventions. The Southern Pacific usually controlled these conventions by means of its notorious Political Bureau, whose machine activities were rivaled only by those of Tammany in New York.[6] Tammany, however, was a political institution, organized by politicians and using business connections for its own political ends. The Southern Pacific's Political Bureau, on the other hand, was primarily an organization that used politics for business ends. Indeed, its sole raison d'etre was to ensure that the company would not have to pay its share of the tax burden, would escape state and local regulation, and could expand its system unhampered by outside influence.[7] Finally, as a consequence of United States Supreme Court decisions such as *Chicago, Milwaukee, and St. Paul Ry. Co. v. Minnesota* (1890) and *Smyth v. Ames* (1898), it was virtually impossible to achieve railroad rate reductions through either legislative or judicial channels. In California, the state Supreme Court, bound by legal precedent and possibly susceptible to Southern Pacific machinations, decided fifty-seven of seventy-nine cases in the company's favor from 1895 to 1910.[8]

Thus, what the Standard Oil Company was to the state of Pennsylvania prior to the turn of the century, the Southern Pacific Company was to California at the same time—and more. Despite the impressive power of the Southern Pacific, George Mowry, an authority on the California Progressive movement, has pointed out that a close examination of California politics in this period "reveals the first faint indications of the coming storm of revolt. . . ."[9] From 1898 on, the Democratic party placed at least one antirailroad candidate on the ticket in every gubernatorial election. In 1898 the Democratic candidate, James G. Maguire, made a good run against Southern Pacific's choice, Henry T. Gage. In 1902 Democrat Franklin K. Lane almost defeated George C. Pardee, the machine candidate for governor. And in 1906 Democrat Theodore A. Bell (who would run again in 1910 against Hiram Johnson) was narrowly defeated for the governorship.

Even within the Republican party there was an effective, if loosely organized, reform element. Prominent among these independently minded Republicans was conservative Thomas Robert Bard of Hueneme in Ventura County. Bard had been active in local politics from the time he came to California in 1865. His business interests included land development, banking, grain, shipping, sheep-raising, and petroleum. Bard founded and was the first president of the Union Oil Company of California.

In 1899 Bard and a few others became convinced that Governor Henry T. Gage was too much a tool of the Southern Pacific to warrant their further support. Their subsequent political activities, and Bard's ultimate election to the United States Senate in 1900 on an antirailroad platform, mark the first major break between "regular" and "antirailroad" Republicans and constitute one of the first effective challenges to Southern Pacific control.[10]

These various elections indicate growing dissatisfaction with, and active opposition to, machine-dominated politics in California. In addition, the Southern Pacific's commercial supremacy in the state was being challenged after 1900 by a number of business enterprises, including two railroads, the Santa Fe and the Western Pacific. The Southern Pacific's Political Bureau could no longer rely upon its strength in the metropolitan areas of northern California. Railroad control was augmented by expanding operations to include county political organizations throughout California, with emphasis on the southern counties. The "organization" thereby continued to control the Republican party in the state, and the Democratic party whenever it was worth the trouble.

## The Genesis of Reform 5

During the first decade of the twentieth century feeling against the machine was strongest in southern California and in the San Joaquin Valley. There was a large reservoir of antirailroad sentiment in Los Angeles as a result of the Southern Pacific's futile attempts in the early 1890's to shift the Los Angeles harbor from San Pedro to Santa Monica Bay, where Collis Huntington had property interests and where his railroad had a monopoly of land control.[11] Resentment against the railroad's activities had been voiced by all segments of political opinion. For example, Charles Dwight Willard, an idealistic, crusading, reform-minded journalist, was outraged by the railroad's high-handed action; but he was no more bitter in his opposition than was the owner of the Los Angeles *Times*, Harrison Gray Otis, a wily, self-made capitalist and staunch conservative whose hatred of the Southern Pacific was exceeded only by his contempt for reformers.

Long-time residents of the San Joaquin Valley remembered bitterly the famous Mussel Slough incident, in which the Southern Pacific's eviction of settlers resulted in the killing of five men.[12] In that part of the state the Southern Pacific received heavy blows from Chester Rowell, who edited the Fresno *Republican*. In his crusade, Rowell was firmly supported by Thomas Flint, a wealthy rancher from San Benito County and powerful antimachine state senator for many years. As in the San Joaquin Valley, so also in the northern counties of the state, newspapers kept antirailroad sentiment before the public. The four leading journals of San Francisco—*Bulletin, Examiner, Call,* and *Chronicle*—ranging in political sympathies from reformer to reactionary, were as one when it came to attacking the Southern Pacific. In Sacramento the McClatchy brothers, owners of the *Bee*, were consistent in their denunciation of the railroad.

Organized business, labor, and agriculture together might have provided effective leadership in the struggle against the Southern Pacific; but these heterogeneous groups were generally and primarily concerned with their own specific economic interests, and were reluctant to participate in statewide political action. "Instead," writes Mowry, "[leadership] was seized by a group of supreme individualists, well educated and bound together by a particularistic point of view, a rememberance of things past, a new code of morality, and more than the normal dash, perhaps, of a sense of indignation and a desire for power. . . ."[13] Most of these men were not initially concerned with battling the Southern Pacific on a statewide basis, but only in cleansing the municipal governments of their own cities. Consequently, the reform movements that eventually would unite against the Southern Pacific were launched in the cities, particularly in the metropolitan areas of Los Angeles and San Francisco.[14]

For many years reform-minded citizens of Los Angeles had been trying to free city government from machine control. In 1898, for example, the Direct Legislation League had been organized by Dr. John Randolph Haynes. Haynes had come to Los Angeles from Philadelphia in 1887, and after observing political corruption in the City of the Angels, had concluded that the only way to achieve civic progress was to broaden participation in government by giving the electorate the powers of initiative, referendum, and recall. The sole purpose of his Direct Legislation League was to transfer political power from the bosses to the electorate.[15]

Efforts at the city level to obtain these three reform measures failed in 1900; but two years later they were endorsed by overwhelming majorities in Los Angeles. After some hesitation on the part of the state legislature, the city charter was ratified in January, 1903. Los Angeles thus became the first city in the United States to write the recall provision into its organic law. Moreover, the recall provision was utilized in 1904 to oust a city councilman on the grounds that he had voted to award a municipal advertising contract to the Los Angeles *Times,* even though the *Times's* bid was from $10,000 to $20,000 higher than those of other newspapers.[16]

In the years immediately following the adoption of the initiative, referendum, and recall in Los Angeles neither the expected chaos feared by conservatives nor the millennium desired by the reformers materialized. Nevertheless, despite cautious use of these political devices by the Los Angeles electorate, men like John Randolph Haynes were convinced that the incorrupt "people" finally had the power and the means to purify city government and to achieve civic progress.

In 1906 a new approach to political reform was undertaken in Los Angeles by a small group of unusually able and determined young men. These were Edward Dickson, associate editor of the Los Angeles *Express,* and three ambitious lawyers, Russ Avery, Meyer Lissner, and Marshall Stimson. Avery had already gained some experience as president of the Los Angeles Voters' League, which supported municipal ownership of public utility corporations. Lissner and Stimson had acquired modest fortunes in the practice of law and in real estate.

These men formed an organization that was ostensibly nonpartisan but was actually dominated by Republicans. They then announced their intention to nominate a complete ticket for the coming Los Angeles election, independent of both major parties. The nonpartisan candidate for mayor was Lee C. Gates, legal adviser for the Title Trust and Insurance Company, personal friend of Harrison Gray Otis, as well as of Otis's son-in-law Harry Chandler, and later a prominent member of the Lincoln-Roosevelt League. Although Gates lost the election, the new organization successfully capitalized upon the fear of potential monopolization of the Los Angeles Harbor by the

Southern Pacific Company, as well as increasing sentiment for municipal ownership of public utilities, winning seventeen of the city government's twenty-two offices, including four out of nine members of the city council. When these men organized the Los Angeles nonpartisan movement and then were successful in the municipal election of December, 1906, the political power of the Southern Pacific had once again been effectively challenged. Subsequently a permanent good government organization was established, and it continued to press for political reforms.[17]

In San Francisco the major targets of reform were Abraham Ruef, boss of the Union Labor party; Mayor Eugene E. Schmitz; and members of the Board of Supervisors. The Union Labor party had been established in 1901 as a result of the struggle between organized capital and organized labor in the Bay City. This industrial warfare had reached a climax in the waterfront strike of that year. Mayor James D. Phelan's use of policemen to protect scab teamsters so provoked union men that they formed their own party in order to elect a mayor favorable to their cause. Ruef, the boss of a distict in San Francisco's North Beach, was alert to the possibilities of such a party. He saw to it that his followers secured the most important offices at the first Union Labor party convention. The party subsequently succeeded in electing its mayoralty nominee, Eugene E. Schmitz, president of a local musicians' union. Schmitz was reelected in 1903, and two years later the Union Labor party swept its entire ticket into office.[18]

If Ruef was ever a sincere believer in advancing the workingmen's cause, he soon gave evidence that he was as cynical a spoilsman as any of the old Southern Pacific stalwarts. During 1906 he served as a confidential attorney for certain public utility corporations that sought special dispensations and privileges from the city government. On one occasion the pliable boss was paid $20,000 by the

Pacific Gas and Electric Company for convincing the Board of Supervisors that a drastic reduction in the gas rate would not be advisable. Ruef used a part of this bribe, some $13,250, to purchase the votes of the supervisors, an additional $3,000 for the support of Mayor Schmitz, and pocketed the remainder as his own fee for the transaction. On two other occasions Ruef received $125,000 from the Home Telephone Company for securing a utility franchise to establish a telephone system, and $200,000 for legal assistance rendered the United Railroad Company (which ran San Francisco's street railways).[19]

The pinnacle of Ruef's power was reached in September, 1906. By then he had gained control of the Republican machine in San Francisco, which was able to secure the election of practically all of that city's delegates to the Republican state convention. Ruef's backing of the Southern Pacific's candidate for governor, James N. Gillett, helped secure Gillett's nomination and subsequent election. "Thus Ruef became temporarily the key figure in the California Republican party," writes Walton Bean, "and ensured the gratitude of William F. Herrin, chief counsel and state political boss for the Southern Pacific. . . ." [20]

The campaign to oust the corrupt Ruef and his cohorts was begun by the crusading editor of the San Francisco *Bulletin,* Fremont Older, who had long opposed Schmitz and Ruef. After consulting with Francis J. Heney, a young attorney who had established his reputation by exposing timber frauds in Oregon, Older went to Washington, D.C. There he secured President Theodore Roosevelt's promise to relieve Heney of his governmental duties as special United States prosecutor if $100,000 could be raised to conduct the graft prosecution. Rudolph Spreckels, the wealthy banker, second-generation rentier, and opponent of the Southern Pacific, guaranteed most of the money. James D. Phelan, wealthy Democrat and former mayor of San Francisco, also made a large contribution. Once the money was raised, Heney was appointed prosecutor by the San Francisco district attorney. The case was prepared during the spring and summer of 1906, with William J. Burns, the famous detective who had worked with Heney in Oregon, conducting the investigation.[21]

The prosecution received enthusiastic backing from the business groups of San Francisco so long as it limited its attack to such corrupt politicians as Ruef, Schmitz, and the supervisors; however, when prominent business leaders—such as Patrick Calhoun, president of the United Railroads, and William Herrin of the Southern Pacific—became implicated, these business groups decided the prosecution had overstepped its proper bounds. "Many wealthy men in San Francisco," writes Bean, "began to believe that the graft prosecution was a socialistic attack upon the institutions of private property. . . ."[22] The conservative press joined officials of the Pacific Gas and Electric Company, the Home Telephone Company, and other leading business organizations in condemning Heney and Burns.

Heney fought back viciously. In ruthless fashion he attacked not only Ruef and his associates, but men of wealth and property as well. The situation became so heated that on November 13, 1907, during a recess in the court proceedings, a prospective juror named Morris Haas shot Heney in the back of the head. Though not fatally wounded, the vigorous young attorney was unable to continue the prosecution, and Hiram W. Johnson, another ambitious and able San Francisco attorney who had joined the graft prosecution in October, 1906, agreed to carry on.[23] Johnson was able to secure the conviction of Ruef; but with the exception of Schmitz and Calhoun, all other indicted politicians and businessmen were found innocent. Moreover, Schmitz's conviction was reversed by the appellate court, while Calhoun's trial in the fall of 1908 ended in a divided jury.[24]

## The Genesis of Reform 11

Anticipating the city elections of 1909, business leaders organized a committee to select candidates who opposed the graft prosecution. This ticket easily won the Republican primaries. Heney, now recovered from his wound, ran for district attorney on the Democratic ticket and was supported by a nonpartisan group headed by Hiram Johnson, James D. Phelan, Rudolph Spreckels, Matt I. Sullivan, and Charles S. Wheeler. The fiery prosecutor was defeated, however, in the subsequent election, and the graft prosecution was thereby halted.[25]

In 1907 Edwin T. Earl, publisher of the Los Angeles *Express*, sent Edward Dickson to Sacramento to cover the legislative session. By chance, Dickson occupied the desk next to Chester H. Rowell, the forceful, intelligent editor of the Fresno *Republican*.[26] Both men quickly became disgusted with the "rawness" of the machine-controlled proceedings. Dickson discussed with Rowell the success of the Los Angeles nonpartisan movement. He suggested that the nonpartisan leaders would be willing to form a nucleus in the south for a statewide organization, if Rowell could gain support from northern reform-minded leaders. Rowell agreed to try; and the two reformers almost immediately discovered a large measure of support among prominent men in their respective regions.[27]

So cordial was the response, in fact, and so emboldened were the youthful leaders, that they decided to call a statewide convention, which was held in Oakland in August, 1907. Thirty-eight delegates attended, most of whom were professional men—lawyers, journalists, businessmen, physicians, and the like. They named their organization the Lincoln-Roosevelt League and drew up a platform that called for the emancipation of the Republican party in California from Southern Pacific domination, the selection of delegates to the next Republican national convention who were sympathetic to Roosevelt's policies, the election of free and honest legislators, the direct election of United States senators, and direct primaries for the nomination of candidates for all state and local offices.[28]

Because of its initial organizational weaknesses, the league was unable to gain immediate control of the Republican party in California, its first victories being local affairs, such as the election of a reform candidate as mayor of Sacramento. Yet by 1908 the infant organization felt strong enough to engage in a statewide struggle with the Southern Pacific. What the reformers lacked in experience they more than made up for in zeal and in timing, as they capitalized on the rising national ground swell of progressivism. The year-old league astonished political "pros" by winning a substantial number of the delegates who would attend the Republican state convention in May of that year.

Although its hold on the party machinery was still precarious, the league managed to send at least as many men to both houses of the 1909 legislature as did the machine. The *California Weekly*, a periodical of progressive leanings, declared that "the anti-machine element is in definite control of the Assembly and nearly in control of the Senate. . . ."[29] According to Franklin Hichborn, to whom students of the Progressive period of California history owe a debt of gratitude for recording the activities of a number of state legislative sessions, "the personnel of the California Legislature of 1909 was, all things considered, better than that of any other Legislature that has assembled in California in a decade or more."[30] The surprising ease with which the league was able to achieve such numerical strength in the legislature suggests that the Southern Pacific's control of state politics had begun to weaken prior to 1909.

Because of poor organization and lack of a definite plan of action, however, the reform elements in both the Assembly and the Senate were unable to take advantage of their political power in the legislature. The well-oiled and smooth-functioning machine easily outmaneuvered the neophytes of the Lincoln-Roosevelt League. In the Assembly the machine element named the speaker, and the speaker selected the committees. The political and parliamentary ineptitude of the league was just as evident in the Senate, where Lieutenant Governor Warren Porter, a machine man, was permitted to appoint all Senate committees in the interests of the Southern Pacific.

The real work of a legislative session, then as now, was done in committee. Two legislative committees scrutinized each piece of legislation before it was put to a vote. It is not surprising, therefore, that the reform measures with which the legislature of 1909 did manage to concern itself were, in their final form, weakened.

A direct-primary measure created the greatest stir. Many reform legislators were dissatisfied with the bill as presented, but concluded that there was no hope of obtaining anything more complete. Almost by default they permitted the machine to amend that part of the measure that dealt with the election of United States senators. Antimachine legislators had wished to follow the Oregon plan of a statewide vote. The machine element, wishing to keep the choices for United States senator within party lines, favored a district advisory vote, and managed to gain amendments to that effect.[31] The passage of the direct primary bill, however, prevented the Southern Pacific from dictating the selection of candidates for all offices in the 1910 election. By abolishing nominating conventions, the bill enabled candidates to appeal directly to the electorate for their nominations.[32]

The administrative instrument chosen by the reformers to redeem the state from railroad control was the Railroad Commission, which for almost thirty years had done little or nothing to safeguard the public interest. The commission had been created under section 22, Article 12 of the constitution of 1879. From 1880 to 1909, however, no remedial legislation relating to railroads had been placed upon the statute books of California. D. F. Pegrum, a careful student of the California Railroad Commission, concluded that the history of regulation during this period was "one of utter helplessness, and often unscrupulousness, on the part of the Commission; and of gross selfishness and lack of public spirit on the part of the railroads." [33]

Contemporary opponents of the railroad machine and historians of the California Progressive movement have accused the Railroad Commission of being subservient to the Southern Pacific. Mowry has written that the Railroad Commission was "decrepit and machine-controlled." [34] More recent studies, particularly those of Gerald D. Nash, paint an entirely different picture. Many railroad commissioners were conscientious and honest in attempting to fulfill their duties. "Their lack of immediate success," writes Nash, "was due more to the complexity of new difficulties which confronted them than to malfeasance. . . ." [35]

Nash believes the chief contribution of early railroad commissions was that of example and experience. While it appeared to many that state regulation of railroads had proved futile from 1880 to 1900, Nash argues that these "two decades of painful trial and error were not barren." By 1899, the railroad commissioners had "recognized the prerequisites for successful regulation—expert aid in rate-making, an enlarged staff and appropriations, and the centralization of administrative power in the hands of the Commission." [36]

The task facing the Railroad Commission in 1909, as it had been since its inception, was to determine the value of the vast railroad properties in California, and then to calculate a fair basis for freight and passenger rates. The existing rates would then be readjusted in the interest of a fair return to the carrier and equitable charges to the public. The Southern Pacific had been able to resist all rate changes the Railroad Commission had sought to impose and to defy it by continuing discriminations. In part, this successful avoidance of public regulation was made possible by institutional weaknesses of the commission itself, but the most important factor was the railroad's political influence. As the legislature made no appropriations for the work of the commission from 1900 to 1907, the commission could not conduct investigations of complaints or even print an annual report.[37]

The impetus for attacking the problem of railroad rate discriminations had already been provided by the federal government. The Hepburn Act of 1906, which was an important precedent for the federal control of private industry, had given the Interstate Commerce Commission the power to set a ceiling on railroad rates.[38] During 1906 and 1907 the Interstate Commerce Commission conducted an investigation of rebating in the United States. Franklin K. Lane, a member of the commission who had urged this immediate inquiry, visited San Francisco to examine conditions on the West Coast. Lane's report revealed that 103 firms in California enjoyed favorable discriminations from the Southern Pacific and Santa Fe railroads. Most of the firms thus favored were large shippers, such as Miller and Lux Incorporated.[39]

The close link between railroad and oil companies was revealed in a report on the petroleum industry made by Roosevelt's Bureau of Corporations in 1906. The railroads, large users of fuel oil owing to the scarcity of coal on the Pacific Coast, had been interested in oil development for many years.[40] The Southern Pacific, for example, had a controlling interest in the Associated Oil Company, a subsidiary of Standard Oil. Generous rebates were granted Associated Oil, and a similar arrangement existed between the Santa Fe and its subsidiary, the Petroleum Development Corporation. In turn, millions of dollars of Santa Fe stock was owned by Standard Oil Corporation directors. Thomas Robert Bard's Union Oil Company was the only major oil concern free from railroad affiliations, a fact that accounts in part for his strong antirailroad attitude.[41]

As a result of these interlocking arrangements, crude oil was sold to the railroads in California by Standard Oil and Associated Oil at rates lower than the market price. These losses were made up by discriminatory rates to small shippers. The Bureau of Corporations also found that in 1904 the railroads in California made more than eighty variations from their published rates in oil shipments to various points within the state. Standard Oil benefited from these discriminations in more than half the cases. "The result of these discriminations," reported the Bureau of Corporations, "has been to exclude the independent producer from securing business which under equal freight rates he would have obtained." [42]

Conditions such as these aroused public anger against the railroads, but, curiously, not against the oil companies. In his excellent study of the Standard Oil Company in California, Gerald T. White points out that "California was far more anti-railroad than anti-Standard, and local followers of Theodore Roosevelt had the Southern Pacific Railroad as their target. . . ." Californians were generally indifferent to the antitrust suit against the Standard Oil Company of New Jersey, and even the sensational report of the Bureau of Corporations aroused little interest.[43] The oil companies had not found it necessary to join the Southern Pacific in its control of state politics, and the average citizen was simply unaware of their power and influence. Only the independent oil producers, some 150 in all, were affected. To combat the oil "octopus," they

*The Genesis of Reform* 17

formed the Independent Oil Producers' Agency and made the Union Oil Company their selling agent; but they were alone in calling attention to the dangers of oil monopoly, and, as a matter of fact, were themselves soon sharing the benefits of monopoly along with Standard Oil, the Southern Pacific interests, and the General Petroleum Company.[44]

Perhaps the Standard Oil Company of California considered itself fortunate to escape public ire, but the railroad lobby soon realized that some law would have to be passed to quiet aroused public sentiment against the railroads. Accordingly, the machine supported the Wright bill in 1909, which would have left the railroads free from effective state supervision while giving the impression of governmental control. Reform legislators backed the Stetson bill, which would have "put teeth" in the Railroad Commission by giving it enough power to regulate railroad rates effectively.

The main difference between the two measures was that the Wright bill provided only for the fixing of maximum rates above which the railroads could not charge, while the Stetson bill stipulated an absolute fixing of rates. Additionally, the Wright bill contained no provision requiring a physical evaluation of railroad properties as a guide to rate-fixing. Railroads would not be hampered in applying their predetermined rates unless a complaint were made by a shipper or by the Railroad Commission. The Stetson bill, on the other hand, provided that the railroads must submit their suggested rates to the commission, which would then approve them or correct them after making a study of the rate schedules.

Judicial review was provided for in both bills, but here again they differed radically. Fines, unless they were made exorbitant, had been found to be of little value in forcing corporations to obey the law. Reformers argued that imprisonment would be a more effective punishment. Only the Stetson bill, however, gave the court the power to choose between fine and imprisonment; the Wright bill limited the punishment to a fine.[45]

Again the machine minority proved too crafty for the reformers. Backed by Southern Pacific attorneys, the minority presented an effective case for the unconstitutionality of any provision permitting the absolute fixing of rates. Peter Finley Dunne (not to be confused with the columnist, Finley Peter Dunne, of "Mr. Dooley" fame) was brought to Sacramento to argue before the Senate Committee on Corporations that the state constitution provided for the fixing only of maximum rates. Several antirailroad legislators were convinced by Dunne's argument, or too confused to counter with an argument of their own. By a series of clever maneuvers the Stetson bill was defeated and the Wright bill passed.

Although an effective railroad regulation bill was thereby cast aside in favor of a less effective one, Mowry has noted that the bill was "the first significant antirailroad measure that the California legislature had passed for many years." [46] The reformers, unsure of themselves in the face of sophisticated legal reasoning, and out-foxed on the floor of the legislature, had nonetheless forced the railroad machine to pass a measure inimical to its interests. Railroads had seen the last of almost total freedom from state control in California.

Later that year in Los Angeles, the nonpartisan forces, led by Meyer Lissner, elected their candidate for mayor. "The political power of the Southern Pacific has been shattered beyond repair," exulted the *Express*. "Its control over the Republican party of Los Angeles has been destroyed. . . ." [47] Lissner wrote an enthusiastic letter about the victory to Robert La Follette, United States senator from Wisconsin, who was greatly respected by California progressive leaders:

## The Genesis of Reform 19

We have met the enemy and they are ours. We put the Southern Pacific push to rout—horse, foot, and dragoons—in our city election held here the 7th of December, electing our entire ticket. If we don't make good now in the city of Los Angeles and hold our ground, it will be our own fault and the general sentiment seems to be that we have gotten the machine on the run and with this beginning . . . we ought to be able to carry the state.[48]

The "machine was on the run," but it had not been entirely defeated. An octopus is a tough creature and the trimming of a tentacle or two was more of an annoyance than a serious injury. The first encounter had yielded some results, but the tempo of attack had to be sustained if total victory over the Southern Pacific and its "allied interests" was to be achieved.

# 2

# "A FIGHT AGAINST THE INTERESTS"

The Lincoln-Roosevelt League would remain but a potentially dangerous irritant to the Southern Pacific machine unless it could place its own candidate in the governor's chair. With so much at stake, only a man of extraordinary merit and impeccable character could be chosen to carry the league's message to the citizens of California. A mistake at this time could bring an inglorious end to reform; for without an attractive and popular leader the movement could easily fall victim to apathy or to disruptive localism.

Francis J. Heney was a first choice of many Lincoln-Roosevelt Leaguers. Had he not achieved national prominence during his conduct of the graft prosecution in San Francisco? Would not his oratorical ability serve him well in a political contest? No member of the league would deny that Heney possessed certain positive attributes; but had not his ruthless conduct of the graft prosecution revealed explosive capacities and an injudiciousness unbecoming a candidate for public office? Was he not just a little too "radical" for the good of the movement? Would his Democratic allegiances "sit well" with Republicans in the state? Chester Rowell, acting-president of the league, felt that Heney's nomination would mean "the immediate disruption of the Lincoln-Roosevelt League. . . ." [1] Meyer Lissner feared that there was "too much latent opposition to him. . . ." [2] Finally, had not Heney stated in a letter to Rowell that he definitely would not be a candidate? [3]

Perhaps Harris Weinstock would evoke a more "respectable" image. Weinstock was the senior member of a prosperous Sacramento business firm, Weinstock, Lubin, and Company. An enthusiastic backer of the graft prosecution, he had an active career in business and a keen interest in public affairs. There was one problem with Weinstock: he absolutely refused to permit his name to be used so long as Hiram Johnson was a possibility. Weinstock, a man of great humanitarian sympathies and yet devoid of political ambition, saw in Johnson the makings of a fine governor and therefore encouraged him to run.[4]

Other leaguers also supported Hiram Johnson, and by early 1910 he had emerged as the most popular choice for many. Yet Johnson adamantly refused to run, and with good reason. His prosperous law practice in San Francisco had enabled him to purchase a homesite in the hills overlooking the Golden Gate, San Francisco Bay, and the lovely countryside of Marin County. Johnson's preference for the quiet, private life of San Francisco over the hectic, public life of Sacramento received the hearty endorsement of Mrs. Johnson.[5]

Yet many leaguers were determined that Johnson should run for governor, considering him the only man with a chance of winning. A special committee headed by Meyer Lissner was named to work on Johnson. Rowell wrote Lissner that he "would be willing to do almost anything short of murder to compel him to [enter the race], but I fear it is hopeless." [6] Rowell, Lissner, Dickson, and Stimson implored Johnson's strong-willed wife to give her consent to her husband's candidacy, and were rebuffed. If her husband were to run for any public office, she stated, she would prefer it be for the United States Senate. Eventually, however, Mrs. Johnson began to change her mind about the desirability of a state position. Some have surmised that she was swayed by Stimson's assurance that the distance from the governorship of California to the United States Senate was not very great.[7]

Meanwhile, Weinstock, assuming Johnson's refusal was final, had permitted his name to be used. When, however, he learned that Mrs. Johnson had finally waived her objections to her husband's candidacy, he immediately informed the league's executive committee of his own withdrawal and unqualified support of Hiram Johnson.[8] His wife now tacitly ranged with a majority of the leaguers, Johnson reluctantly gave in and agreed to "sacrifice himself" to the cause. Having once committed himself, however, Johnson informed the league's leaders that he would conduct a vigorous campaign.[9]

Son of a tough, wily, conservative lawyer and politician, Grove Johnson, Hiram Johnson was an attractive candidate. Born in Sacramento in 1866, he had attended the University of California, but left during his junior year to marry Minnie McNeal, the daughter of a Sacramento contractor. After studying law in the family office for a brief time, he was admitted to the bar in 1888 and soon became well known and respected in Sacramento.

While Grove Johnson had long been a chief spokesman in the state legislature for the railroad machine, Hiram had taken a different course on political and economic issues. This led to a gradual alienation from his father. The family law firm was dissolved, and in 1902 Hiram moved his practice from Sacramento to San Francisco.[10] There he was soon involved in several sensational trials and was Francis J. Heney's right-hand man during the graft prosecution. Johnson's reform background and progressive outlook were enhanced by an eight-year association with organized labor as an attorney for the teamsters in San Francisco.[11] Yet he had always been careful, unlike Heney, not to exacerbate the sensibilities of wealthier citizens.

As an orator, his strong speeches in support of the Lincoln-Roosevelt League attracted much attention. Johnson had a positive flair for generating not only public interest, but public enthusiasm as well. As a stirring, if not mellifluous, speaker, he was particularly effective before large crowds. Chester Rowell once referred to him as an "aggressive advocate," just the type needed for the "first fight." [12] A sort of western Theodore Roosevelt, Hiram Johnson invested the cause of political reform in California with a similar brand of dynamic righteousness.

The Lincoln-Roosevelt League placed a full state-ticket on the primary ballot, including candidates for the Senate and Assembly. Johnson's running mate for lieutenant governor was a southern Californian, Albert J. Wallace, president of the Anti-Saloon League of California and a devout Methodist. Wallace had extensive oil interests in Kern County, was a member of the Independent Oil Producers' Agency, and owned considerable areas of farming land in the San Joaquin Valley and in Contra Costa and Monterey counties. He was one of the first men to urge the establishment of a federal line of steamships on the Pacific Coast, to be operated in competition with vessels controlled by the railroad and steamship trusts.[13] For its United States senatorial candidate the league selected John D. Works, a former justice of the California Supreme Court. Upon retirement from the bench, Works had practiced law in Los

Angeles, serving as president of the Good Government League there.[14]

Conservative newspapers and periodicals were quick to point out that the league, after having dedicated itself to direct legislation and democratic reforms, had proceeded to use machine methods in selecting its candidates.[15] Chester Rowell, for one, admitted the undemocratic nature of the league's operations. As he explained to Mark Sullivan, editor of *Collier's Weekly,* the theory of the league had been to organize clubs everywhere to conduct local campaigns and to elect delegates to a state convention. This state conference would then substitute an elected central organization for the provisional one. But the theory had not worked out in practice. It had been impossible to organize local clubs everywhere. The provisional organization had remained intact. A state conference for reorganization had elected Rowell president and authorized him to appoint the rest of the organization. That organization had selected the primary ticket and thereafter was accepted by the rest of the reform forces as representing them. Rowell wrote that this was "about the nearest thing to popular government the people are yet willing to accept. We have been as democratic as the people will let us be, which has been shockingly autocratic. Curiously, nobody has been shocked, except the involuntary autocrats." [16]

To oppose Johnson, the railroad backed State Superintendent of Banks Alden Anderson. Others running for governor in the Republican primary were Secretary of State Charles F. Curry, State Engineer Nathan Ellery, and former Speaker of the Assembly Philip Stanton. When Curry, Ellery, and Stanton refused to withdraw under pressure from the railroad, Johnson's chances soared.

As Chester Rowell wrote Johnson shortly before the campaign for the primaries began, the league had "the candidate, the issue, and the opportune time." [17] While in letters to close friends Johnson was uncharacteristically confident about his chances, and while he was very gratified by the press's enthusiastic response to his candidacy, he also expressed concern about public support, the amount of money available for the campaign, and the lack of publicity arrangements. In Johnson's opinion, the Lincoln-Roosevelt organization was simply not prepared to wage a statewide campaign supporting a ticket of nearly fifty candidates.[18]

Later on, after several blunders on the part of the league's campaign organization (such as the improper handling of news stories), the testy and decisive Johnson declared: "Of all the Damn Fool Leagues that ever existed, the LINCOLN-ROOSEVELT REPUBLICAN LEAGUE not only is the worst, but the worst that could ever be conceived. . . ."[19] Resolving that the only chance of success was personal control of his own campaign, Johnson set up his own organization, independent of the league's. For his manager he chose Al McCabe, a superb organizer who remained with him in that capacity for years thereafter. Assisting McCabe was Harriet Odgers, who had worked in Johnson's law office. This combination provided the Johnson campaign with the central direction and organization it needed.

Johnson even refused to travel with the other Lincoln-Roosevelt League candidates, explaining his decision with characteristic bluntness: "This fight is very serious as well as sentimental with me and I do not wish it cheapened by a mere scramble for office. . . ."[20] Rowell warned Lissner that it was best to let Johnson have his way, because it was imperative "to protect Johnson's nerves, which are, for this campaign, our most valuable asset. . . . We need not deceive ourselves," Rowell continued, "Johnson is the strength of this campaign. He is winning it, not we. Our function is to organize and finance the fight. . . ."[21] In order to calm the easily aroused candidate, Rowell assured Johnson that he "didn't need to be bothered with the eighty-six [other] candidates." Johnson was winning the fight, Rowell wrote reassuringly, and should not be upset when things went wrong.[22]

To gather material for his speeches Johnson sent letters to various businessmen and shippers, asking for confidential information regarding the unjust rate exactions of the Southern Pacific.[23] Early in the campaign he expressed his intention to connect his efforts in California with those of the insurgent Republicans in the East, such as La Follette in Wisconsin, and Cummins and Dolliver in Iowa. "They are making the same fight that we are making in California," he wrote to a member of the staff of the San Francisco *Daily News*, "a fight against the interests and the system, and for true democracy. . . ."[24]

Touring the state in a brand-new crimson Locomobile, with his son at the wheel, the gubernatorial candidate of the Lincoln-Roosevelt League waged a unique and colorful campaign. In the larger cities Johnson spoke to packed houses, harping on the same theme—"Kick the Southern Pacific out of politics." Ringing a cowbell to attract listeners in the smaller towns, he would excoriate the Southern Pacific to the evident delight of those in attendance. Some leaguers advised him to broaden his campaign to include other pressing issues, but Johnson had selected his main theme and would accept no other.[25]

In late May, after an exhausting and discouraging tour of southern California, Johnson turned his attention to the rural areas of the state. Writing to Al McCabe, his campaign manager, Johnson related that the "past week has convinced me that my sphere of action is north of the Tehachapi, and that my every effort in this campaign must be devoted to the *farmers et al.* of the rural counties."[26]

What appeal did Johnson think he would have in the rural counties? Would his major campaign slogan reach responsive ears there? Undoubtedly he was aware of the uniqueness of the agricultural pattern and social structure in California's rural areas. He also fully realized that many residents of these counties had special grievances against the Southern Pacific.

As Carey McWilliams, a former chief of the state's Commission of Immigration and Housing, has pointed out, California differs from other states because it skipped the frontier phase of land development. Because of early Spanish and Mexican grants, California began with land monopoly.[27] After 1860 the federal government and the state began to sell California land to private individuals, and by 1880 most of the valuable parcels had been taken. In addition, the federal government also granted nearly 11,500,000 acres to California railroads. Millions of additional acres were sold for cash, warrants, or scrip. Altogether these grants and transfers of land amounted to nearly 36,000,000 acres, well over one-third of the total area of the state.[28]

The immense holdings thus acquired thwarted the operation of the Homestead Law in California because the best land had been taken off the open market before homesteaders came to settle. One of the first publicly to decry this situation was Henry George, whose famous book *Progress and Poverty* was published in 1879. Earlier, in 1871, George had published a remarkable, brief booklet entitled *Our Land and Land Policy,* in which he had vividly described California as a land of plantations and estates, not of farms. Arguing that land monopoly was the greatest obstacle to settlement by small independent farmers, he pointed out that early agricultural development in the state had resulted in large-scale farming units worked by wage laborers, and not in extensive private farm tenancy.[29]

Important social consequences resulted from this unique agricultural pattern. McWilliams summarizes the most important of these consequences as follows: ". . . a marked degree of social instability; the existence of a long-standing and cancerous farm labor problem; the continued existence of an unresolved land problem; and the development of a most exceptional social structure." [30] This agrarian social structure was sharply divided into four classes: absentee corporate owners, a managerial class to operate the large farms, a working class of small farm owners, and a large group of migratory farm laborers.[31] A report released by the Commission of Land Colonization and Rural Credits in 1916 recognized the abuses inherent in such a social and economic system: ". . . We have at one end of the social scale a few rich men who as a rule do not live on their estates, and at the other end either a body of shifting farm laborers or a farm tenantry made up largely of aliens, who take small interest in the progress of the community. . . ." [32]

An important aspect of this "body of shifting farm laborers" was that they were primarily Orientals or Mexican-Americans, and therefore the majority could not vote. Many who were American citizens did not vote because they had neither social status nor stake in the community. Furthermore, after 1894 the state constitution required literacy in English as a voting requisite.[33] Thus when Hiram Johnson wrote McCabe that "my every effort in this campaign must be devoted to the *farmers et al.* of the rural counties," he was concerned with a very select group —the large farmers and ranchers of the state. To these influential men Johnson could appeal most effectively. A majority of them had an economic reason for despising the railroad machine. They transported their products on Southern Pacific lines, but few received favorable rate discriminations. While they had a legitimate reason for complaint about high rates, still they had *not* been impoverished by such arbitrary railroad policies. Rates may have been unjust and excessive, but the crucial fact was that substantial profits were made under the existing rate system. Population increase, ever rising demand, and a superb climate insured their continuing prosperity. Johnson had to make his case by demonstrating that even more profits would be made by forcing the railroad to charge equitable rates. He had to appeal to the rich farmers' well-developed entrepreneurial instincts. In his decision to stake the campaign on the railroad issue, Johnson displayed both a shrewd insight into the farm economy and an understanding of an important power structure. Johnson was also well aware that as influential molders of public opinion in the rural areas and as a source of campaign funds, these relatively few wealthy farmers and ranchers were of inestimable value.

It seems clear that the conflict in 1910 was only to a lesser extent between oppressed migratory farm laborers and aggressive agrarian capitalists. It was far more importantly a conflict between one group of capitalists (the large farmers and ranchers) and another group of capitalists (the railroad interests). The former group did not wish to *displace* the Southern Pacific, but only to *share* its privileges and stature. These acquisitive agrarian entrepreneurs wanted more than anything to end the tapping of their incomes by a predatory railroad. Johnson's campaign slogan—"Kick the Southern Pacific out of politics" —thus had a very special appeal to them.[34]

Even though Charles Curry carried San Francisco and Sacramento counties in the August primary, he still ran a distant second to Hiram Johnson, who won a total of 101,666 votes, only 12,273 less than the combined total of his four Republican opponents.[35] Johnson had greatly underestimated his vote-getting ability in the urban areas of southern California, for it was Los Angeles County that provided his margin of victory, delivering him one-fifth of his entire statewide vote. Other league candidates fared equally well, sweeping all contested offices in the southern counties and enough offices in the north to give the statewide Republican ticket a distinct reform flavor.

Such large returns for Johnson from Los Angeles

County, and such impressive successes on the part of league candidates in the south, were due in large measure to the "dry" vote. The temperance movement was much stronger in the less urban south than in the industrial northern part of the state. This may be accounted for by the ethnic and religious contrast between Los Angeles and San Francisco residents. The inhabitants of Los Angeles were mainly migrants from the Middle West and Northeast, while the population of San Francisco was composed for the most part of foreign immigrants or their children.[36]

Chiefly responsible for linking the temperance cause to the Progressive movement in California was Daniel M. Gandier, appointed legislative superintendent of the Anti-Saloon League in 1909. Without permitting the name of the league to be connected with the Johnson campaign in 1910, for fear of alienating northern "wets," Gandier had been able to bring many of the state's church organizations into the Johnson camp. The Anti-Saloon League concentrated mainly upon the election of Albert Wallace, Johnson's running mate, for it feared that a vote for Wallace, a prohibitionist, substantially smaller than that for Johnson, a "wet," would discredit the temperance movement. However, while the campaigns for the two candidates were conducted separately, both men profited from the support of the temperance people.[37]

Johnson was extremely pleased with his success in the primary election but realized that in Democratic primary winner Theodore Bell he faced an experienced and capable opponent. Bell, like Johnson, was a progressive. Robert Hennings, an authority on California progressives of Democratic persuasion, has reminded us: "Because of a tendency to associate all progressives with the party of Theodore Roosevelt, one is apt to forget that Wilson Democrats were also fond of styling themselves progressives. . . ." Progressive Democrats in California had much in common with their Republican counterparts, and the major difference was a "matter of traditional ties and personal ambitions. . . ."[38]

Bell had begun his political career as district attorney of Napa County. He was one of three Democrats from California in the House of Representatives in 1902, but had been defeated for reelection in 1904. Bell had run unsuccessfully for governor in 1906, emphasizing the old Democratic theme of the 1880's—the railroad's domination of politics. He was repeating this antirailroad campaign in 1910.[39]

So far as the Republican party was concerned, the Lincoln-Roosevelt League had proved itself the predominant power in California. Of the 428 delegates at the Republican state convention in September, only a small minority were "regulars." The Republican platform prepared at that convention was similar to the Democratic, except that the Republicans endorsed woman suffrage and the national income tax. As the San Francisco *Chronicle* editorialized: "For the first time in history . . . the Republican platform is rather more radical than that of the Democrats."[40]

Because of the similarity of the platforms, the campaign turned largely on the personalities of Johnson and Bell. Both men denounced the Southern Pacific; in fact, Bell's campaign was virtually a duplication of his 1906 effort. But the Democratic candidate could not match Johnson's ability to delight crowds and to arouse enthusiasm among his supporters. Even though he and Johnson were in perfect agreement on the major issue of the day—railroad domination of state politics—Bell was charged repeatedly by Johnson with accepting railroad support. In Santa Barbara on October 6, for example, Johnson accused his opponent of "using the soft pedal" on Herrin and the railroad interests. With masterly skill, Johnson painted a picture of a pliable Bell seeking to placate the machine by toning down his attacks.[41]

These were serious allegations, but it *was* apparent that

Herrin and his cronies preferred Bell to win, believing him easier to manipulate than the intractable Johnson. In fact, among Bell's supporters were the San Francisco *Globe*, the personal organ of Patrick Calhoun; Jere Burke, Herrin's right-hand man; and George A. Knight, a Southern Pacific attorney. Furthermore, Walter Parker, chief political agent of the Southern Pacific in southern California, worked actively for Bell.[42] Nevertheless, a perceptive student of the campaign has concluded that there "is not a shred of evidence to indicate that Bell sought, welcomed, or encouraged this following or that he would have listened to it if elected." [43]

Johnson's chances received a boost in late August when W. H. Porterfield, editor-in-chief of the Scripps chain, announced that all the Scripps newspapers in California would endorse Hiram Johnson for governor.[44] There could, however, have been little doubt about the outcome of the election, for the Republicans were a distinct majority in the state. Despite this fact, Johnson's victory in November was not particularly resounding. Although he carried San Francisco by a narrow margin, he lost twenty-one of the remaining forty-nine northern counties. Again piling up decisive majorities in southern California, he won all nine counties there.[45]

California now had an attractive and popular reform spokesman. Would his grandiose promises be translated into legislative reality? Fundamental improvements and reorganizations of state laws and agencies had already been made in the fields of banking, insurance, and transportation.[46] Yet many problems still existed and much remained to be accomplished. Progressive Californians of all parties were confident that the Johnson administration would continue the task of making the government of California more responsive to the popular will and more attuned to the needs of the people.

Had these Californians known, however, that their newly

elected governor possessed very few specific ideas about reform legislation, their confidence in him would have been badly shaken. In order to gather information about reform possibilities, Johnson traveled East after his election to consult with Theodore Roosevelt, Robert La Follette, and Lincoln Steffens. During his absence the Republican State Central Committee, fearing that the new administration would enter office with no program of any consequence, appointed several subcommittees to draft measures in accordance with the 1910 platform pledges. During the week preceding the opening of the 1911 session, these committees presented their proposals at a general meeting of members of the new legislature.

This activity greatly perturbed Johnson, who was not consulted about the plan and who completely failed to appreciate the importance of the work done by these committees. Indeed, without their preparatory efforts in the areas of railroad legislation, conservation, direct legislation, suffrage, and labor legislation the record of his first administration would undoubtedly have been much less impressive.[47]

Only a relatively few legislators and close advisers, however, knew of Johnson's disapproval of the Republican State Central Committee's course of action. Most Californians were certain that they had chosen as governor a man of courage and conviction, ingenuity and incorruptibility. They eagerly awaited his inaugural address, fully expecting to be inspired by his call to arms. They were not to be disappointed.

# 3

## ONWARD CHRISTIAN CAPITALISTS

"In some form or other," declared Hiram Johnson in his inaugural address of January 3, 1911, "nearly every governmental problem that involves the health, the happiness, or the prosperity of the State has arisen because some private interest has intervened or has sought for its own gain to exploit either the resources or the politics of the state. . . ." His audience, accustomed to such caustically sweeping statements by disillusioned muckrakers but not by governors of California, was fascinated. For most of those persons listening attentively to Johnson's address, California's major problem was quite clear-cut: "the interests" were choking off political and economic opportunities from "the people." There were thus nods of approval when the new governor pledged that his first task would be to eliminate every private interest from government and "to require from our officials the highest efficiency and an undivided allegiance." Here was a man who meant business, a man who was more than a match for "the interests."

Johnson's goal, as outlined in his speech, was to develop an efficient public service that reflected the public good and not the good of special interests. The power or wealth of a particular politician did not matter to him; but if that politician were dividing "his allegiance to the State with a private interest," thereby impairing his efficiency, he would be attacked and ousted. The emphasis on efficiency and the repudiation of private interests' exploitation of politics and resources constituted the two major themes of Johnson's inaugural address. His belief in efficient and rational approaches to social and economic problems—in what might be called "scientific management" of state affairs—was coupled with a desire to *use* the immense resources of California "rationally and equitably" on behalf of all and not to *exploit* them ruthlessly for private gain.[1]

The governor's specific legislative recommendations demonstrated his intention to "return the government to the people" and to give them honest public service untarnished by corruption and corporate influence. Briefly, his recommendations were as follows: adoption of the initiative, referendum, and recall, the last to include elected judicial officials; appropriation of $75,000 to enable the Railroad Commission to make a physical evaluation of railroad properties as a basis for fixing absolute rates; amendment of the direct primary law to incorporate a statewide advisory vote on United States senators; adoption of the short ballot to reduce the number of elected officials; elimination of partisan designation on ballots after the names of judicial candidates; utilization of the merit system for public servants and the enactment of a civil service law; conservation laws; and an employers' liability law.[2]

In the months that followed, the legislators hastened to carry out these recommendations, and added numerous measures of their own. By the end of the first week of the legislative session, 156 Senate bills and 159 Assembly bills had been referred to the appropriate committees, now firmly in the hands of the progressives.[3] On January 10 John D. Works was named United States senator by an overwhelming majority of both houses. Three days later State Senator Stetson introduced virtually the same railroad bill that had been defeated in 1909. Hopes rose for the enactment of a prodigious body of reform legislation.

These hopes were not frustrated. Despite an ingrained American distrust of administrative power lodged in the state, the Johnson administration launched an impressive program based upon the exercise of state responsibility.

To the reformers, one of the greatest evils of the Southern Pacific machine was that it represented and advanced the interests of a limited and privileged number of citizens. Hiram Johnson and his followers sought to eliminate this evil, and largely succeeded. Determined that business opportunities should not be limited to a special few, they capitalized on the spirit of the times to score notable successes. Under progressive leadership, California extricated itself from Southern Pacific machine control. This liberation was applauded most heartily by those who benefited most—the entrepreneurs of this immensely rich state. Large farmers, independent oil producers, and other rising businessmen knew they could make substantial amounts of money more easily once the Southern Pacific's influence in the business life of California was sharply curtailed.

Some of the applause accorded California's liberation from railroad rule should rightly have been reserved for Hiram Johnson himself; for seldom has a governor so dominated the political life of his state. By means of public and private persuasion, effective utilization of the California press (Johnson numbered among his closest friends and acquaintances many leading newspaper editors, including Chester Rowell, Fremont Older, C. K. McClatchy, Irving Martin, and E. T. Earl), and by the sheer force of his compelling and dominant personality, the vigorous and able governor pursued his goals. It is true that the reforms favored by Johnson also found widespread public acceptance. Yet it was he who here convinced a legislator, here influenced an editor, there delivered a forceful speech on behalf of a particular legislative measure. While he alienated many people, there is no denying his political effectiveness.

Hiram Johnson was fully aware that the success of his administration depended largely upon effective railroad regulation, the issue upon which he had pegged his entire campaign. When the Stetson-Eshleman railroad bill was introduced in January, therefore, he sent a special message to the legislature, praising the bill and urging its adoption. Extensive private efforts of persuasion were unnecessary, for the bill had strong support in both houses.

Approved February 9, 1911, this act gave the Railroad Commission power to establish rates for the transportation of freight and passengers by all railroads and other transportation companies. Furthermore, if the commission felt a particular rate charge was unreasonable or discriminatory, it could assign a board of inquiry to investigate. The "long-and-short haul" principle was to be followed, unless permission was granted to do otherwise. The commission was also authorized to ascertain the actual value of all property owned by transportation companies within the state.[4]

Shortly after the passage of the Stetson-Eshleman bill, three constitutional amendments were framed by the newly strengthened Railroad Commission. They were designed to authorize the legislature to give the commission broader powers of regulation over railroad rates and control over public utilities as well.[5] The powers conferred to the Railroad Commission by these three amendments, adopted at a special election in October, 1911, included the enforcement of financial restrictions and standards of service and safety, as well as rates and accounting. Transportation companies were forbidden to raise their rates without the commission's assent. Finally, the legislature was authorized to extend the commission's jurisdiction to include utilities other than railroads.[6]

While the electorate was altering the constitution, the Railroad Commission was busy collecting information to be used for future legislative purposes. The new commission consisted of three members elected in November, 1910: H. D. Loveland, a former traffic manager and wealthy San Francisco shipping agent, the only survivor of the pre-Johnson commission; John Eshleman, a bright young attorney from El Centro; and Alexander Gordon, a Sacramento fruit grower. During the summer of 1911 the commission sent its legal counsel, Max Thelen, previously employed by the Western Pacific Railroad Company, to investigate the leading railroad and public service commissions of the United States. Thelen spent two months visiting eleven states and the District of Columbia. He spoke with officials, observed their methods, and gathered information to be used in writing California's public utility laws.[7]

In his formal report, Thelen advocated the creation of a new railroad commission to regulate public utilities in addition to railroads.[8] Thelen, Eshleman, and State Senator Stetson worked together in the writing of a public utilities act. Upon its completion the bill was submitted to members of the legislature and to officers of the leading public utilities in California. Accepting the concept of regulation without dissent, the corporations nevertheless hired a score of attorneys to raise objections to specific clauses. From their previous work on the bill, however, Eshleman and Thelen had gained an unsurpassed knowledge of the law relating to public utilities and were ready to answer any query and to defend any section. Some minor changes were made, but in its final form the bill retained its vital provisions.[9]

Introduced on November 28, 1911, the Public Utilities Act was passed unanimously by both houses and was signed by Governor Johnson on December 23. It provided for an increase in the number of railroad commissioners from three to five, to be appointed by the governor rather than elected, as before. Johnson retained the three members elected in November, 1910: Eshleman, who served as president; Loveland; and Gordon. The two appointed commissioners were Max Thelen, who served in the dual capacity of legal counsel and regular member, and Edwin Edgerton, prominently identified with the investigation of public utility corporations and rate fixing as a member of the Los Angeles Municipal Commission.

Jurisdiction of the reorganized Railroad Commission was extended to all public utility companies within the state, except those in incorporated cities and towns, which were given the privilege of turning over their powers to the Railroad Commission if they wished. Under the provisions of the act, public utilities were defined to include common carriers, gas, electricity, telephones, telegraph, water distribution, pipelines, and warehouses used in connection with the transportation of property by common carriers or vessels.[10]

Although the new Railroad Commission retained authority to enforce its orders, the Public Utilities Act provided for prompt judicial review. Any appeal of a decision made by the commission was to be taken directly to the state Supreme Court for review, but no issues could be raised at that time which had not been presented to the railroad board. This procedure eliminated costly delays of injunctions and writs of review. Between March 23, 1912, when the act went into effect, and October 1, 1914, the Railroad Commission rendered more than 1,500 formal decisions. Yet only eight times was the Supreme Court asked to review any of these decisions.[11]

These various rate cases resulted in a statewide reduction of passenger and freight charges. For example, the commission forced the Southern Pacific and Santa Fe railroads to reduce their rates in the San Joaquin and Imperial valleys. It was estimated that by the end of June, 1912, the Railroad Commission had saved the shippers, consumers, and traveling public of California more than $2,000,000 in railroad tolls. Most of these savings went to large farmers and shippers, but in spite of the reductions, transportation companies continued to prosper and the predicted ruin of business never materialized.[12]

The Johnson forces had reason to be proud when the act went into effect in March, 1912. Prior to that time the public had had practically no means of securing fair rates from any utility other than railroads. Control over the rate charges of utility companies had been given to municipalities and county boards of supervisors. These supervisors had often proved corrupt, as in the case of San Francisco and Boss Ruef. The arrangement had proved expensive and unworkable, enabling the efficiently organized utility corporations to wield excessive power in local affairs. As municipal regulations broke down, the provisions of the Public Utilities Act became imperative.

It is interesting to note that in the formal complaints filed with the Railroad Commission under the provisions of the Public Utilities Act the large public utility corporations were plaintiffs nearly as often as they were defendants. The Pacific Gas and Electric Company, the largest electricity corporation in the West, was one of the first to take advantage of the new act. It lodged a complaint against the Great Western Power Company, demanding that the latter be prevented from operating in territory exclusively served by the Pacific Gas and Electric Company. The Mount Whitney Power Company, a large corporation in Tulare County, also instituted action against rival companies in that part of the state. The Postal Telegraph Company protested before the commission that it had been discriminated against by the Pacific Telephone and

Telegraph Company. The Central California Traction Company filed suit against the Santa Fe Railway, and the Northern Electric did the same against the Western Pacific, each seeking to force an interchange of traffic.[13]

It thus becomes evident that the Johnson administration was determined not only to reform abuses in railroad and public utility rate structures, but also to achieve equitable competition among California corporations. Companies filing complaints and suits with the Railroad Commission were not utilizing for their own ends legislative machinery designed for other purposes. Instead, they were accepting the Johnson administration's implicit invitation to share in the economic growth of California under the beneficial aegis of the state government. An attempt was thus made to assist all business units so that the larger did not wax rich at the expense of the smaller. This economic policy—the entrepreneurial as opposed to the vested—enhanced the future development of California industry by giving all business interests a chance to prosper, and at the same time prevented unhampered and extortionate rate charges. The legislation of 1911 was regulatory, but certainly not antibusiness.[14]

No better example may be found of the Johnson administration's stress on efficiency than the Board of Control, an innovation in California government. This agency was created by the legislature of 1911 to provide for close supervision of the state's finances. One of the many duties of the new agency, which replaced the old Board of Examiners, was to examine at least once a year the accounts of the state prisons, reformatories, hospitals, and other institutions, commissions, and bureaus of the state. Some member of the three-man board was to visit each public institution as often as possible to determine the conditions therein. The board was to have complete control of purchasing by state agencies and was to receive all claims against the state, settlement of which was not otherwise provided by law.

For chairman of the Board of Control, Johnson selected a tall, handsome Irishman, John Francis Neylan. Born in New York City in 1885, Neylan was educated at Seton Hall College in New Jersey. Moving West in 1903, he worked at various jobs, including teamster, bank teller, and newspaper reporter. In 1910, as a reporter for Fremont Older's San Francisco *Bulletin*, he had covered Johnson's gubernatorial campaign. Johnson had developed a great respect for Neylan's ability and honesty. As one of his first executive appointments, the governor chose the shrewd reporter as head of the new agency. Neylan did not disappoint him.[15]

Neylan's Board of Control ripped into virtually every state agency, exposing graft, obtaining confessions of illegal actions, reorganizing departments, installing new accounting and budgetary systems. By 1913 sixteen state officials, from hospital superintendents on down, had been exposed, discharged, and forced to repay all money embezzled from the state.[16] The accounts of California's twenty-two state institutions had been audited, something that had not been done for a period of fourteen years prior to the Johnson administration. The first comprehensive state budget had been submitted, and an inventory of all state property was under way.[17]

Opponents charged that the Board of Control was an extravagant and unnecessary waste of the taxpayers' money. Neylan admitted that the board cost approximately $42,000 a year to operate, as compared with $19,000 for running the Board of Examiners, but pointed out that the net saving to the state was $750,000 as of January 1, 1913. Nearly $300,000 had been saved in the reduction and correction of claims against the state.

As a result of its extensive fumigating efforts and its efficient management of financial affairs, the Board of

Control enabled the Johnson administration to provide honest, economical service, and converted an inherited deficit of $250,000 into a surplus of more than $4,500,000 by the beginning of 1917.[18]

Among progressives in the United States there were major differences of opinion regarding popular democracy and direct legislation. Most progressives believed that "the people" were fundamentally wise and good. If freed from institutional restraints, such as nominating conventions, partisan designations, and formal party structure, "the people" could be relied upon to provide their elected leaders with trustworthy guidance. This guidance would manifest itself in direct primary elections and initiative, referendum, and recall procedures. In other words, the cure for democracy was more democracy.

Some progressives, however, disagreed with this appraisal of "the people," arguing that the cure for the problems of the day was not more democracy but better leadership. Society would be better off, in their opinion, with less "procedural" democracy (i.e., fewer opportunities for popular choice) and with more "substantive" democracy (i.e., better decisions enunciated by trained and experienced leaders). Herbert Croly, a critical supporter of the Progressive movement, was perhaps the foremost proponent of this view, although he later modified his position. Croly argued that in an age of organization, political democracy could not be improved simply by more democracy. Rather, in his *The Promise of American Life*, published in 1909, and in other publications, he stressed the need for strong executive leadership in reform as a necessary counterbalance to the initiative, referendum, and recall, and spoke of a "democratic elite" possessing patriotic disinterestedness.[19]

California progressives, in the main, shared the former view. Believing strongly that democratic processes would generally produce correct and wise decisions, they trusted "the people" and distrusted formal party organizations. Progressive legislators broadened their concept of "the people" in late January, 1911, by overwhelmingly approving a woman suffrage amendment. The legislature of 1911 also demonstrated its enormous disdain for party structure by placing the elections of candidates for nonpolitical offices on a nonpartisan basis. Proposals were approved which made the election of judges and school officials nonpartisan. Parties were further weakened in 1913, when the legislature made all county and township elections nonpartisan, leaving only the governor, several state officials, and members of the state legislature to be elected on a partisan basis.[20] The session of 1911 also amended the Direct Primary Law of 1909 so that the voters could state their preference for United States senator. In addition the amended law made provision for a presidential primary election and removed the party designation from the ballot.

In 1913 the famous cross-filing provision was instituted —candidates were thereafter allowed to file for nomination in the primaries of parties other than their own. The adoption of this provision was motivated by more than a desire for nonpartisanship in state elections. Progressives, not wishing to run independently for fear of losing, wanted to maintain their ties with the Republican party (by running on both tickets) in case their own Progressive organization, launched in late 1913, should break apart.[21]

While the California progressives were demolishing party organizations they were also providing the electorate with the tools of direct democracy. These new instruments—initiative, referendum, and recall—were to be used to "return the government to the people." In 1911 State Senator Lee C. Gates headed a committee to draft initiative, referendum, and recall amendments. One of the major problems that arose was the number of signatures required to invoke initiative and referendum. The general opinion was that 30,000 signatures should be required for initiative and 20,000 for referendum. Because 8 percent of the vote for governor in 1910 (385,713) was 30,858 and 5 percent of that vote was 19,286, it was decided to use the number of votes for governor as the basis of computation and to retain those percentages.

Senator Gates reminded the committee, however, that as the population of the state increased, those percentages might surpass 50,000. This number would be prohibitive to ordinary citizen groups, Gates argued, while large corporations would find it relatively easy to finance signature campaigns. Consequently, the committee agreed that when 8 percent of the vote for governor reached 50,000, or when 5 percent of that vote reached 35,000, the requirement would be frozen.

The measure was then introduced into the legislature. After the bill had passed the Senate and was pending in the Assembly, Franklin Hichborn, legislative correspondent for the Sacramento *Bee,* had occasion to give it a careful reading. "To my astonishment," writes Hichborn, "I found that the 50,000 signature limitation for Initiative and 35,000 for Referendum had been omitted. . . ."[22] Hichborn felt that the measure should be amended in the Assembly to restore the limitation on signature requirements, and then be sent back to the Senate for concurrence. Others feared that such a move might endanger the entire direct legislation program and argued that an appropriate amendment could be made at a later date.

Such an amendment was never passed, however, and future difficulties became evident in 1914 when the vote for governor reached 926,689.[23] The signature requirement for initiative then became nearly 75,000 and for referendum more than 46,000. Hichborn concludes: ". . . Most of the evils that have developed in the use of direct legislation in California can be traced to the failure of the progressives to meet the signature issue squarely when the question was before them at the 1911 session." [24] Others would contend, however, that a high signature requirement prevents the ballot from being overloaded with a confusing multitude of initiative proposals.

In November, 1911, the initiative, referendum, and recall amendments were to be submitted to the electorate. In the months preceding the election, conservative newspapers in the state voiced their adamant disapproval of the measures. Warning fellow Californians of the dangerous results of such undermining of the republican form of government, they urged rejection of such "radical" proposals.[25] Hiram Johnson, determined that the measures should pass, embarked on a strenuous speaking campaign on their behalf. Largely as a result of his efforts, the constitutional proposals were approved and another of his campaign pledges was redeemed.

From organized labor's point of view the legislative session of 1911 was a remarkable one. The unprecedented number of bills enacted on behalf of the workingman (thirty-nine of the forty-nine advocated by labor spokesmen) reflected a new concern for the plight of urban workers. Representatives of labor were aggressive in their demands and the legislators were responsive to their needs. Such related problems as workmen's compensation, the limitation of working hours, child labor, and public employment exchanges were dealt with in a constructive fashion.

Until 1911 no attempt had been made to introduce a workmen's compensation law in California. As the state's economy became more industrialized, however, the use of new machines in manufacturing resulted in many serious accidents. Prior to 1907 California employers could draw from three common-law defenses in cases of employee injuries: (1) contributory negligence on the part of the employee, (2) negligence of a fellow employee (the fellow-servant rule), and (3) injury arising from the ordinary hazards of the occupation, if the employee had been aware of these hazards (the doctrine of risk). If the employer could prove one of these defenses, he was not liable for damages.[26]

In 1907 two limitations had been placed upon such common-law defenses: "the employer was made responsible for the negligence of a co-employee who had the right to direct the person injured," and "the fellow-servant ruling was no longer to apply to employees working in different departments, or on some other machine or appliance than that where the injured employee was working." [27]

During the session of 1909 four attempts had been made by organized labor to reduce further the employers' common-law defenses, but each of the bills had died in committee. In 1911, the State Federation of Labor endorsed a model Employers' Liability Act. Under pressure from labor unions and officials, both the Assembly and the Senate passed this workmen's compensation measure. Those California employees who did not wish to accept the voluntary compensation provisions of the act were still subject to the law of liability for damages resulting from negligence; however, the old common-law doctrine of risk and the fellow-servant rule were abolished. The doctrine of contributory negligence was also modified. The Industrial Accident Board was created to prepare more thorough legislation and to "provide professional, specialized, and coordinated leadership in the application of complicated legal rules." [28]

Labor unions in California had also fought many years for the limitation of hours during the working day. Moderate successes in the 1860's had been virtually wiped out by the depression of the 1870's, which resulted in heavy unemployment. The depression of 1893 again called attention to the need for legislation, yet it was not until

1901 that a bill to provide an eight-hour limitation on public works was passed.[29]

After the famous Lochner case in 1905, in which the United States Supreme Court refused to uphold a New York law limiting the hours of employment in bakeries and confectionery establishments on the grounds that it would violate the right to work, legislators were reluctant to impose an eight-hour limitation on women's labor. New impetus was given the maximum-hour legislation in 1908, however, when the Supreme Court in *Muller* v. *Oregon* upheld a ten-hour state law for women workers in factories and laundries.

At its annual convention in 1910, the State Federation of Labor, the state branch of the American Federation of Labor, pledged its support to an eight-hour bill for women. The eight-hour proposal had been made by W. A. Vanna, a delegate from the Los Angeles laundry workers' union. Vanna's proposal was supported by the Los Angeles Central Labor Council and the Building Trades Council, both of which sent telegrams urging southern California legislators to vote for the bill.[30]

Assemblyman Thomas F. Griffen, long an advocate of such reform, introduced the eight-hour bill in the 1911 legislative session. The Griffen bill passed the Assembly without a dissenting vote but met opposition in the Senate, where powerful farm interests, including packers and cannery owners, were able to have themselves exempted from the act. The Senate finally passed the bill thirty-four to five, and Governor Johnson subsequently signed it into law.[31]

In addition to the workmen's compensation act and the eight-hour law for women, the legislature of 1911 passed an act providing that no employer could withhold wages longer than fifteen days after they were due. The State Bureau of Labor Statistics assumed responsibility for enforcing the act. During its first year of operation the bureau was deluged with nearly 2,000 claims for wages, but managed to settle approximately 1,300 grievances involving $25,000 in due wages.[32]

Several other labor measures were approved, including restrictions on child labor, but two important bills failed to pass. The first of these was the Weinstock compulsory arbitration bill, which would have forbidden strikes against utilities and other public service corporations until after a thorough investigation of the unresolved issues by a state commission of inquiry. Organized labor objected to the settling of labor disputes by an outside official body and used its influence to defeat the measure. Another bill, which would have curbed the use of injunctions in labor disputes, passed the Senate, but died in the Assembly. This time it was the votes of southern California legislators which defeated the measure—reflecting the antiunion sentiment in the Los Angeles area. The defeat of the anti-injunction bill was organized labor's greatest disappointment of the 1911 session.[33]

Nevertheless, the legislative agent of the San Francisco Labor Council, John I. Nolan, was very pleased with the legislature's labor enactments and with Hiram Johnson's support of those measures. Commenting on Johnson's role, Nolan concluded:

> The present Governor of this State is entitled to and should receive the unanimous support, without any exception, of the entire labor movement of the State of California, and it is to be hoped that labor, when the time comes, will show that they appreciate the square deal accorded to them at the hands of Governor Johnson.[34]

Such impressive successes in the field of labor legislation were not matched in the area of conservation, however, as a conflict among the ranks of conservationists precluded effective action.

In his important book dealing with conservation, Samuel P. Hays has made it abundantly clear that the political implications of conservation in the early years of the twentieth century were subordinate to the scientific. Historians who have cast the struggle for the preservation of natural resources in terms of "the people" versus "the interests" have ignored the basically technical nature of resource management. They have ignored as well the absence of any real grass-roots protest against the encroachment of private interests on valuable land. The real issues were debated by hydrologists, foresters, and geologists, not by politicians.[35]

Nevertheless, politicians often find it convenient to draw battle lines between "good" and "evil," and drastically to oversimplify complex questions. Hiram Johnson was no exception to this general rule. As Elmo Richardson, an authority on the politics of conservation in the West, has pointed out, the "adoption of a federal policy for the conservation of natural resources was, by 1909, one of the most publicized results of the Progressive movement. . . ."[36] Johnson recognized the value of such a political plum. Given the desire to link his struggle "against the interests" to similar struggles being waged by progressives in the Midwest and East, it was natural that Johnson should inject the issue into the campaign of 1910.

Johnson's supporters invited Gifford Pinchot, who had been chief forester during Theodore Roosevelt's administration, to speak on behalf of their gubernatorial candidate. During the course of his visit to California in 1910, Pinchot praised Johnson and William Kent, progressive candidate for Congress, for their support of conservation measures. Johnson himself was not a crusading conservationist of the Pinchot variety, but he skillfully employed the symbols of the conservation controversy.[37] By aligning himself with Roosevelt and Pinchot against Taft's policies, Johnson clearly identified himself as an insurgent Republican.

Another of the many commissions established during Hiram Johnson's governorship was designed to deal with the problems of natural resources conservation—the Conservation Commission. Composed of three persons appointed by the governor to work without compensation, the commission received an appropriation of $100,000 for the purpose of hiring experts and assistants to conduct studies and prepare reports. Former Governor George Pardee was selected chairman, and Louis R. Glavis became the commission's secretary. Glavis had been an investigator in the General Land Office of the Department of Interior, under Secretary Richard A. Ballinger. There he had helped Gifford Pinchot expose Ballinger's alleged misdemeanors with respect to withdrawals of public land in Alaska.[38]

Ironically, within a year of his appointment to the California Conservation Commission, Glavis found himself accused of profiting from the sale of public lands to several lumber concerns. Glavis strongly defended his activities as legitimate, but to avoid a public scandal Johnson and Pardee requested his resignation. ". . . I could not see my way clear to tolerate in one of our people what we so loudly denounced in one of our opponents," a disappointed Johnson reported to Lissner.[39] Elmo Richardson, reflecting on the potential impact of Glavis's conduct on national conservation policy, comments: "It is interesting to speculate on the way in which conservation and the progressive revolt might have gone if Glavis's integrity had been similarly muddied two years before." [40]

It is not surprising that the session of 1911 did not produce any significant conservation legislation, for it would take time for the Conservation Commission to investigate the situation and make its recommendations. The commission's major accomplishment was to provide a background of information upon which future legislative sessions could draw.[41]

During the remainder of the Johnson administration, however, a conflict between the Conservation Commission and the state forester prevented the passage of much significant legislation.[42] The greatest success was in the field of water control and use; in 1913 the legislature preserved the state's water rights from encroachment by private interests by passing a law that provided for the establishment of a state agency to control and distribute California's water. Otherwise, except for laws regarding fire protection and reforestation of cutover lands, little was accomplished.[43]

The major conservation controversy of the Johnson administration involved the Hetch Hetchy project. In 1905 Chief Forester Pinchot had approved a project submitted by the city of San Francisco requesting permission to flood the beautiful Hetch Hetchy Valley in Yosemite National Park for use as a reservoir. A bitter controversy arose between those who believed in "conservation *for* use," as did Gifford Pinchot, and those who favored a more "aesthetic" concept. The most important member of the latter group, the "nature lovers," was the famous California naturalist and writer John Muir, an ardent supporter of conservation policies in forest and mountain areas, but an equally strong opponent of the utilitarian approach. Muir waged a nine-year battle against the Hetch Hetchy project.[44]

Despite Muir's efforts, in 1908 James R. Garfield, secretary of interior, granted San Francisco permission to use the valley for its water supply system. When William Howard Taft assumed office in 1909 he appointed Ballinger as the new secretary of interior. Ballinger, perhaps aware of the opportunity to oppose Pinchot's policies and yet still appear as the defender of strict conservation, displayed some sympathy for Muir's struggle; but while Muir received token support from Taft and Ballinger, the grant of 1908 was never revoked and the matter was left unresolved. Finally, in 1913 a bill was introduced by Representative John E. Raker of Alturas calling for the confirmation of the Hetch Hetchy grant. Muir then enlisted the aid of Robert Underwood Johnson, conservationist and editor of *Century Magazine* in New York. Johnson spearheaded the fight in the East against the Hetch Hetchy project and sought to influence members of the United States Senate to oppose the bill [45]; however, Pinchot's and Garfield's utilitarian interpretation of conservation policy predominated in the Senate. "The apostles of the gospel of efficiency subordinated the aesthetic to the utilitarian," writes Samuel Hays. "Preservation of natural scenery and historic sites, in their scheme of things, remained subordinate to increasing industrial productivity. . . ."[46]

John Muir's long campaign against the Hetch Hetchy project and Robert Underwood Johnson's letter-writing to various United States senators were of no avail, as the Senate subsequently approved the bill confirming the grant of 1908. It is significant that Muir was unable to enlist the support of Hiram Johnson in his cause. Although references in Johnson's correspondence to conservation matters are rare, it is unlikely that the governor had much sympathy for Muir's aesthetic approach to the preservation of natural resources. Pinchot's concept of "conservation *for* use" most likely seemed to Johnson the more sensible approach, and he never came to Muir's defense.

Regulation of public morals also received the careful attention of the 1911 legislature. The Anti-Racetrack Gambling Act had been passed in 1909, but had been rendered ineffective by the courts of the state. In 1911, therefore, a remedial law was passed, designed to correct the defective features of the 1909 act, and race-track gambling in California remained outlawed for more than twenty years. In addition, a measure to abolish slot machines easily passed both houses.

Of all legislation relating to public morals, it was the prohibition problem, however, that aroused the most interest. The drive for prohibition was a significant factor in the California Progressive movement, as it had been in virtually every major reform movement in the state's history; but despite the vigorous efforts of the Southern California Anti-Saloon League, by 1911 the temperance forces had been fought to a standstill by the well-organized "wets." It was during the Johnson administration that the temperance people won their most impressive victories; by 1916 there were three and one-half times as many dry towns and cities in California as there had been in 1910.[47]

Although the Anti-Saloon League found little sympathy for prohibition among northern progressives, it was able to gain their support for more limited temperance measures, particularly local option. The league was able to accomplish this goal by singling out the saloon, rather than liquor itself, as the major evil.[48] Even "wet" progressives who were by no means prohibitionists, like Hichborn, McClatchy, and Rowell, found themselves in agreement with the Anti-Saloon League on the question of the connection between organized vice and the saloons; and Hiram Johnson had gained the Anti-Saloon League's support in 1910 by promising to fight for a local-option measure if elected.[49]

Daniel Gandier's local-option measure, as originally introduced in 1911, provided that people of any county outside the jurisdiction of cities and towns could compel the board of supervisors, by means of initiative procedures, to hold a special election that would decide whether saloons could be licensed in that area. After some revision, which substituted the supervisorial unit for the county unit as the basis for local option, it passed the legislature and was approved by Johnson. The immediate effects of the new law were remarkable, and "no-saloon" areas spread across the state. Gilman Ostrander informs us that by 1912 one-fifth of the supervisorial districts of northern California's forty-eight counties had gone dry. This figure rose to one-half within two years after the law went into effect. In addition, about 400 incorporated and unincorporated towns had outlawed the sale of liquor in saloons.[50]

The Anti-Saloon League did not immediately press for prohibition, realizing that such a move was premature and would only antagonize those who were not prohibitionists. Instead, it deferred further action until the local-option law had gained acceptance by the majority of California's citizens. The league could now devote its energies to the extension of dry areas throughout the state.

The Stetson-Eshleman railroad bill; the Public Utilities Act; the reorganization of the Railroad Commission; the Board of Control; nonpartisan election measures; a woman suffrage amendment; the preferential vote for United States senators; adoption of the initiative, referendum, and recall; a workmen's compensation act; an eight-hour law for women; the establishment of the Conservation Commission; and a local-option law—these were the major accomplishments of the legislature of 1911.

A more sophisticated society might question the value of an antiracetrack gambling law, the abolition of slot machines, or a local-option measure; but to reformers of an earlier era, this was progress. This penchant for probity, this moral absolutism, was part and parcel of the progressive mind. Had such legislation constituted the main thrust of progressive activities in California, the entire movement could be dismissed as feeble indeed. But there was more, much more. In a face-to-face confrontation with the major problem of the day—railroad domination of state politics—progressives in 1911 capitalized on previous reform efforts and on aroused public opinion to achieve success. Never again was the railroad so politically powerful. The astounding record of the legislature of 1911 in this and other areas attracted national attention and praise. Hiram Johnson, the "aggressive advocate," the western prototype of Theodore Roosevelt, was suddenly thrust into a predominant position among progressives throughout the country.

# 4

## THE "BULL MOOSE" CAMPAIGN

After Hiram Johnson was elected governor of their state, California progressives became anxious to find another Republican who could replace President Taft in 1912. Taft, personally selected by Roosevelt to carry on in the progressive tradition, had failed to achieve the pending shift in party control from the Old Guard to the insurgents. By finally aligning himself with the reactionaries he had alienated progressives across the nation.[1]

Like most progressives, those in California were astonished by Taft's desertion of the insurgents on the tariff question and were outraged when he signed the Payne-Aldrich tariff bill of 1909.[2] Taft was further discredited in the eyes of California's progressives when, in the Alaskan lands controversy of 1910, he supported his secretary of the interior, Richard A. Ballinger, rather than Gifford Pinchot, leader of the anti-Ballinger forces and a man of immense popularity in California.

Moreover, Taft's visit to California in October, 1911,

had convinced progressive leaders that he would be an impossible candidate. Johnson reported to Roosevelt that "every man who thinks or believes in political righteousness in the state was elbowed aside" during the President's trip.[3] In addition to their disappointment with Taft's performance as President, California progressive leaders feared that the stature of regular Republicans in the state would be enhanced by Taft's renomination.

Roosevelt had been their choice to replace Taft, but his attempt to fuse the progressive and conservative wings of the Republican party after his return from Africa in 1910 had disappointed them. Momentarily cheered by his "New Nationalism" speech at Osawatomie, Kansas, California progressives were dismayed by his persistent denials that he would be a candidate in 1912.

With Roosevelt out of the running by his own choice, many California progressives, identifying themselves with the insurgent-progressive bloc in the national Congress, began to line up behind "Fighting Bob" La Follette. In late November, 1911, more than 600 men and women met at San Francisco's Palace Hotel to launch the La Follette League, the purpose of which was to insure an overwhelming vote for the Wisconsin senator in the coming presidential preference primary. Elected temporary chairman of this league, Chester Rowell declared: "This movement, to restore the government to the people, . . . must be nationwide, and the way to succeed is to stand for La Follette for President." [4]

When the National Progressive Republican League was formed at the Wisconsin home of Senator La Follette in January, 1912, many Californians, including Hiram Johnson and Francis Heney, were among its charter members. The ostensible purpose of this league was to spread progressive doctrine throughout the nation, but its real purpose was to nominate and elect a progressive Republican President in 1912.

## The "Bull Moose" Campaign 59

Early in 1912, bored with private life, prodded by friends, Roosevelt began to change his mind about a presidential candidacy. George Mowry believes a crucial factor in this change of attitude was that "his irritation with Taft, which had been almost continual since 1909, had broken all bounds with the institution of the steel suit [against United States Steel Corporation]. . . ."[5] John Morton Blum adds two other Taft policies that especially aroused Roosevelt:

> . . . The treaties of arbitration which the President negotiated violated Roosevelt's conception of the proper bases for the conduct of foreign policy; the President's administration of Alaskan public lands reversed . . . Roosevelt's program for the conservation and use of natural resources. . . .[6]

It was not surprising that Roosevelt should consult Hiram Johnson, with whom he had formed a personal friendship and whose progressive record in California he had followed closely.[7] On January 14, he asked Johnson to come East and "consult on the political situation." Johnson accepted with alacrity, but before he entrained for Oyster Bay he met with two of his closest friends, Chester Rowell and Meyer Lissner. They discussed means of persuading Roosevelt to seek the presidential nomination, and their firm decision was to wait until Roosevelt had clearly established his intentions before formally declaring themselves for La Follette.[8]

Johnson lunched with Roosevelt on February 2 and afterward wired California that Roosevelt would definitely run. That evening, worried about his daughter's serious illness and close to the point of physical collapse, La Follette delivered a rambling and confused speech in Philadelphia. The next morning the nation's papers reported his "breakdown." This unfortunate incident was a blessing for those who had pledged themselves to La Follette but who had since transferred their allegiance to

Roosevelt, for the Wisconsin reformer's candidacy was subsequently withdrawn.[9]

While Johnson was consulting with Roosevelt at Oyster Bay, Edwin Earl, owner of the Los Angeles *Express,* was launching a drive to make Johnson the vice-presidential nominee of the Republican party in 1912. Earl directed Edward Dickson, then his Washington correspondent, to obtain publicity for the governor. Dickson was to seek the support of nationally prominent men, such as Gifford Pinchot, Mark Sullivan, and Medill McCormick. With this groundwork prepared, Earl later informed Roosevelt that a Roosevelt-Johnson ticket, with a campaign slogan of "Hands Across the Continent," would be unbeatable.[10]

Progressive Republican newspapers and periodicals throughout California joined in Earl's crusade. The *California Outlook,* unofficial voice of progressivism in the state, placed Roosevelt's and Johnson's pictures on the covers of its February 24 and March 2 issues. California progressive leaders also carried on their campaign for Johnson outside the state. Fellow progressives in Oregon, Washington, Arizona, New Mexico, and Nevada were urged to advance Johnson's candidacy in their respective states. Editorials were sent to eastern newspapers and were published with favorable comment. Dickson's contacts with Washington correspondents proved helpful, as many agreed to support a Roosevelt-Johnson ticket.[11]

On March 11, in Los Angeles, Hiram Johnson opened the California campaign for Theodore Roosevelt. Not even a heavy downpour that day could dissuade hundreds of Roosevelt admirers from attending the governor's address. In typical fashion, before a packed house, Johnson proclaimed that "this battle is the age-long battle of privilege against common welfare." After acknowledging Roosevelt's devotion to the common good, and after stressing his own administration's impressive reform record, Johnson added:

"Remember, it is a cause that is at stake. It is a great movement that is in the balance. . . ."[12]

Emboldened by the successes of his first year in office, a confident Hiram Johnson was pleased by the prospects of the Colonel's campaign in California. It would give him a superb opportunity to link the victories of his administration with those of Roosevelt while President. And his advocacy of Theodore Roosevelt could not help but strengthen his own political position within the state.

Roosevelt did not come to California during the primary campaign but sent letters to Johnson for publication in the press. Johnson himself carried on a whirlwind statewide speaking tour on Roosevelt's behalf, and was joined in early May by Gifford Pinchot and Senator Albert Beveridge of Indiana. Their efforts paid dividends. In the state's first presidential preference primary of May 14, 1912, and the first California election at which women could vote, Roosevelt showed great strength, polling double the votes received by Taft and more votes than Taft and La Follette combined.

To express his gratitude to Johnson, Roosevelt asked the governor to make the first speech seconding his nomination at the Republican convention to be held the next month in Chicago. Nor did Johnson's effective advocacy of Roosevelt go unnoticed in the nation's press; he continued to be promoted for the vice-presidential nomination in many editorials. The *Times* of Washington, D.C., for example, came out strongly for him:

> Geography no longer counts in determining the availability of a candidate. The only questions worth discussing relate to personal fitness and proved worth. In these respects, no name that may be placed before the Republican national convention can eclipse that of California's Governor.[13]

Hopes for a Roosevelt nomination at the Republican convention waned, however, as it became apparent that the Taft forces would dominate the delegates. Johnson could smell trouble brewing, and his last telegram to Lissner before departing for the convention contained this prophetic statement: "I THINK WE MAY PRESIDE AT THE HISTORIC BIRTH OF THE PROGRESSIVE PARTY." [14]

Colonel Roosevelt had decided to attend the Republican convention at Chicago in 1912, thereby breaking the precedent that a presidential candidate did not show his face at a convention until after nomination. Heightening the jubilee atmosphere, this announcement provoked the distribution of 100,000 handbills declaring that Roosevelt would walk on the waters of Lake Michigan at 7:30 Monday evening. The streets were packed when he arrived, and the police had to clear a path to his hotel.[15]

Bitter disagreement between the contending factions had developed well before the convention began. One area of dissension involved the California delegates. The Republican National Committee, headed by two conservatives, William Barnes of New York and Senator Boies Penrose of Pennsylvania, awarded two of California's delegates to Taft, despite the overwhelming Roosevelt victory in the state. Francis J. Heney immediately objected to this "steam-roller" tactic, and the battle was on.

Another major dispute occurred over the convention's temporary roll call, prepared by the National Committee. The California delegation favored rejecting it altogether. Johnson, who had already proposed a walkout on the old party, announced in a speech: "No porch-climbing political burglars in the national committee can establish regularity for the rank and file of our party. . . ." [16] During the first day he led the Roosevelt men out of the convention hall in protest over the unfavorable decision rendered by the Taft majority on the selection of a temporary chairman. The next day the volatile governor led the Californians out for the final time. Johnson's bold actions at the Republican convention thus paved the way for the founding of the Progressive party.[17]

As soon as it became clear that enough delegates would be seated to ensure his defeat, Roosevelt gathered his lieutenants together for a strategy meeting at the Congress Hotel. There he received assurance of financial support from Frank Munsey, the millionaire newspaper and magazine editor, and from George Perkins, an associate of J. P. Morgan and the holder of large blocks of stock in the United States Steel Corporation and the International Harvester Company. In the early morning hours of June 20, 1912, after a thorough discussion of the pros and cons, a major decision was made—Roosevelt would run on a national Progressive party ticket.

The next day the Republicans nominated Taft. Nearly 350 delegates, however, had not voted for him; those delegates were in Orchestra Hall listening enthusiastically to Hiram Johnson sound the initial charge for the new Progressive party:

> We came to carry out . . . not the will of a rotten boss in Pennsylvania or a crooked one in New York, . . . but to carry out the mandate of the people to nominate Theodore Roosevelt. By a fraudulent vote he has been robbed of what was his. We propose that Mr. Roosevelt, having won his fight, shall have his reward.[18]

Roosevelt then announced that he would accept the nomination of the party if it were offered by a traditional presidential convention. Accordingly, the first Progressive convention was scheduled for that August in Chicago. Meanwhile, Hiram Johnson was named chairman of a temporary committee to manage the new party until convention time.

As William Henry Harbaugh has pointed out, the Progressive party convention of August "was destined to prove a failure of politics and a triumph of ideals. The practical politicians upon whom success depended were notable for their absence. . . ." [19] Nevertheless, if many regulars deserted Roosevelt, scores of volunteers, having apotheosized their leader, came forth to carry on the fight. Determined and militant delegates streamed into Chicago from every part of the country, eager to nominate their hero and then to work feverishly for his election.

Senator Albert Beveridge's keynote address, bristling with the most advanced progressive ideas, opened the convention. The next day Theodore Roosevelt delivered what he called a "Confession of Faith," which amounted to an attack on the traditional two-party system in America and a call for radical reform. Frequent bursts of applause and a thunderous roar of approval at the conclusion of the speech indicated that he had voiced the wishes of the majority of delegates. Although a serious conflict broke out over the contents of the extremely bold platform, in its final form it closely followed Roosevelt's recommendations in his "Confession of Faith." [20]

The only remaining business was the formal nomination of the party's presidential and vice-presidential candidates. On August 7 Senator Beveridge announced that Roosevelt and Hiram Johnson had been chosen to lead the battle against Taft and the Democratic nominee, Woodrow Wilson. The long campaign of Edwin Earl and other California progressives to put Johnson on the national ticket had succeeded. In his acceptance speech the vice-presidential nominee declared: "I would rather go down to defeat with Theodore Roosevelt than go to victory with any other Presidential candidate." [21]

The secession of the Progressives, combined with Roosevelt's immense popularity, ruined Taft's chances for reelection. Consequently, Roosevelt and Johnson were excoriated in the standpat newspapers. "Worse than Aaron Burr" and "a Benedict Arnold" were typical of the editorial diatribes hurled at the Progressive "outcasts and traitors."

A major decision faced California progressive leaders after the formation of the new national party: whether to maintain control of the existing Republican machine in the state or to organize a new Progressive party. It seemed to some that because there was a new national party there should also be a new state party. But important political considerations could not be ignored. In late July, Johnson wrote a confidential letter to Meyer Lissner, his closest friend in southern California. A careful examination of California's election laws, Johnson reported, had revealed that if a new party were formed, its candidates would have to run independently, as would a prohibitionist or any other splinter party nominee. Johnson sensed defeat if Progressives ran with these independent candidates against Democrats and Republicans. The situation looked very bad to him.[22]

After much soul-searching, expediency finally triumphed. Progressive leaders decided to remain Republicans within the state, while joining the national Progressive party. The election laws of California provided that men nominated for presidential electors were to be selected at party conventions composed of all nominees for state offices. Thus, all the progressives had to do in order to retain their control of the state Republican party was to nominate at the September Republican primary a majority of assemblymen and senators pledged to name Roosevelt electors.

Understandably, "regular" Republicans raised a great commotion about this and described the progressives' strategy as "bald-faced robbery and sheer dishonesty." The Old Guard demanded that Lissner resign as chairman of the Republican State Committee and ordered progressives to leave the party. To their cries of rage and anguish Lissner responded with the impudent suggestion that the impending primary provided them the opportunity to regain control.

Because the Old Guard no longer had any power within

the state organization, the outcome of the primaries could easily have been foretold. Of the one-hundred legislators nominated, at least eighty pledged themselves to vote for Roosevelt electors. After failing to obtain a writ of mandamus from the state Supreme Court to compel the listing of Taft electors on the ballot, the regular Republicans gave up. They even declined to make use of the right of petition, which might have succeeded. Thus, Californians wishing to vote for Taft in 1912 had to write his name on the ballot. Johnson publicly justified the situation with an explanation of dubious logic:

> ... Neither morally nor equitably is Taft the nominee of the Republican party. ... The Republican party of California is progressive and in this state the party was redeemed and made respectable by progressives. ... It has therefore been determined that those candidates for the legislature in the Republican party who are progressive shall agree, if they are successful, to nominate candidates for Presidential electors who will vote for Roosevelt. ... [23]

George Mowry tells us: "To all intents and purposes the Republican party had removed itself from the 1912 California elections." [24] It would appear, however, that the progressives had given it a mighty shove. They had exacted revenge for their harsh treatment at the national Republican convention in June.

The campaign of 1912 was an exciting affair. Although somewhat subdued in comparison with his earlier days, Roosevelt was still a vigorous candidate. Not even a bullet fired at his chest during a campaign trip to Milwaukee could keep him off the election trail; he insisted upon delivering his address as scheduled. Nor was Johnson a less vigorous campaigner. In August he left California for a highly successful, ten-week, cross-country tour, during which time he delivered 500 speeches in twenty-two states.

During Johnson's absence Roosevelt visited California and criticized Woodrow Wilson's proposals as constituting a return to an outmoded Jeffersonian laissez-faire. "His theory was a theory which if ever applicable was applicable to some primitive community at the end of the eighteenth century," explained the Progressive presidential candidate. "It is one inapplicable to the United States in the beginning of the twentieth century. . . ."[25] Roosevelt argued that only by recognizing the inevitability of consolidation in big business, and by expanding the powers of the central government to regulate big business, could the social and economic evils of the day be resolved.

Just as there was sharp ideological disagreement among Progressives regarding popular democracy and direct legislation, so too were there differences of opinion over the trust issue and the desirability of consolidation in big business. Roosevelt had recognized this dichotomy in the basic economic program of progressivism as early as 1911, and at that time had lamented:

> Half of [the progressives] are really representative of a kind of rural toryism, which wishes to attempt the impossible task of returning to the economic conditions that obtained sixty years ago. The other half wishes to go forward along the proper lines, that is, to recognize the inevitableness and the necessity of combinations in business, and meet it by a corresponding increase in governmental power over big business; but at the same time these real progressives are hampered by being obliged continually to pay lip loyalty to their colleagues, who, at bottom, are not progressive at all, but retrogressive.[26]

Certainly there were many California progressives who *were* representative of that "retrogressive rural toryism" which Roosevelt had earlier criticized. Yet the presidential candidate was well aware that the Johnson administration, in strengthening the Railroad Commission and creating a Board of Control, had made practical application of New Nationalism's demand for government control over large, efficient, corporate enterprise. Indeed, there were some California progressives who enthusiastically shared Roosevelt's attitude toward the trusts. Senator John D. Works, for example, was quoted as saying: "It is not the size of the business or the fact of the combination that is wrong and constitutes a crime, but the kind of business, or the use that is made of it, or the nature of the combination or power that is wielded as a result of it." Works favored "effective regulation" rather than "ineffective prohibition." [27] Fremont Older, in several editorials in the *Bulletin*, commented favorably on Roosevelt's solution to the trust problem.[28] Charles Dwight Willard, as well, wrote that "the whole tendency of the organizing of business for efficiency is toward combination and co-operation. To ignore that fact is to fly in the face of our country's advancement." [29]

It is not surprising that Californians, including Hiram Johnson, were much more concerned about the farmer and about agrarian problems than was Roosevelt, whose philosophy of government was essentially urban in its appeal. Furthermore, the Colonel's New Nationalistic disdain for direct-democracy measures was not shared by most California progressives. Yet Mowry may be overstating the case when he contends that Roosevelt "was supported in the West not because of his New Nationalism but in spite of it." [30] It appears that Roosevelt's economic views, at least, may have been more commonly held in California than has been recognized.

Although Roosevelt received more votes than Taft in 1912 (a remarkable showing considering the traditional plight of third parties in United States history), his party carried only Pennsylvania, Michigan, Minnesota, South Dakota, Washington, and California. Wilson won in a landslide, receiving 435 electoral votes. The Democrats also captured both houses of Congress. Within California,

The "Bull Moose" Campaign 69

Wilson carried San Francisco by more than 10,000 votes, but was narrowly defeated in the state by the large Roosevelt-Johnson returns from Los Angeles.

John Morton Blum has written that the Progressive party was "a politician's Gothic horror." Its ranks were filled primarily with disgruntled Republicans, reformers, men of wealth who shared Roosevelt's attitude on consolidation of big business, and a few professional politicians. "It was a party," Blum continues,

> with only three assets, all transitory: enthusiasm, money, and a Presidential candidate. The enthusiasm and the money vanished with defeat. The candidate understood political organization too well to expect a group of ardent amateurs—even wealthy amateurs—running an incomplete ticket, to provide the stuff of victory in 1912 or continuity thereafter. . . .[31]

However, Johnson's ability to carry California for the Progressives greatly impressed American political leaders. Roosevelt recognized this ability, and commented to a friend: "Try to keep in touch with Hiram Johnson, for of all public men in this country, he is the one with whom I find myself in most complete sympathy. You are perfectly safe to follow his lead."[32] Roosevelt's admiration was fully reciprocated by Johnson.

Outmaneuvered by Johnson and the progressive organization, the regular Republicans in the state became more openly hostile after the election. They demanded insistently that the progressives leave the party or renounce their national Progressive affiliations. Perhaps Johnson and his followers could no longer honestly call themselves Republicans; but practical politics required that they remain Republicans within the state or jeopardize their success in California. Consequently, the regulars' demands were ignored.

# 5

## ACCEPTANCE AND REJECTION IN 1913

Having devoted most of their energies to the national campaign in 1912, Hiram Johnson and his advisers turned their complete attention the following year to state matters. Originally their reform goals had been three: "turn out the railroad villains," "purify" the administration of governmental affairs, and "democratize" the political system. Such a general program had offended few people and had received enthusiastic endorsement by a large majority of the state's citizens. In fact, the great strength of the reform movement of 1910–1911 was due to the relatively uncontroversial nature of its "ideology" and to its consequent broad appeal.[1]

Yet even before the end of the legislative session of 1911 Arthur J. Pillsbury, an editor of the *California Outlook* who was later appointed to Johnson's new Industrial Accident Commission, had counseled caution. Writing under the byline "The Watchman," he had advised the Johnson administration and the reform forces in the legislature to be careful not to "outrun the consensus of opinion of the people of California and so induce revulsion of feeling. . . ."[2] Even Chester Rowell, for many years in the vanguard of the California Progressive movement, had written, late in that memorable year, that the Public Utilities Act completed the reform program of the Lincoln-Roosevelt Republican League.[3]

After the political catharsis of the Bull Moose campaign, many progressives had simply had enough of reform. The pledges of the 1910 campaign had been fulfilled: the Southern Pacific had been kicked out of politics, the people had been given additional power through direct-legislation measures, and state agencies had been fumigated by the Board of Control. Was there more to be done? Could more be asked of them?

Before the legislature of 1913 convened, therefore, it had become quite clear that the basic unity characterizing the California Progressive movement in the earlier years no longer existed. Conflict was inevitable between those legislators who felt reform had gone far enough and those who recognized the necessity for additional legislation. Johnson's opening address to the session seemed designed to pacify the former element, as he requested only two specific measures: higher corporate taxes and the creation of an administrative board that would manage all state institutions and would have powers commensurate with the financial jurisdiction of the Board of Control. If Johnson did not publicly urge the 1913 legislature to enact sweeping reforms, and if he had no well-formulated legislative program of his own, it is, however, to his credit that he supported and helped push through the legislature many progressive measures advocated by various pressure groups and influential citizens.

The session of 1913, though less memorable than that of 1911, considered and passed a significant body of legislation. Among the most important was the establishment of three new state agencies—the Industrial Welfare Commission, the Industrial Accident Commission, the Commission of Immigration and Housing—and the passage of the Alien Land Law.

The growing number of unskilled workers in California after 1900 had made it difficult for labor unions to maintain even the minimum wage levels of the national average. Several pressure groups, including the California Consumer's League and the California Federation of Women's Clubs, attempted to persuade the legislature to assume responsibility for maintaining wage standards.

Leader in this fight was Mrs. Katherine Philips Edson, head of the California Federation of Women's Clubs and prominent suffragette and reformer from Los Angeles. Daughter of an Ohio politician, she and her husband had moved to Los Angeles in 1899. There she was active in civic affairs, and during the next ten years enlisted in numerous reform causes, including pure milk laws, charter revision, and woman suffrage. In 1912 she was appointed special agent for the Bureau of Labor Statistics in southern California—the same year Massachusetts enacted the country's first minimum-wage law. With the Massachusetts experience in mind, Mrs. Edson began her own campaign for a similar measure in California.[4]

The San Francisco Labor Council, and the organized labor movement generally, opposed Mrs. Edson's campaign and condemned the idea of fixing a minimum or a maximum wage for either men or women by legislative enactment. The Labor Council specifically feared that a law would later be passed compelling workers to receive the minimum wage as a maximum wage. The Labor Council further argued that the standard fixed by law would be lower than that of the unions and would thereby undermine union scales. Furthermore, labor was concerned that there would be no incentive for women to join unions if a minimum wage were set for them.[5]

To counter the arguments of organized labor, Mrs. Edson consulted Florence Kelley, a prominent national leader of the minimum-wage movement. From her Mrs. Edson received advice, pamphlets, statistics, and encouragement. Governor Johnson promised his support. In May, 1913, the state Senate, by a vote of twenty-six to eight, endorsed the Assembly's approval of a minimum-wage statute.

The legislators also established the Industrial Welfare Commission, composed of five members, one of whom was to be a woman. The members were to be appointed by the governor for four-year terms and were given broad powers to investigate wages, hours, and working conditions of women and children in California. To ensure compliance with the law, the bill included a provision making it a misdemeanor for any employer to refuse to obey the commission's orders.[6] Selected by Governor Johnson as the woman member, Mrs. Edson served for seventeen years, during which she dominated the Industrial Welfare Commission and more than anyone else made it a powerful force in the economic and social life of the state.[7]

The first task, according to the commission's first biennial report, was to "ascertain the wages paid, the hours and conditions of labor and employment in the various occupations, trades and industries in which women and minors are employed in the State of California, and to make investigations into the comfort, health, safety and welfare of such women and minors." [8] Investigators were immediately sent out to gather information. Conferences were held with representatives from various industries in order to gain their cooperation. The budgets of working women throughout the state were carefully examined by the commissioners, who paid particular attention to the costs of food, housing, and clothing. Mrs. Edson then correlated this data for use by the commissioners. Her findings revealed that the minimum standard of living for a single woman was approximately $500 a year, or nearly $10 a week. A special study of laundries made in 1913 revealed that more than half the women of the state engaged in that occupation were earning less than the minimum standard as determined by Mrs. Edson.[9]

Throughout the period of Johnson's governorship, the Industrial Welfare Commission examined labor conditions in the garment, laundry, and canning industries. In 1916 a modest minimum-wage rate of sixteen cents an hour was set for women working in the canning industry, which was the largest employer of women in the state. Action was also taken to eliminate sweatshop conditions in manufacturing concerns.[10] In 1918 there were in operation nine orders of the Industrial Welfare Commission: eight established minimum wages for the major industries employing women, and one prescribed sanitary working conditions. The minimum wage for these industries was set at $10 a week.[11] By 1920, 50 percent of women workers in California were receiving more than the minimum standard-of-living wage. While these accomplishments were less than many progressives hoped for, in Mrs. Edson's opinion the commission had done an excellent job, justifying her efforts and her belief in its possibilities.[12]

The creation of the Industrial Accident Board has been discussed above.[13] This board's function was to collect and disseminate information about the workmen's compensation act passed in 1911. As they became more and more acquainted with the subject, however, members of the board were convinced that existing compensation insurance facilities were inadequate and that the state should administer an insurance program. Revising a successful New Zealand law to fit California circumstances, the members prepared a bill entitled "The Workmen's Compensation, Insurance, and Safety Act."

It was to be expected that private industrial accident insurance companies should oppose such legislation; however, with the backing of most of the state's labor unions, Johnson was able to secure the bill's passage. Charles McConaughey, legislative agent for the San Francisco Labor Council, reported that the act was "one of the greatest victories that labor has ever attained at the hands of any Legislature. . . ."[14] Paul Scharrenberg, secretary of the California State Federation of Labor, hailed it as "the greatest achievement of the fortieth session" and added: "[Governor Johnson's] uncompromising attitude for an effective Workmen's Compensation Act . . . should ever endear him to the men and women of labor."[15]

The act of 1913 created the Industrial Accident Commission, which had four major functions: (1) to administer and enforce the Workmen's Compensation Act of 1911, (2) to administer the state insurance fund, (3) to promote safety in industry, and (4) to collect and publish statistics relating to industrial accidents.[16] Commissioners A. J. Pillsbury, Will J. French, and Harris Weinstock divided the commission into four separate departments: the Medical Department, the Permanent Disability Department, the Compensation Department, and the Department of Insurance. Such rationalization of administrative functions simplified the execution of compensation laws, drastically reduced court costs, and shortened the time required for consideration of cases.[17]

The program proved to be a great success, reducing by one-third the employers' compensation insurance costs and providing fair treatment for injured employees. In addition, because of lower overhead costs, an average of 15 percent of the yearly premium was refunded to policyholders at the end of each operating year. At the same time, the State Compensation Insurance Fund, while charging the same rates as private liability insurance companies, made substantial amounts of money. These profits were invested in municipal, state, and liberty bonds. So successful was this voluntary insurance program, in fact, that by 1919 the state of California was handling about 40 percent of the compensation insurance policies.[18]

California's agricultural system, always dependent upon a large, mobile supply of cheap labor, attracted thousands of unskilled aliens to the state and dictated the substandard living conditions of a large part of this population. Chinese, Japanese, Mexicans, and native migrants followed the harvests, living in camps or "jungles." Inadequate housing conditions and poor sanitary facilities resulted in sporadic uprisings in California's "factories in the fields," such as the famous Wheatland hop fields riot of 1913.[19] In addition, thousands of immigrants from southern and eastern Europe flocked to California, lured by the advertised promise of wealth, health, and happiness. Once there, however, they often found that for the immigrant the Golden State was a kind of hell. For them life was dismal; they were underfed, underpaid, exploited, ignorant of the language and of their rights under American law. Many returned to their native lands, but many stayed, hoping for a better future.

These aliens, whether living with their families in rural labor camps or in urban slums, constituted a serious challenge to an administration concerned with social amelioration. The Johnson administration accepted the challenge, and a liberal reformer named Simon Lubin provided the main thrust. The result was the creation of the third, and perhaps the most important of the social welfare agencies —the Commission of Immigration and Housing. Launching a program of immigrant assimilation unparalleled in the United States at the time, this agency was a pioneer in immigrant housing and education, and in labor camp inspection.

"To Simon Lubin more than any man," writes Samuel E. Wood, a specialist on problems created by immigration, "must be credited the creation of the Commission of Immigration and Housing. He insisted upon an independent agency, invested with powers adequate to cope with the complexity of the immigration problem in this state. . . ."[20] Lubin selected the personnel of the commission, and as its president was instrumental in determining the policy and charting the activities of the agency for ten years.

Simon Lubin, born in Sacramento in 1876, was the son of David Lubin and the nephew of Harris Weinstock, both prosperous Sacramento merchants and crusaders for industrial and agrarian reform.[21] Educated at Harvard, Simon Lubin spent his college vacations working in the Lower East Side of New York. From 1903 to 1904 he was a resident of South End House, a Boston social settlement. During his last two years at Harvard he made special investigations of immigrant problems in New York and Boston. In 1906 he returned to California. From then until his death in 1936 he was secretary and manager of Weinstock, Lubin, and Company of Sacramento. The employee-employer relationships of this company were characterized by advanced schemes of management-employee representation, credit unionism, and retirement systems. Much of California's social legislation during this period was drafted by Lubin at his desk in the company offices.[22]

Lubin's first conversation with Governor Johnson regarding a state program directed at the immigrant problem was just prior to the Bull Moose convention in 1912. Johnson discussed Lubin's suggestions with "some of those in whom I have confidence" during the convention and after his return to California.[23] The social worker–businessman continued to urge immediate action and finally prevailed upon Johnson to appoint a special committee that would submit a report to the next session of the legislature. On August 21, 1912, Lubin received his appointment to this committee. At the same time, Johnson wrote

Lubin his own personal thoughts on planning for the future. "My hope," explained the governor,

> is that by timely action on our part, even if the immigration diverted to us by the opening of the Panama Canal shall be as great as that which in recent years has come to the Atlantic Coast, we may prevent the dreadful conditions of poverty that prevail in the great cities there. . . .[24]

The temporary agency recommended legislation to create a permanent commission rather than attempting to strengthen existing state agencies. Lubin prepared a rough draft of an act creating an unpaid commission of industries and labor consisting of five members appointed by the governor. This commission was to direct and supervise a bureau of industry and immigration and appoint all its employees.[25]

Lubin met with Johnson in late November, 1912, after which he reported to a fellow committeeman that he was sure the governor had "caught the spirit of the act." Johnson liked the idea of an unpaid commission that would determine policy and hire paid experts to administer the program. He advised Lubin to prepare a memorandum for the Board of Control, explaining the organization and proposed expenditures of the commission. In this memorandum Lubin recommended an appropriation of $50,000 a year to support the commission.[26]

While Governor Johnson officially sponsored the measure and chose specific legislators to lead the fight in the Senate and Assembly, he left the mobilization of pressure and the handling of the opposition to Lubin and his fellow committeemen. During the spring of 1913 Lubin remained in Sacramento to press for the passage of his bill. He arranged for witnesses to appear at committee hearings. He convinced C. K. McClatchy to wage an editorial battle for the bill in the Sacramento *Bee*. He prepared articles for newspapers and saw to it that letters were written to key legislators.[27] The legislature, responding favorably to this, and other, pressure, passed the measure (which included a $50,000 appropriation for the gathering of information and data) and sent it to the governor in June.[28] Members of the new Commission of Immigration and Housing were well aware of the general conditions under which aliens lived in California; but they lacked factual data upon which to base a specific remedial program. The first order of business, therefore, was to employ housing experts and special investigators to make field surveys. Between April 1 and August 11, 1914, 641 labor camps in every county of the state, housing more than 41,000 laborers, were inspected. Of the total number, 188 were found to be in dangerous sanitary condition, and only 195 met the modest minimum sanitation standards established by the commission. Rapid improvements were made, however, so that by 1915 Austin Lewis, the attorney for the workers who organized the strike at the Durst hop-ranch in Wheatland, could report:

> With regard to the actual cleaning up of hop camps and construction camps, the change has been so great in the state of California, as to be almost revolutionary. Where formerly places were filthy in the extreme, and the livers in them were subjected to all manners of risky infection and the like, as well as the unmentionable results of crowding both sexes indiscriminately in vile and unsanitary surroundings, the camps have now been transformed into decent places. . . .[29]

In addition to labor camps, the commission's experts investigated lodging houses and tenements in the larger cities, into which were packed newly arrived Spanish, Mexican, Portuguese, and Italian families. These various surveys resulted in thirty-five special reports, three of which were eventually published.[30]

The commission's *Report on Unemployment*, published in December, 1914, called for the creation of a state bureau of labor exchanges with branch offices in major cities. It urged the passage of adequate camp sanitation laws and a complete revision of the state's housing laws. It also recommended legislation to prevent and punish fraud and misrepresentation in the sale of agricultural land. Governor Johnson was very enthusiastic about this report, and Lubin described the governor's reactions in a letter to Mrs. Frank Gibson, a fellow commissioner:

> In all my contact with the Governor I never saw him so enthusiastic. He asked a great many questions, and then began to give again his opinion of the value of our work in the state, saying that he thought the real fruits of our efforts would not be seen until most of us had passed away. . . . He said that we could expect his cooperation at every stage of the game, and that he wants us to know that he is in entire sympathy with all we are trying to do.[31]

It was not until 1915 that the legislature authorized the Bureau of Labor Statistics to establish free employment bureaus in specific cities; passed the Labor Camp Act requiring proper bedding, bathing, and eating facilities in all labor camps; and created the State Colonization and Rural Credits Committee.[32] Nevertheless, a substantial beginning was made during the years 1913–1914 to ameliorate the conditions under which immigrants in California were forced to live. Californians had invited the world to share the blessings of their state. The least the legislature could do was to ensure that those blessings could be enjoyed by all who accepted that invitation.

It may seem strange that an administration so concerned about the plight of the immigrant would at the same time support legislation designed to restrict the activities of a large number of the state's alien population, the Orientals. Yet twice within a period of seven years, Californians, by their actions against the Japanese, embarrassed the national government and involved it in international difficulties.

There had been no significant anti-Japanese legislation passed in California prior to 1913, but there had been a long struggle for Japanese exclusion.[33] While most California exclusionists eventually opposed all immigrants except those from northern Europe, they pressed initially for Japanese exclusion only. Anti-Japanese feeling in the state increased after the turn of the century. In 1900, James D. Phelan, then mayor of San Francisco, had declared to a number of labor groups gathered to protest further Japanese immigration:

> The Japanese are starting the same tide of immigration which we thought we had checked twenty years ago. . . . The Chinese and the Japanese are not bona fide citizens. They are not the stuff of which American citizens are made. . . . Personally we have nothing against the Japanese, but as they will not assimilate with us and their social life is so different from ours, let them keep at a respectable distance.[34]

It is significant that Phelan, who played a major role in the anti-Japanese movement until his death in 1930, was a progressive Democrat and a man of strong reform sympathies.[35] Even Chester Rowell, an extremely broad-minded individual on most issues and later an intellectual exponent of California progressivism, had early expressed his opinion on the Japanese question. Rowell editorialized: ". . . Japanese coolie immigration is of the most undesirable class possible, and we are quite right in objecting to it and in demanding that something be done about it. . . ."[36]

After the Chinese Exclusion Act was renewed in 1902, anti-Oriental agitation in California subsided for several years. The Russo-Japanese war of 1905 caused great concern, however, as many feared a "stream of Japanese immigration" once the war with Russia was over. Although no significant anti-Japanese legislation was introduced at the 1905 session, such bills were presented to the legislature periodically for the next forty years.

Until 1906 the anti-Japanese movement in California had attracted little attention outside the state. In 1905, however, two events occurred which focused the national spotlight on California. First, on May 14, 1905, the Asiatic Exclusion League was formed in San Francisco—the first organization in the state which held as its sole purpose the exclusion of Japanese. Secondly, the San Francisco school board announced its intention eventually to segregate Japanese pupils so that American students would not suffer from such "harmful association." In October, 1906, the Board of Education, under pressure from the Asiatic Exclusion League, made its decision to segregate Japanese and Korean students from American.

Although the Board of Education's segregation order was never enforced, the Japanese government immediately protested this action. President Roosevelt sent Secretary of Commerce and Labor Victor H. Metcalf to investigate. Californians expected Metcalf, a former Republican congressman from Oakland, to see things their way. Metcalf's report to President Roosevelt surprised them; it stated that Japanese residents deserved "the fullest protection and the highest considerations."

The legislature of 1907, succumbing to Roosevelt's pressure and to his promise of relief through a "Gentlemen's Agreement" with Japan, adjourned without passing an anti-Japanese measure. Under the terms of the Gentlemen's Agreement, skilled and unskilled Japanese laborers, except those who had formerly been residents of the United States or were relatives of residents, were not granted passports by the Japanese government. This agreement permanently decreased Japanese immigration, but it did not completely satisfy West Coast exclusionists.

So long as the Japanese remained wage laborers, agitation against them came largely from nonfarm groups that feared competition from "cheap labor." Farmer-employers, on the other hand, welcomed this source of mobile, cheap labor. As one Fresno fruit grower explained in January, 1907: ". . . we are wholly dependent upon [Japanese] labor. If they are excluded, we shall have to give up our farms and go out of business. . . ."[37]

A shift of Japanese population from urban to rural areas after 1908, however, increased anti-Japanese feeling in those districts, especially in the Central Valley. The Japanese began to acquire land and to employ as workers members of their own race exclusively, thereby reducing the farm-labor pool. As Japanese landowners began to monopolize such cheap farm labor, they incurred the animus of large growers, who had previously favored the presence of Orientals. Smaller growers were also aroused. The Japanese were no longer merely a convenient source of manpower, but had gradually become active competitors for farm labor, farmland, and agricultural markets.[38]

Yet in 1909 there were still approximately 30,000 Japanese agricultural laborers in California. They were employed chiefly during cultivation and harvest, but were far more difficult to manage than the Chinese had been. Their characteristic independence was bemoaned by large growers, one of whom expressed his dismay in this manner:

> The Chinese when they were here were ideal. They were patient, plodding, and uncomplaining in the performance of the most menial service. They submitted to anything, never violating a contract. The exclusion acts drove them out. The Japanese now coming are a tricky and cunning lot, who break contracts and become quite independent. . . . One trick is to contract work at a certain price and then in the rush of harvest, threaten to strike unless wages are raised.[39]

These feelings of irritation at the continued threat to the existence of large units of production and dismay at the decrease in the supply of cheap, manageable labor were manifested in increased anti-Japanese activity in the California legislature. When such economic pressures were merged with latent social and racial hostility, the issue was sure to become of prime political importance.

Five discriminatory measures were introduced in the 1909 session, including an alien land act, a school segregation bill, and a municipal segregation ordinance; but none was passed. Again President Roosevelt intervened successfully to block all anti-Japanese legislation. Additionally, the Los Angeles and San Francisco chambers of commerce petitioned the legislature not to pass these measures because the "Oriental trade passing through the ports of this State has assumed large proportions and is likely to be seriously crippled by such proposed action." [40] The Merchants' Association of San Francisco also protested the passage of the measures, stating that "they will put a restriction upon the development of the resources of California. . . ." [41]

During the 1910 campaign, Democrats monopolized the anti-Oriental issue. Hiram Johnson decided not to take a public stand on the question and turned down invitations to speak to the Asiatic Exclusion League; but he did assure A. E. Yoell, the league's secretary, that he favored exclusion.[42] Once elected, however, Johnson informed Philander Knox, President Taft's secretary of state, that he would do everything he could to prevent the passage of anti-Oriental legislation in 1911. Johnson successfully bottled up such legislation in committee and no measures passed.[43]

In 1913, California business leaders in charge of organizing the Panama-Pacific International Exposition, to be held in 1915 to celebrate the opening of the Panama Canal, worked to quash further discriminatory legislation for fear it might impair trade and business relations with Japan and China. Chester Rowell, a member of the exposition's advisory council, explained to Johnson in January, 1913, that the Japanese Diet was about to convene and would be debating its proposed budget. Included in that budget was an appropriation of some $1,500,000 for the exposition. Rowell and his fellow commissioners feared that if that item were defeated or slashed, it might seriously harm the exposition. Johnson was urged to press for postponement of anti-Oriental legislation. "There is no immediate urgency in passing the bill at all," Rowell declared. "The law must be passed ultimately, if California is not to be Hawaiianized, but there is no emergency so long as Japan continues in good faith to carry out the present arrangement. . . ."[44]

Johnson, in turn, suggested that a committee from the exposition come to Sacramento and address a conference of the legislators. The commissioners were initially reluctant, fearing that such action might overdramatize the issue and provoke adverse reaction.[45] Eventually they agreed to accept the governor's suggestion, however, and met with him prior to the opening of the legislative session. Johnson assured the nine-man delegation that he would support their efforts to head off an alien land act. The delegation then met individually with nearly every senator and assemblyman in an effort to quash any legislation dealing with aliens.

Their efforts were in vain, for when the session opened anti-Japanese measures were submitted by Democrats and Republicans in both houses. Johnson later explained to Theodore Roosevelt that the exposition officials might have succeeded in their task had not many legislators, up to that time uncommitted, been persuaded by the impressive testimony of farmers from various communities in the state. "These farmers insisted that an alien land bill was absolutely essential for their protection, and necessary for the future welfare of California," Johnson reported.[46]

Perhaps as important as the farmers' testimony was the challenge presented to Hiram Johnson and California politicians by the federal government's intervention in

April, 1913. For Johnson, this intervention was a major event, marking "the breaking down of the barrier that has heretofore existed between the national government and legislation in the states. . . ."[47] After Woodrow Wilson had taken office, Johnson informed Chester Rowell of his suspicions that such pressure would be exerted to block discriminatory legislation.[48] Much to Johnson's surprise, however, Wilson did not immediately intervene to thwart anti-Oriental measures. In fact, the President even encouraged Democratic politicians in California to continue their course: ". . . I have never been inclined to criticize," Wilson wrote James D. Phelan. "I have only hoped that the doing of the thing might be so modulated and managed as to offend the susceptibilities of a friendly nation as little as possible."[49]

Rather than intervene directly in California's affairs, Wilson chose to express his point of view to Representative William Kent, a progressive from northern California. During an interview held the first week of April, 1913, Wilson suggested to Kent that California legislators might frame their bill in less offensive form by excluding from landownership those persons who had not applied for American citizenship, without singling out the Japanese. Kent relayed this suggestion to Hiram Johnson, and the doughty governor replied that Wilson should communicate with him directly if he had anything to propose.[50]

Diplomatic historian Thomas A. Bailey has surmised that Wilson would not have intervened further in the California situation had not the Japanese held a mass protest meeting in Tokyo in mid-April, 1913.[51] Arthur Link, the Wilson biographer, also mentions this outburst and the consequent necessity for action in the face of a possible break in relations between Japan and the United States. Link stresses, however, Wilson's belief in states' rights and his reluctance to use federal coercion.[52]

The President's dilemma was temporarily resolved when

Johnson agreed to his request that Secretary of State William Jennings Bryan consult with the California governor; but Bryan's mission was hopeless from the beginning, for the California legislature was more than ever determined to pass an anti-alien measure. On April 21, a few days prior to Bryan's arrival, the state Senate amended the pending bill to permit European corporations to own land, while denying the same privilege to Oriental corporations and individuals. By the time Bryan arrived in Sacramento, substantial progress had been made in preparing the bill for passage.

Secretary of State Bryan was given the use of the lieutenant governor's office during his stay in Sacramento. During a period of one week he summoned various senators and assemblymen for personal interviews, discussing with them the diplomatic consequences of anti-Oriental legislation and urging them to reconsider their views. He also met with the legislators in a remarkable closed executive session, but his overtures were completely disregarded. In early May the alien land bill passed the Senate by a vote of 35 to 2 and the Assembly 72 to 5.[53] Setting maximum terms of three years for leases of agricultural land to Japanese, the law barred further land purchases by aliens ineligible for citizenship. Aliens eligible for citizenship, on the other hand, could own property without limitation.

Johnson promised Bryan that he would not sign the bill until the Secretary had conferred with President Wilson. On May 11, 1913, Bryan sent Johnson a telegram suggesting that the bill be vetoed. In his lengthy reply, Johnson clearly stated California's position, stressing the fact that, in his opinion, the federal government had established the precedent for Oriental discrimination. It was California, not the Oriental, which was being discriminated against. Accordingly, on May 19, 1913, Johnson signed the bill.[54]

The Asiatic Exclusion League immediately announced

that it intended to invoke direct legislation against the Alien Land Act and to substitute a law prohibiting Japanese from either owning or leasing any land in California. Despite some dissatisfaction with the bill, however, most Californians seemed to feel that the problem of Orientals had been laid to rest. As a result, there was very little anti-Japanese agitation for the remainder of Johnson's tenure in office. (Johnson himself prevented the passage of a stricter alien land law introduced in 1915.) [55]

What role did Hiram Johnson play in the passage of the Alien Land Act of 1913? What beliefs and political calculations motivated him? In late March of 1913 he had assured the Panama-Pacific Exposition delegation that he would support their efforts to head off the alien land bill. Yet Roger Daniels, author of a detailed study of the movement for Japanese exclusion in California, reports: ". . . it is now quite clear that from the middle of March Johnson was the behind-the-scenes manager of the alien land bill. . . ." [56] In support of this statement Daniels cites a telegram of March 23 from Johnson to Rowell: "HAVE INFORMED [Assemblyman E. S.] BIRDSALL [sponsor of a general antialien bill] THAT HE MAY ACT IF HE DESIRES." [57] What caused Johnson to so instruct Birdsall? What prompted him to renege on his promise to the Panama-Pacific Exposition delegation? Daniels does not discuss the reasons for Johnson's switch from opposition to support for the bill, but several may be advanced.

Johnson obviously enjoyed his skirmish with the federal government, although he admitted afterward that he had never "skated on thinner ice than . . . in the contest with Mr. Bryan. . . ." [58] Writing to Theodore Roosevelt, Johnson exulted: ". . . we have shown the Democratic doctrine of 'State's rights' to be sham and pretense, insisted upon when it is their state that is affected but denied when they represent the federal government and our State is affected." [59] In waging a victorious battle against the federal government on behalf of "State's rights," Johnson not only succeeded in embarrassing the Wilson administration but also in attracting national publicity.

It is also probable that Johnson saw the handwriting on the wall: If the legislature was bound and determined to pass the alien land law, why should he risk his political neck to fight for its defeat? What must be stressed is Johnson's belief that passage of the bill was essential for his own political survival. In a particularly revealing letter to Meyer Lissner, Johnson commented on recent progressive defections:

> ... You can not make people be good faster than they want to be good. ... Communities will stand just so much reform legislation at one time, and wise is the man who intuitively has some conception of just how far he can go. ... Indeed, our legislation had brought us to the very verge of disaster. ... The alien land bill rehabilitated us north of Tehachapi; but aside from the right of the alien land bill, its necessity etc., it was the most fortunate thing that ever occurred from a political standpoint. ...[60]

Anti-Oriental legislation thus became the means by which Johnson could regain the esteem he felt had been lost by his support of "excessively radical" legislation. Such demagoguery was not uncharacteristic of Johnson, but the fact that he was willing to involve the United States government in international difficulties mainly to enhance his own political position was unusually irresponsible. Daniels has pointed out that Johnson's support of the alien land bill was particularly wanton because he "knew well that Japanese land tenure in California would not be seriously affected by it. ..."[61] As Californians quickly discovered, the Alien Land Act was rendered ineffective when the Japanese continued to buy and lease land in the names of their children who were American citizens. Orientals also formed corporations and bought or leased land in the corporate name, after issuing a majority of the capital stock to American citizens, who served as trustees. In 1920 a new land law remedied these "defects": Japanese were thereafter prohibited from buying or selling land in the names of their children or through the medium of corporations.[62]

While it was possible to evade the law, it must not be assumed that Japanese farmers were not seriously affected by the Alien Land Act. Occasionally the Japanese would win their court cases and be impoverished in the process. The antialien laws made landownership uncertain and subject to the whims of politicians and district attorneys.[63] Progressives of both major parties were responsible for this unfortunate affront to the dignity of the Japanese people. Ostensibly dedicated to the principles of democracy, yet blinded by racial prejudice, these "reformers" were so influenced by unfounded fears of Oriental inundation that they participated in an essentially undemocratic act.

Despite the reluctance of many progressive legislators to proceed farther along the reform path, the 1913 legislature established an impressive record, marred only by the Alien Land Act. Social welfare legislation set the pattern for the session, and individuals such as Katherine Edson, Harris Weinstock, and Simon Lubin provided the main impetus for the passage of these measures. Characteristic of the California progressives' "scientific" approach to social and economic problems was the creation of numerous commissions: the Industrial Welfare Commission, the Industrial Accident Commission, and the Commission of Immigration and Housing. Their reliance upon scientific evidence and expert testimony is nowhere better illustrated than by the activities of these various agencies— hiring investigators to collect data on wages and working conditions, collecting and publishing statistics relating to industrial accidents, employing housing experts to make field surveys.[64]

## Acceptance and Rejection in 1913

When discussing social welfare legislation of the Johnson administration it is possible to confuse accomplishment and aspiration. It is true, for example, that Simon Lubin's Commission of Immigration and Housing, like many other commissions of that day, lacked power to accomplish sweeping reforms. Nevertheless, by first spotlighting the migratory labor problem in California that agency expressed a deep concern for the plight of the immigrant, especially the immigrant of European stock. It is unfortunate, though perfectly in character, that the progressives' concern was not coupled with a sympathy for the aspirations of nonwhite aliens.

# 6

## MUTINY AND PARTY DISCORD

Like an unseasonable snowfall on a spring day, the national Progressive party quickly melted away after the brief election flurry of 1912. When Frank Munsey, the millionaire newspaper and magazine publisher, deserted the camp, there seemed little hope left for the party's continued existence. California progressive leaders debated whether it would ever be worthwhile to leave their secure political position to embark upon the unknown seas of national Progressive politics.

Efficient and astute Meyer Lissner was the most determined to break away from the California Republican party.[1] Johnson and Rowell also wanted to organize a new party. Dickson and Stimson, on the other hand, were not so adventurous. Additionally, a majority of important state leaders and almost all of their friends in the state legislature were against any radical departure. "I find three classes of people among our supporters," an annoyed Johnson wrote:

First, the tread-softly, pussy-footed politicians who want to retain their "Party regularity" and who in the past couple of years in our state have been progressives from necessity, and not from conviction. Secondly, those good, but timid, people who want to maintain an anchor to windward politically, and shrink at the public break from the Republican Party; and thirdly, those who conscientiously believe they have some duty or obligation because they ran as Republicans and were elected as Republicans to continue as such until the close of the session. . . .[2]

Despite Dickson's and Stimson's conservative belief that progressives in California should retain control of the Republican party for at least another year "to see which way the cat jumped," the ultimate decision was left to Johnson; he joined the radicals, Lissner and Rowell. To become Progressives in the state as well as in the nation, he believed, was the only consistent course they could take. "The longer we continue as Republicans," Johnson explained to Lissner, "the more difficult it will be to make the break and the greater prestige we add to the old name."[3] Accordingly, the progressive-dominated Republican State Central Committee disbanded on December 5, 1913. On the following day, in San Francisco, the California Progressive party was formed.

United States Senator John D. Works, for one, objected to this course of action. Writing to a friend in Fresno he declared: ". . . We have been deserted by our former friends who have gone into the Progressive party. . . ." Like Dickson and Stimson, Works contended that progressive Republicans had gained complete control of the party in California and in several other states. He believed that by 1916 they would control it as a national party. "This accomplishment was destroyed," Works continued, "and the prospect of future conquest lost by Progressive Republicans going off into a new party. . . ."[4] He later wrote Rudolph Spreckels that progressives within the Republican party must prevent that party from being carried back to the "old standpat Republicanism."[5]

California conservatives lost no time in attempting to recoup their lost power in state politics. During the latter part of 1913 regular Republicans began to reorganize their wing of the party. The Republican State Central Committee, established by a minority group of Taft Republicans in 1912, still existed. It was reorganized by the Republican National Committee as the official party organization in California, even though it had not been legally appointed according to the state's laws. In late November, 1913, conservative Republicans gathered in San Francisco to discuss ways of breathing new life into their party. Leadership of the resurrected Republican party was assumed by three young men: Philip Stanton, a Republican National Committeeman; Gustav Grenner, chairman of the Republican State Central Committee; and Francis V. Keesling, newly elected vice-president of the Republican State Central Committee. With renewed vigor and high hopes these men selected a committee to launch a reorganization and recruiting drive in the counties and precincts.[6] Conservative Republicans retained control of the party in California from late 1913 until a few months before the end of the fateful Hughes campaign of 1916.

The California Progressive party had a most difficult time during 1914 and 1915. By the end of 1913 substantial unemployment in San Francisco and many other parts of the state had aroused considerable concern. One estimate placed the number of unemployed somewhere between 20,000 and 25,000 during the winter of 1913–1914. More than 1,000 of these unemployed persons paraded in front of Governor Johnson's San Francisco home on New Year's Day, 1914.[7] So concerned was Johnson about the problem of unemployment that he instructed John P. McLaughlin, commissioner of the Bureau of Labor Statistics, to make a study of the situation. McLaughlin's report concluded that migratory workers from other states, seeking the warm winter climate of California, had swelled the number of unemployed. He foresaw no change in the situation until the spring season, when new jobs would be available.[8]

In addition to a seasonal industrial depression within the state, and the tensions that existed between labor and capital, Hiram Johnson was finding it increasingly difficult to remain the sole leader of his faction. In the northern part of the state, outside Johnson's own immediate circle of supporters, the strongest elements of the party gathered around Francis Heney, wealthy Congressman William Kent, and Fremont Older.[9] The relationship between Johnson and Heney, never very amicable, grew worse after 1913. William Kent, in turn, was annoyed with Johnson because the governor had not intervened when the boundaries of Kent's congressional district were changed in 1911. Moreover, he had given Kent little support for his renomination in 1912 and in 1913 had disagreed with Kent over the issue of anti-Oriental legislation. Older was disappointed in Johnson for not urging more significant labor legislation and for not supporting him in his campaign to get Abraham Ruef released from prison.[10]

Writing to Theodore Roosevelt in August, 1914, Johnson expressed his exasperation with Older and his disgust with those who would challenge his leadership:

> ... [Older] has gone so far that he has made a God of Haywood and the McNamaras and others of this sort, and he cannot understand why I stop short with sane legislation such as Child Labor Laws, an Eight Hour Day for Women, Workmen's Compensation, and the like. He wants me to abolish all Prisons, free all convicts, and incarcerate society alone. ... These gentlemen would have driven me upon the rocks long ago, and because I would not wreck the whole Progressive cause by going to extremes no sane man could justify, their ardor for

Progressivism has cooled, and while still they claim to be with me, their advocacy this year is wholly perfunctory.[11]

In southern California, relations between party leaders were even worse than in the north. Ever since Johnson had been elected governor, Lissner had "represented" him in Los Angeles, and along with Rowell had dominated the state party machinery. Dickson and Edwin Earl, publisher of the Los Angeles *Express*, resented this; they accused Johnson of ruining the party's prestige in the southern part of the state. Lissner and Earl were not on friendly terms. Earl was annoyed with Lissner, Stimson, and Russ Avery for not conferring with him before they organized a municipal conference in the spring of 1913 to heal a rift sequently reproached by Rowell.[12] Lissner and Dickson eventually managed to patch up their personal squabble, but were never again really close friends. There was no reconciliation between Earl and Lissner, nor between Earl and Rowell. The self-important Earl was also at odds with Johnson. Their relationship finally came to a break in 1916 when, according to Lissner, Johnson refused to "flop over in praise of the Earl papers" in his campaign speeches.[13] It is apparent that after 1913 the progressive machine was no longer functioning so smoothly.

In addition to their personal grievances with the testy, difficult Johnson, ambitious progressive leaders must have found his dictatorial control hard to endure. Throughout his life, according to George Mowry, Johnson had been unable to play a coordinate, much less a subordinate, role among reformers. Earl published a lengthy diatribe against the three progressive leaders in his *Express*, and was sub- in anything:

> Whether as prosecutor, governor, or senator, he had to stalk the center of the stage. If he could not be the hero of a piece, he seemed compelled to be the hero's chief antagonist. . . . All through his progressive years he

was apparently determined to be "The Boss," the number one man in California. Whoever threatened that position was likely to incur his wrath. . . .[14]

And anyone who felt the lash of Johnson's temper could never forget it. Nor did Johnson forget him. Some years later, Senator William Borah of Idaho (who backed Johnson for President in 1920) confirmed this conclusion. Borah was quoted as saying of the then United States senator:

> The difference between Johnson and me is that I regard questions from the point of view of principles while he regards them from the point of view of personalities. When a man opposes me I do not become angry at him. On the next issue he may agree with me. When a man opposes Johnson he hates him. He feels that the opposition is directed personally against him, not against the policy that separates them.[15]

Chester Rowell once commented upon Johnson's inability to consider the abstract merits of a proposition, apart from the persons involved. According to Rowell, once Johnson had made up his mind about a matter in which he was very knowledgeable he could be swerved by no one. In other matters he sought the judgment of whatever expert possessed his personal confidence. Advising Katherine Edson on how to interest the governor in one of her ideas, Rowell wrote that "the thing to do is to get him interested in the persons involved, or in the personal results which will come from these measures. If you try to make an abstract argument on the merits of the measure itself, he will be merely amused at your thinking. . . ."[16]

Robert Glass Cleland, another historian of California, has also concluded that those who crossed Johnson "later found that it was safer to trust a broken reed than to rely on Johnson's loyalty and good faith, for the man's self-interest was too highly developed to leave much room for gratitude."[17] If Mowry, Cleland, and Borah have been rather harsh in their appraisals of Johnson's character and personality, others have come to his defense. In February, 1953, after reading Mowry's *The California Progressives,* Edgar A. Luce, a prominent San Diego attorney, wrote Mowry a long, critical letter. Luce explained that in 1907 he had helped organize a Lincoln-Roosevelt league in San Diego which was instrumental in overthrowing the machine in that city. Luce later worked in Johnson's 1910 campaign, became the governor's close friend, and was elected a state senator in 1914. In challenging Mowry's and Cleland's estimates of Johnson, Luce wrote:

> The charges seem to have been made by Professor Cleland and by yourself that Johnson was disloyal to his friends and supporters. I believe that I knew him very intimately, as I have said, and I found him to be very warm-hearted, appreciative, and extremely loyal to his friends and supporters. . . . I do not believe a greater libel could be printed than to say that Hiram Johnson was disloyal. . . .

In Luce's opinion, Mowry and Cleland relied too heavily upon personal interviews with Edward Dickson, who "was so bitter that he planned little tricks to embarrass Johnson at his meetings and other places when Johnson was on his campaigns. . . ." Admitting that Johnson, like "any intense fighter," was "emotional, temperamental, sensitive, and quick-tempered," Luce pointed out that he always had a large group of loyal and steadfast friends who supported him.[18]

Others interviewed in recent years who were progressives and close friends of Johnson have corroborated Luce's testimony.[19] The evidence is therefore conflicting, as it is bound to be where the judgment of a man's personality and character is concerned. It is clear that Johnson made strong friends and enemies, engendered deep loyalties and bitter hatreds. If he was emotional and sensitive, he was also courageous and incorruptible. If he was temperamental, he was also public-spirited. If most of the reform legislation during his administration was conceived by others, he was highly successful in pushing through the legislature those bills he felt would serve the general welfare and at the same time enhance his own political position. Conversely, Johnson was more than anything conscious of public opinion, and no measure that failed to gauge correctly that opinion received his support. Publicly, he was an idealistic crusader who viewed issues in terms of good versus evil; privately, he was a politician of consummate skill who was constantly manipulating the chessboard of politics so as to counter in advance any move he regarded undesirable.

The struggle for Progressive leadership came near to open rebellion when in the mid-summer of 1913 Heney talked with Johnson, indicating that he planned to run for either senator or governor in 1914. He did imply, however, that he would not oppose Johnson in either race. Johnson obviously did not want him to run at all, and when Heney asked for the governor's advice, Johnson refused to commit himself. Heney waited several months for Johnson's advice, which was not forthcoming, and then formally announced his candidacy for United States senator without again consulting the governor. This action infuriated Johnson, as did the support Heney received from such old associates as Earl, Dickson, Stimson, Older, C. K. McClatchy, and former Governor George Pardee. In Johnson's mind, such support bordered on political, and therefore personal, treachery.

Meanwhile, the irate governor, whose very leadership of the party was in jeopardy, began planning a political counterattack. To head off the Heney candidacy, Johnson threatened to run against him for the Senate. Employing a tactic that must have outraged Johnson, Heney announced that if Johnson did so he would then run for governor.

This "either-or" declaration produced the final split. Johnson would probably have preferred to run for the Senate, and he certainly felt a great resentment against the men who had launched the Heney movement. Considering Johnson's sensitive and suspicious nature, it is obvious that he thought they were trying to unseat him and make Heney the central figure in the California Progressive movement.[20]

How could Johnson prevent mutiny? How could he remain in command and avoid the intrusion of a second commander? First, he encouraged Rowell to run against Heney in order to "meet the one candidate movement" and to make "it known that the field is open." Rowell balked. He did not want to enter the race, and wrote Johnson and Lissner that he would do so only if they considered it a "serious party emergency." [21] Some of Heney's enemies, including Johnson's personal secretary and campaign manager, Al McCabe, joined in persuading the reluctant journalist. Rowell was finally convinced that the situation was perilous and entered the race to save the day for Hiram Johnson and the California Progressive party.

The strategy failed miserably. In spite of the support of the Johnson faction, Rowell was easily defeated by Heney for the Progressive nomination. This was due in large part to Rowell's phlegmatic campaign and to the fact that his heart simply was not in the fight.[22] Yet it also seems that insurgency within the Progressive party in California was more widespread than Johnson had anticipated.

The situation was serious. The failure of Rowell's candidacy had discredited Johnson, and Heney's impressive success had increased his own stature in the party. It was now up to the governor himself to reassert his leadership, and the gubernatorial campaign of 1914 gave him his opportunity. As his running mate, Johnson selected one of the most popular and capable of all California Progressives, Railroad Commissioner John Eshleman. Repeating his tactic of 1910, when he had broken from the Lincoln-Roosevelt League to set up his own campaign organization, Johnson now organized numerous independent, nonpartisan Johnson-Eshleman clubs. When Heney vigorously protested this action, fearing that the Progressive organization would be greatly weakened by the departure of the Johnson forces, the governor explained: "Neither of us can win with the Progressive vote alone. Each of us, to be successful, must have Democrats, Republicans, and others. . . ." Johnson assured Heney that there was no intention on his part to eliminate the Progressive organization or to hamper it in making the fight for all the Progressive candidates.[23] More candidly, however, he informed Lissner: ". . . I propose to conduct my campaign as I see fit. I know that it is necessary for my success to break down partisan lines in the state, and that non-partisan organizations in my behalf can contribute greatly to that result." [24]

This time Johnson's strategy was successful. Despite the revolt within party ranks, there was no doubt that he remained immensely popular with the electorate. Running for reelection as a Progressive, he won an overwhelming victory, the first governor in more than forty years to succeed himself. Alas, poor Heney, running for the United States Senate on the same ticket, lost to James D. Phelan, a Democrat from San Francisco.

After comparing his own senatorial returns in the general election with Johnson's gubernatorial margin of 190,000 votes, Heney protested that he was a victim of an understanding between Johnson and Phelan. He angrily charged that Progressive support was given to the latter in return for Democratic money and support for the former.[25] Evidence supporting this "knifing" charge was Heney's defeat in San Francisco and Johnson's large majority in that city. Insinuations were made by Heney and his supporters, but they were never substantiated. After all, once before when he had run for district attorney of San Francisco, Heney had been defeated; he was not very popular there. Furthermore, even though Johnson *was* popular in the Bay City, he had been unable to swing its predominately Democratic votes to Roosevelt in 1912.

Two scholars who have studied this election, George Mowry and Robert Hennings, have acquitted Johnson of making a trade with Phelan or with San Francisco labor. Both admit, however, that Johnson and many of his followers were hostile to Heney; and Hennings does suggest that some covert agreements were made between the Johnson and Phelan forces at the lower organizational levels. Hennings analyzes the situation in this manner:

> . . . Whether or not anything really came of these talks is unknown; nor is it known whether or not Johnson was aware of their existence; but in Phelan's files are two letters which show that Phelan at least knew that such plans were afoot. In both cases Phelan supporters around Sacramento were hoping to make mutual aid pacts with local Johnson men. . . .[26]

There is another relevant letter, mentioned neither by Mowry nor Hennings. It indicates the thoughts that had once run through the minds of Johnson and Rowell. On December 18, 1913, Rowell had written Johnson, expressing concern that Heney might be elected United States senator. Rowell offered the following plan:

> If we run Eshleman against Heney for Governor we have thereby staked our all on that contest and cannot afford to risk anything less than one hundred per cent certainty, which is, of course, unattainable. On the other hand, if Heney were to run for senator, even without opposition, he could easily be isolated during the campaign, so that the rest of us would have no responsibility for him, and his victory at the primaries, and either his probable defeat or his possible victory at the polls, would leave the California situation no worse than it is now. . . .[27]

Johnson's probable guilt, as charged by Heney, is less important than the fact that the simmering politics of California were not cooled by the 1914 elections. It is interesting to note that the charge of betrayal in 1914 by members of Johnson's own party was the same one that would be made two years later by the conservative supporters of Charles Evans Hughes.

Although Johnson had achieved an important personal victory, Heney's defeat by a Democrat was a most damaging blow to Progressive prestige. And there were other indications that the Progressive machine was faltering. Johnson had won easily, but many of the party's candidates for minor state offices were not so fortunate. The electorate also turned down by referendum a statewide eight-hour law and a minimum-wage law for women and children.

The fall and winter of 1914 were gloomy for Hiram Johnson. It seemed that the national reform movement was losing impetus. It was clear to him now that the California Progressives' decision to create their own party instead of retaining their control over the Republican organization had been ill-timed, for all across the nation there was a noticeable movement of Progressive "prodigal sons" returning to the Republican house.

# 7

# THE DECLINING YEARS

Sensing the temper of the times, Hiram Johnson delivered a moderate inaugural address in January, 1915. The governor placed major emphasis on past performance, not future reform. After proudly listing an impressive number of accomplishments achieved during his first term of office, he declared that it was not his purpose at that time to set forth any definite program. Johnson shared the attitude of a majority of members of the 1915 legislature, described by the *California Outlook* as being influenced strongly "by the nationwide impression that there has been enough, if not too much, legislation in recent years. . . . The present desire . . . is to take time to digest and assimilate the new laws now on our statute books." [1] The number of bills introduced in both houses during the first session, smaller by 1,000 than in 1913, reflected this attitude as well as anything could.

The failure of orthodox Republicans and Democrats to develop an effective anti-Johnson bloc before the opening of the legislative session left Johnson in absolute control of the legislature. He had a clear working majority in the state Senate on the basis of Progressive senators alone, and C. C. Young, candidate of the administration forces, was elected overwhelmingly as speaker of the Assembly. In the Assembly, members of all parties joined in a nonpartisan coalition, which gave Johnson mastery of that body. The Sacramento *Bee*'s account of the opening session summarized the situation: "The key-note to the action of the Legislature will be the Governor. Pretty much what he wishes done will be done, and little that he doesn't want done will be accomplished." [2]

Administration forces in the legislature centered their efforts upon bills to establish a system of rural credits, designed to give the farmer the same access to credit that the average businessman enjoyed. While many believed the social ills of California were rooted in the state's agricultural pattern, characterized by large holdings of land farmed by wage laborers or held out of use for speculative purposes, little had been accomplished in the way of concrete legislation to remedy the situation. In 1914 the Commission of Immigration and Housing had recommended the creation of a state land bureau that would publish information for prospective purchasers of agricultural land, but nothing further had been done.

During the legislative recess of February, 1915, a committee appointed by Governor Johnson began a thorough study of land colonization and rural credits. Members of the committee were Harris Weinstock, Chester Rowell, and David Barrows of the University of California. Weinstock was perhaps best qualified of the three to recommend such legislation. Concerned and involved with agricultural problems for many years, and motivated by a belief that the small landowning farmer was a basic element of democracy, he had been appointed by Governor Johnson in 1913 to the American Commission on Credit and Co-operation. This federal commission, an inspiration of David Lubin, was composed of seventy agricultural experts from the United States and Canada and was organized to study European achievements in cooperative marketing and related matters. According to Grace Larsen, a specialist on agricultural economics, the information gathered by that commission "helped shape future rural credits legislation, including the Federal Farm Loan Act of 1916." [3]

When appointing his committee to study the problem of rural credits, Johnson had given the members explicit directions that no plan involving a large expenditure of money would be advisable.[4] Owing to this budgetary restriction, Weinstock, Rowell, and Barrows decided it would be impossible to do anything during that legislative session, other than to make specific recommendations that would pave the way for future legislation.

The committee approached the problem from two directions, land colonization and the actual financing of existing farmers. Weinstock explained that his proposed system of land colonization would make it possible for the "fit farm laborer or the farm tenant to become a farm owner." Once the prospective purchaser had demonstrated his need for state cooperation, the land, selected by the state, would be sold to him at cost, with liberal repayment provisions. His proposed system of rural credits, on the other hand, would enable the man already on the farm "to borrow money from a State fund at a low rate of interest and to repay it gradually during a period of thirty years. . . ."[5]

Rowell assured Johnson that the Weinstock rural credits bill would meet the governor's conditions: ". . . it won't disturb the budget by calling for an appropriation, and it will be conservative; in fact, damned conservative. . . ." While the bill would not accomplish "any very large or visible results," Rowell continued, it *would* redeem Johnson's pledge to the state. In Rowell's opinion, however, the land colonization measure was much more important than the rural credits bill because it would do more to stimulate the public imagination and would cost practically nothing. Furthermore, the scheme would be a "sort of social safety-valve." [6]

Rowell, Weinstock, and Barrows finally proposed, and in September, 1915, the legislature established, the State Colonization and Rural Credits Commission, headed by agricultural specialist Elwood Mead.[7] While Weinstock had grandiose ideas about the possibilities of such a commission, Johnson thought in more limited terms of forty to eighty families settling on a single tract of land.[8] Without Johnson's enthusiastic backing, the program bogged down, and in 1916 it was concluded that the Federal Farm Loan Act would provide California farmers with terms as favorable for borrowing money as the state could. Action on the state level was therefore temporarily abandoned. It was not until 1917 that the legislature created the State Land Settlement Board, with functions similar to those proposed by the Commission of Immigration and Housing in 1914.

If little was accomplished with respect to rural credits and land colonization during 1915 and 1916, some progress was made in efforts to achieve statewide marketing of agricultural produce. California growers had been pioneers in cooperative marketing arrangements, as a result of early exploitation by commercial packers. In the 1860's and 1870's, when there were no price guarantees to growers, commercial packers had demanded and received a guaranteed profit for shipping produce. They operated on the growers' capital and required the growers to take all the risks. If a carload of fruit did not bring enough to pay packing and freight charges, the grower was billed for the difference. There were frequent delays in remitting proceeds, and occasionally remissions to the grower were omitted entirely if a packer went bankrupt. By the 1880's and early 1890's, growers in southern California had had enough of this consignment system. In an attempt to market their produce more efficiently, they organized various "co-operatives"—the California Fruit Growers' Association, the California Fruit Union, the California Fruit Growers' Exchange (now Sunkist)—and by 1915 there were six different associations.[9]

For a cooperative to succeed, its members had to agree to sell through it exclusively, and the cooperative had to be able to enforce those agreements. This was no easy task, given the traditional individualism of American farmers and growers. Many refused to "co-operate." Defections left loyal growers with an increased burden of fixed cost. In addition, growers of various deciduous fruits—oranges, apricots, lemons, raisins—preferred to "go-it-alone" rather than coordinate and unite in a federated statewide organization owned and controlled by them. Consequently, as agricultural specialists Erich Kraemer and Henry Erdman have pointed out, "the majority of farmers continued to ship through the independent dealers whose activities they had criticized and condemned. . . ."[10]

For many years Harris Weinstock continued his efforts to combine growers and shippers in order to regulate fresh-fruit shipments to the East. In 1910 he had been made a member of a committee organized for the purpose of uniting the shipping agencies of the state into a collective body. Although his plan failed, he did not give up. Finally, in 1915, Hiram Johnson and many legislators were sufficiently impressed with the need for marketing reform that they created a state marketing agency. Weinstock was appointed state market director. Assemblyman H. E. McPherson of Santa Cruz, who had introduced the act creating the new agency, stated that it was designed to "end the exploitation of both the producer and the consumer at the hands of the commission merchant."[11]

Weinstock undertook the administration of the State Market Bureau in November, 1915, and immediately set out to organize the state's agricultural producers. As he saw it, the farm problem was essentially one of finding markets and eliminating waste in distribution.[12] He traveled throughout California in an attempt to gain the growers' support for his program. The age of individualism was over, he told them repeatedly. Only through collective action, Weinstock urged, could they get better prices for their goods.[13]

To assist him in his statewide campaign, Weinstock turned to Aaron Sapiro, a brilliant young San Francisco attorney. Weinstock had known Sapiro for many years and in 1913 had recommended him highly to Governor Johnson, who was considering Sapiro for a state position. Because the small appropriation to run the Market Bureau did not provide for a lawyer's salary, Weinstock paid Sapiro from his own pocket.[14]

Sapiro prepared himself for his new job with great enthusiasm, reading all he could find on cooperative marketing. Larsen and Erdman have commented upon the fact that Sapiro and his law firm profited greatly from his work with cooperatives, because the new associations established under the direction of the Market Bureau usually became his clients.[15] Yet the fact remains that he provided invaluable assistance to Weinstock by talking with growers who sought the Market Bureau's advice and by going on speaking tours to sell the idea of cooperative associations. He drafted articles of incorporation and bylaws for new groups, and he prepared contracts requiring growers to sell only through their respective cooperatives. As a result of his activities, Sapiro received requests for information and assistance from all parts of the country.[16]

Meanwhile, Weinstock was finding it increasingly difficult to induce citrus-fruit growers to establish a state clearinghouse, as various groups of retail grocers, packers, manufacturers, and canners vigorously opposed him. He was never able to win over the powerful California Fruit Growers' Exchange, which fought his plans for a state bureau of distribution because it feared possible political influence in the distribution of fruit and was concerned that eastern buyers might benefit from the market information released publicly in California.[17]

Weinstock finally resigned in 1920, frustrated and dejected over the failure to achieve his goals of rural credits, land colonization, and statewide market distribution. The story of his courageous efforts warrants discussion here, however, for it illuminates some important characteristics of the Progressive era in California. First, farmers and growers were essentially conservative and their self-help philosophy prevented them from seeking political remedies or state assistance for their marketing problems. Furthermore, local pride and rivalries among various citrus industries precluded extensive cooperation. Finally, it is very clear that Hiram Johnson and his advisers, particularly Harris Weinstock and Simon Lubin, shared a sincere concern for the plight of the state's farmer entrepreneurs. Perhaps they were concerned too much with marketing and distribution rather than with the twentieth-century notion of curbing production; yet they recognized the existence of land and agricultural problems and attempted some practical solutions.

With the exception of the action taken to solve agricultural problems, a nonpartisan election law, and a revision of the state's tax laws, the session of 1915 was relatively unproductive. The legislators were satisfied to confine their activities to the perfection and modest extension of those measures that had been passed in previous sessions. The *California Outlook* noted that the legislature of 1915 had established "a reputation as one of the most conservative bodies of lawmakers in the history of California. Not a single measure thus far passed can be properly called radical. . . ." [18]

Labor, however, praised the results of the 1915 legislative session, while at the same time acknowledging that it was not so fruitful as were the sessions of 1911 and 1913. The major labor legislation of 1915 included a better workmen's compensation law (applying to occupational diseases as well as to industrial accidents), the removal of property qualifications for jury service, a $50,000 appropriation for the establishment of free state employment bureaus under the control of the state labor commissioner, improved child-labor and labor-camp inspection laws, a semimonthly pay-day law, and an antiusury law. Commenting on this legislation, the *Labor Clarion* editorialized:

> There seems to be more or less pronounced opinion among the working people of California that the session of the Legislature just closed has been reactionary in thought and deed. This is far from the truth; and a mere reference to the principal labor and humanitarian measures approved at this session will clearly demonstrate the falsity of such opinion.[19]

And the San Francisco Labor Council's legislative agent, A. W. Brouilett, reported: "Compared with any session of the California Legislature prior to 1911, the session just ended was certainly friendly to labor. . . ." [20]

Johnson's prolabor reputation was thus further strengthened by the 1915 session, but later that year he suffered a major defeat at the hands of the electorate. Painfully aware of his party's minority status in terms of registration, Johnson had worked perserveringly to erase party lines. His plan to make the election of all state offices nonpartisan had been approved by the legislature. When the act was submitted by referendum to the voters Johnson urged their approval of the measure, contending that it would constitute the last necessary step to complete popular rule in California. But, in a very light turnout, the scheme was defeated.[21]

This setback was accepted graciously by Johnson in public—"Long ago men who have been on the firing line in California learned not only how to give a punch, but how to take one"—but that punch hurt more than Johnson would let on. Except for Rowell's defeat by Heney in the senatorial primary of 1914, it was the first real political setback that Johnson and his followers had experienced in five years. The defeat was enormously gratifying to conservative anti-Johnson Republicans, itching for an opportunity to regain their lost power. An editorial in the *California Outlook,* probably written by Chester Rowell, declared: ". . . The conservatives have been afraid to trust the people, because, like the radicals, they supposed that the people were radical. It is a good thing for both of them to learn that the people are conservative." [22]

Outside California the actions of the state's voters were cited in standpat newspapers as an example of the same conservative reaction evident in elections in eastern states. The Kansas City *Journal* reported proudly:

> The news from the Coast is in conformity with reports that come from all of the so-called Progressive states. Reaction has set in against any further experiments along the lines of so-called "Progressivism." . . . Governor Johnson remained for many months the only avowed Progressive State executive. California was the surviving stronghold of a species of political hysteria that disappeared rapidly from other parts of the country. Now California has risen to the necessity of ousting the Progressive incubus from administrative domination. . . .[23]

California Progressives would have been angered by that editorial, but most of them would have agreed that the future looked grim. By mid-1915 Roosevelt had become vehement in his demands for an adventurous and vigorous foreign policy. On the other hand, California Progressive leaders advocated peace with Mexico and Germany. Desiring to avoid militarism, they feared a vast preparedness program would hinder domestic reform. After the war had begun, Mowry writes, "the average California Progressive desired a policy of strict neutrality and argued that both sides to the struggle were guilty of perpetrating this offense against mankind." [24] Thus, Wilson's foreign policies were praised, while most California Progressives found they could not agree with Roosevelt when he criticized the Democratic administration as cowardly.

Conscious of the precarious position of the national Progressive organization, California Progressives were concerned about their future within the state. Should they renounce the national party and attempt to regain control of the state Republican organization? Chester Rowell explained the problem to the Progressive National Committee at a meeting in January, 1916. It was decided to accept the following strategy: maintain the Progressive organization and hold a nominating convention simultaneously with the Republicans. The purpose of this strategy was to nominate a compromise presidential candidate, with Johnson as the vice-presidential nominee. This provided a much safer road for Johnson. After all, he *had* been defeated in the nonpartisan attempt of 1915, and under prevailing conditions it was better to rely upon negotiations with party leaders than to trust the whims of the electorate.

After the Progressive National Committee had decided on its strategy, Johnson publicly suggested that the two parties would unite in Chicago if candidates sympathetic to progressive principles were nominated. In February, McCabe and Lissner met the chairman of the Republican State Executive Committee and proposed that the Progressive and Republican parties in California send a joint delegation to Chicago, one half "regular" and one half "progressive." Lissner conditioned the offer by requiring that the delegates be bound to Johnson for the vice-presidential nomination.

Such an incredible proposal could not but be rejected by the Republican Executive Committee. When the attempted plan was divulged to the public, Johnson denied knowing anything about it. Three months later, commenting on the attempted fusion, old Grove Johnson wrote to Francis Keesling: ". . . Harmony is a good thing, but do not for the sake of a harmonious party put traitors in power. Let these prodigals return, let them eat of the fatted calf of repentance and when they show by their works that the poison is out of their system, then give them a seat at the table. . . ." [25]

The next attempt to capture the California delegation was made by Progressives and some leading Republicans. These Republicans did not want to be labeled "Progressives," but they realized the political advantages to be gained from sending a joint delegation. Calling themselves the "United Republicans," the two groups met in San Francisco on February 27, 1916, and selected a list of uninstructed delegates.

Worried lest these delegates be elected to attend the Chicago convention, the Republican State Central Committee then offered to accept the original Progressive proposal. The Progressives held a stronger bargaining position by this time, however, and vetoed the offer. Finally, Republicans named their own delegates for the May primaries, while the United Republicans did likewise.

Progressives were asked by their leaders to enroll in the Republican party and support the "united" ticket. Rowell explained to Lissner that the public must understand that the United Republicans stood for two things: first, the union in a revived Republican party of Republicans and Progressive-Republicans (notice the hyphen) who had supported Johnson policies for the past five years;

and second, support at the Chicago convention of a ticket and platform that Progressives would find acceptable.[26] Johnson of course realized it would be very difficult to obtain a Progressive victory within the Republican party while most of his followers remained in the Progressive party. Rowell sent Johnson an unnecessary "reminder" of the seriousness of the matter. The governor must have nodded his head in worried agreement as he read the following words:

> ... In the popular mind you are already so far identified with the United Republicans and they with you that if they are defeated, whether you say anything about it or not, that defeat will be regarded in large measure as your defeat. ... Moreover, your enemies will gloat over that defeat as your defeat.[27]

The effort to deprive the standpat Republicans of representation in their own convention failed. With about 30 percent of the electorate voting, Johnson received his second major defeat in six months and the regulars were in absolute control of the Republican delegation.[28] Just as Rowell had predicted, the California Old Guard concluded that Johnson's political power had waned, that the Progressives were on their way out, and that both Johnson and his followers could therefore be ignored. The conclusion was not unwarranted, but it proved extremely costly to the Republican presidential nominee of 1916, Charles Evans Hughes.[29]

Johnson's political correspondence after the defeat of the United Republicans, and before the conventions in Chicago, reflects his rebellious attitude and his intense desire to utilize Roosevelt as a device to prevent the Republicans from nominating a reactionary. The embattled governor felt that Roosevelt had no chance of receiving the nomination and could not understand upon what grounds Roosevelt supporters based their confidence. He was, however, adamant about one thing: he would not tolerate a "pussy-footed reactionary"; he would rather support Wilson. Johnson confessed to Irving Martin, publisher of the Stockton *Record*, that he did not know whether it would be necessary to "deliver" California to Wilson in order to regain the Progressives' prestige within the state.[30] Writing to Fremont Older several days before departing for Chicago, Johnson expressed a similar attitude:

> . . . As a Progressive, I want first to see Roosevelt nominated by the Republicans. I would take the mysterious, stuffed prophet Hughes. I will not accept a rotten reactionary. And I have the fear, perhaps unfounded, that Perkins and Roosevelt may want to put over on the Progressive convention some rotten reactionaries. I am going to Chicago to prevent that very thing, if it should be attempted. . . . I look upon [Wilson] as a mere opportunist, without a conviction in the world . . . , but from the broad national standpoint, I think it would be better for the country to have four more years of his faltering and wobbling and changing, than to have fastened upon us a generation of reactionary standpat government. . . .[31]

Johnson's blood began to boil when he arrived in Chicago and found George Perkins in complete control of the Progressive convention. Johnson and Rowell had tried for years to nudge the Wall Streeter out of party control, but because of Roosevelt's fondness for the man, had failed. Johnson's initial discomfort turned to rage when he discovered Perkins' strategy was to hold off nominating a Progressive candidate until the Republicans acted. Then an incredulous Johnson discovered Roosevelt was in back of this "stall and dicker" strategy. After being defeated for permanent chairman of the convention, Johnson realized he no longer wielded a big stick in the party. Roosevelt's desertion to the Old Guard was the lowest blow of all. Johnson had begun his political life in opposition. He could see no reason for backing down now.

*Hiram Johnson in 1886 at age 20.*

*Hiram Johnson arriving for Ruef trial after the shooting of Francis J. Heney—1908.*

*Relaxing with Sunday paper after exhausting 1910 campaign.*

*Mr. and Mrs. Johnson at Lake Tahoe—1910.*

*Hiram Johnson and California delegation to Republican Party Convention in Chicago, June, 1912.*

*The "Bull Moose" ticket—1912.*

*Drafting a speech.*

*Senators Borah and Johnson in Washington, D.C.*

# 8

## DISINTEGRATION AND DEADLOCK

In June, 1916, two presidential nominating conventions were held simultaneously in Chicago. The Coliseum was the scene of the Republican convention, while a smaller Progressive convention was housed in the auditorium adjoining the old Congress Hotel.

Despite disavowals of his candidacy, Charles Evans Hughes was the leading contender for the Republican nomination. The Old Guard would have preferred to nominate conservative Elihu Root of New York, but even they realized it would be politically expedient to nominate Hughes. The tall, distinguished New Yorker had compiled an excellent record as his state's chief executive. He had gained national fame in 1905 as a result of his investigation and exposure of lax management in the great insurance companies of New York.[1] Resigning the governorship in 1910, he had become an associate justice of the Supreme Court, where he was still serving in 1916. Hughes had won a place of leadership among the liberal minority of the court and appealed to many Republicans as the man who might persuade wayward Progressives to return to the fold.

Hopes for reuniting the two parties grew dimmer as convention time approached. The Progressives, with their 2,000 delegates and alternates, were much more difficult to manage than Progressive National Chairman George Perkins had anticipated. There was only one man who could easily control them, and he remained at Oyster Bay. At a cost of $1,000 a day, a private long-distance telephone line was installed to keep Colonel Roosevelt in close contact with the Progressive leaders.[2]

On June 8 the Progressives received a message from Roosevelt which tempered their ardor to rush through his nomination. He urged Republicans and Progressives to unite. A joint conference committee assembled but could reach no agreement on a candidate.[3] The deadlock remained unbroken. The belief persisted, however, that Roosevelt would head the Progressive ticket, especially if the Republicans nominated Hughes. Roosevelt's dislike for the Justice because of his equivocal stand on preparedness was well known.[4]

In the early morning hours of June 9, when all hope for agreement had been abandoned by the joint conference committee, the members telephoned Oyster Bay and asked Roosevelt point-blank for his recommendation. His reply astounded everyone. He urged both parties to unite on Senator Henry Cabot Lodge of Massachusetts, a staunch, old-school reactionary who, as representative of New England's industrial interests, had been fighting progressivism for twenty years.

At the Progressive convention that day, the delegates listened in unbelieving silence as Chairman Perkins recounted the conference committee's talk with Roosevelt. They suddenly realized that the jig was up, that the founder of their party was leaving it, and at the same time was administering its final and harsh coup de grace. Most of the delegates were frantically loyal to Roosevelt, and believed he would be equally loyal in return. As the guillotine fell, it was almost too bizarre to be believed. Taken by surprise, some sat stunned, while others could not keep back the tears that streamed down their cheeks.[5]

The crowd then suddenly surged from astonishment to anger. Amid a deafening tumult of cheers and yells, Hiram Johnson, one of the most intransigent of all Progressives, stepped to the platform. His face flushed and his hands characteristically extended toward the delegates, he urged the nomination of Theodore Roosevelt and promised to attempt to convince the Colonel to accept. Swayed by Johnson's persuasive appeal, the crowd roared its approval.[6]

When the Progressives had finally quieted down, they greeted with grim silence the announcement that the Republicans had just nominated Hughes. Hiram Johnson's urging of Roosevelt's nomination had come too late to affect the action of the Republicans.

That evening the Progressive delegates reassembled to hear Chairman Raymond Robins read Roosevelt's answer to their nomination:

> I am very grateful for the honor you confer upon me by nominating me President. I cannot accept it at this time. I do not know the attitude of the candidate of the Republican party toward the vital questions of the day. Therefore, if you desire an immediate decision, I must decline the nomination. . . .[7]

"For a moment there was silence," recalled William Allen White. "Then there was a roar of rage. It was the cry of a broken heart such as no convention had uttered in this land before."[8] Sullen, puzzled, dismayed, overwhelmed, a party without a leader, the Progressives filed slowly out of the auditorium. Undoubtedly few of them realized that they had participated in the last official drama of the national Progressive party. Those who had followed Roosevelt and the Progressive movement for many years with great hopes and who had served in the rank and file of the national Progressive party for four years were crushed. Abandoned in their hour of potential triumph, many left the Progressive party for good, and carried thousands with them. They were insurgent; they were united. But the Bull Moose was left at the post without a rider.[9]

Irascible Hiram Johnson summed up the Progressive situation prior to his departure from Chicago: "We are in a difficult position, but we are used to fighting. We will continue to fight on the West Coast. . . . Many of our party will support Mr. Hughes if it is the Colonel's desire, but they will not do it enthusiastically." [10] Johnson also told reporters: "I positively would not accept the Presidential nomination if it were offered to me. My time in the future will be fully occupied by my work in California." [11]

It is not difficult to imagine the humiliation Johnson must have felt after the convention. Determined not to crawl back to the Republican fold on his knees, he felt immensely bitter toward his beloved Colonel for sanctioning the "stall and dicker" strategy. Roosevelt, on the other hand, desired to heal the rift and to dissuade Johnson from doing anything drastic.

Johnson, Rowell, and several other disgruntled Progressives had gone to New York after the Chicago fiasco. There they hoped to devise some way of keeping the Progressive party alive. Roosevelt met with Rowell and told him: "I don't want anyone to infer that Hiram Johnson refused to see Teddy Roosevelt." Such an inference came very near to being the truth. Rowell finally persuaded the seething governor to meet alone with Roosevelt in a quiet hotel where the latter was hiding from reporters. During their meeting, Johnson made it very plain that he found Roosevelt's company "most uncongenial," and therefore the Colonel did not attempt to force reconciliation.[12]

Before departing for California on June 22, Johnson paid Hughes a visit at the Hotel Astor and pledged his support.[13] He also formed a "pact" with Gifford Pinchot. The two Progressives agreed to make an effort to keep the Progressive movement alive in their respective states, to keep in touch with one another, and in whatever manner possible to amalgamate the party into a national organization. The governor returned to California with these thoughts in mind.[14]

After Johnson left New York, Rowell met with the Republican steering committee to discuss the California senatorship. He received what he thought to be a promise from Senators Murray Crane of Massachusetts and Boies Penrose of Pennsylvania (speaking for the committee) that they would support Johnson, even to the extent of soliciting a similar endorsement from Hughes.[15] Hughes had decided after his nomination not to turn over exclusive management of his campaign to the Republican National Committee controlled by Crane, Penrose, and Reed Smoot. Consequently, he set up a new campaign committee composed of eleven Republicans and six Progressives.[16] Rowell managed to secure membership on this committee. The regular Republican William Crocker was also appointed. California was thus represented on the campaign committee by two national committeemen, one from each of the warring factions.

As his campaign manager, Hughes selected William R. Willcox. Willcox had been an able administrator of the New York City Public Service Commission during Hughes's second term as governor, but was a complete novice in managing a presidential campaign. Hughes's biographer, Merlo Pusey, observes that "the Willcox appointment was to prove candidate Hughes's first major mistake." [17] It would not be his last.

One can now see, with wisdom born of hindsight, that the Republican party's political future depended a great deal upon Hiram Johnson.[18] The drama enacted on the California stage during the summer of that year had national, indeed, international, significance. It was a period of restless uncertainty for Johnson. He had senatorial aspirations, but was not at all confident he could win. The disintegration of his party in Chicago and the turmoil within California seriously impaired his chances.

On June 27 the governor issued a public statement. He declared that *he* intended to vote for Hughes; yet he made no demands that Progressives follow his lead. Conceding that the formal Progressive party was dead, he advised his followers to register in the major parties and "progressivize them." "He as much as intimates," suggested an editorial in the Sacramento *Star*, "that he could vote for Wilson with a clear conscience." [19]

Johnson stated publicly that he would vote for Hughes, but in a confidential letter to Katherine Philips Edson he revealed his private attitude. Having attended the Progressive convention as a delegate, she had written the governor expressing her disappointment over the miscarriage of their hopes and her attempt to "intellectualize" herself into supporting Hughes.[20] Johnson's reply expresses an attitude that became more inflexible and unyielding after Hughes had come to California and gone.

> This is confidential and private. . . . I haven't any objection to the Hughes Alliance or anything else of that sort. I don't know any reason, however, why we should break our necks in this campaign. According to Rowell and Dickson we should do so for the honor of being a part of it, and a very small part—so minute and vanish-

ing that it would ever be at the beck and call of the big Republican bosses. I have made my choice for Hughes, but during the campaign, I am going my own way as usual. I don't propose to be ordered about by Mr. Wm. H. Crocker or any other man calling himself a Republican in the nation or in the state. According to these gentlemen, our help is to be accepted and during the very period we are helping, we are to be disciplined. I never did submit to discipline and I am not going to now, politically or otherwise. . . .[21]

To his Progressive friend in Ohio, James Garfield, Johnson confessed that under the circumstances, there was nothing for men with their views to do but support Hughes; however, Johnson qualified his support: "I will not stand side by side upon the same platform with men who are demanding the destruction of those who have fought so faithfully with me for the past five years. . . ." If the present situation continued, warned Johnson, "the enthusiasm of many Progressives in this state for Mr. Hughes will naturally be very greatly dampened." [22]

Progressive leaders felt it absolutely necessary to perpetuate the gains made under Johnson's leadership. To achieve this, more than five hundred Progressives were summoned to San Francisco in early July for a meeting. Johnson reminded them of their party's suicide in Chicago, caused by the stalling tactics of Perkins and Roosevelt. Warning them of the attack on liberalism being organized by reactionaries, he urged all progressives to fight to protect California politics from greed and corruption. Johnson offered to run for senator on the Progressive *and* Republican tickets, and a motion to endorse his candidacy was carried unanimously. Rowell's motion to support Hughes was hissed and booed down. Reiterating that his choice of Hughes was a personal one, Johnson recommended that each Progressive judge the presidential candidates and then make his own decision. Then, as the meeting divided into factions supporting either Wilson or Hughes, both groups pledged their support of Hiram Johnson for United States senator.

The regular Republicans entered two highly respected candidates in the race against Johnson. "After eight years without political pap," George Mowry writes of the conservatives' frenzied activity,

> the hungry Republicans in California saw Johnson's announcement as a brazen attempt to steal what they felt was honorably theirs. Righteously indignant, William H. Crocker and Francis V. Keesling, the regnant standpatters, soon managed to obtain the withdrawal of one of the Republican candidates so as to concentrate all conservative strength behind Willis H. Booth and defeat the interloper Johnson. With that move the political fat began to fry.[23]

Johnson and his party lieutenants knew he faced a tough battle. Many expressed grave doubts about the possibility of his election.[24] It was a crucial time in the history of California progressivism. Since Johnson's attempt to make all state elections nonpartisan had failed, there were still approximately 45,000 registered Progressives and an additional 300,000 without party affiliations. So that these important voters would be able to participate in the Republican primary it was mandatory that they be reregistered. Most Progressive leaders agreed that it was necessary to concentrate on Johnson's candidacy; the national contest could wait until after the state primaries.[25] Johnson opened his campaign in Los Angeles on July 15, declaring: "I am, in this campaign, for Charles Evans Hughes, and to the best of my ability, I shall loyally support him." [26]

The Progressive meeting in San Francisco on July 8, 1916, also marked the commencement of the "battle of the telegrams." Chairman Willcox importuned Progressives and Republicans to strive for a united backing of Hughes. He sent Francis Keesling the following telegram:

DISQUIETING RUMORS ARE CURRENT HERE OF LACK OF
COOPERATION LOOKING TO GENERAL SUPPORT IN YOUR STATE
OF ALL FORCES OPPOSED TO WILSON ADMINISTRATION. PAR-
TICULAR ATTENTION HAS BEEN CALLED TO ATTITUDE OF LOS
ANGELES TIMES AND A REPORTED POLITICAL BLACKLIST.[27]

In response to a similar request from Willcox for unified and cooperative effort, Rowell met with Republican National Committeeman Crocker and State Central Committee Chairman Keesling to determine how the Hughes meetings should be conducted. Rowell thought Johnson should be present to introduce the presidential candidate, especially since the Republican steering committee had promised in June to support Johnson. Crocker and Keesling had never heard of such a promise. Crocker flatly told Rowell that he wanted only to defeat Johnson and to nominate Booth. No agreement was reached on the governor's proposed introduction of Hughes.

A few days later, after requesting national headquarters to send Crocker confirmation of the promise to support Johnson, Rowell again sought joint action. Crocker and Keesling, meanwhile, had also demanded clarification of the "promise" Rowell claimed to have received from the Republican steering committee.[28] Although Willcox knew about Rowell's meeting with Crane and Penrose, he chose to deny knowledge of it. Thus Willcox in effect stamped Rowell a liar, and merely solidified opposition to Johnson.

Rowell, certain he had been betrayed by the national organization, finally wired Perkins that California Republican leaders could have sole responsibility for Hughes's tour. He explained that unless the deadlock were broken, it would be fatal to Hughes in California.[29] Perkins quickly responded, pleading with Rowell to ask Hughes for help.

The final decision—an important one in which Hughes must have acquiesced—was made by Willcox. It was to disregard the promise made by Penrose and Crane and to permit the regular Republicans to assume control of the campaign in California. Perhaps this decision was warranted, considering the fact that Johnson seemed to be losing control of his own party machinery. "Since any action was calculated to alienate one side or the other," comments Mowry, "it must have seemed the better part of politics to play with what looked to be the winning side. . . ."[30]

Evidently Crocker was confident that Willis Booth would win the primary election, for he asked Willcox to delay Hughes's trip to California until after the primaries were concluded.[31] According to Merlo Pusey, Crocker's suggestion was disregarded because there were two imperatives of the campaign: first, to have Hughes travel widely and speak frequently in order to emerge from his cocoon of judicial seclusion; and second, to confine his major efforts to the big cities of the East during the final weeks. If the western trip were postponed, reasoned Hughes and Willcox, it could not be made at all. Pusey claims "this decision was reached without any real understanding of the intense hatred between the Johnson and Crocker factions."[32] One wonders just how much notification Hughes and his campaign manager needed. Many influential politicians had warned Hughes about the bitter rivalry in California; he was also advised not to let either group monopolize him during his tour of the state.[33] Additionally, Rowell had peppered Willcox with warnings and suggestions. On July 29 he had written the campaign manager a sixteen-page letter in which he argued strongly that Progressives should share in the organization and conduct of the Hughes tour. "Whatever recognition is granted or denied to Governor Johnson personally," Rowell warned, "is regarded by Progressives as granted or denied to the Progressive movement. . . ."[34]

Finally, in exasperation, Rowell wired Willcox the following message, also sending a copy to Hughes: "HAVE MADE EVERY EFFORT DURING PAST TWO DAYS TO ACCOMPLISH

TRUCE FOR PERIOD OF HUGHES VISIT AS YOU REQUESTED, BUT REGRET TO ANNOUNCE TOTAL FAILURE. . . ." [35]

It seems impossible that Hughes could have been ignorant of the political faux pas he would be committing if he did not at least cast an approving nod in the Progressives' direction. Perhaps he felt that if he recognized western Progressives, he would risk the loss of conservative votes in the East; but certainly the decision to enter California before the primaries, and then to disregard Progressives, must have been made with full understanding of the existing political ferment. This decision could *not* have been made "without any real understanding of the intense hatred between the Johnson and Crocker factions," as Pusey claims. Evidently Hughes felt he could handle the combatants. Moreover, it must have seemed apparent to him that the regular Republicans would win the primaries. The more logical conclusion is that Hughes knew full well what he was doing. He was taking a calculated risk and felt he could afford to be manacled by regular Republicans.

By the end of July, all efforts to reach agreement had failed. Crocker, certain he had succeeded in gaining complete control of Hughes's tour in California, placed Keesling in charge of all further arrangements. Keesling would prove to be even less cooperative with the Progressives.

While the campaign managers of the warring factions waged their telegram battle and engaged in accusations and denunciations, Johnson worked diligently to consolidate his forces. Near the end of the month he sent a political forecast to a friend in Washington, D.C.: "I don't envy Hughes when he comes here in August. He will have to be an exceedingly clever man, as well as a courageous and just one, to get through the state without difficulty." [36] The stage was set. The Progressives awaited Hughes's grand entrance.

# 9

## BLUNDER BEGETS BLUNDER

Hughes spent the month of July diligently poring over magazines, newspapers, reports, and the *Congressional Record*, storing up facts for his campaign and generally acquainting himself with the contemporary situation. Even though his duties on the bench had served as a buffer between him and the practicalities of politics for the past six years, the Justice had thought deeply about current political problems and had read widely in the political literature of the day.[1]

Hughes's major task as he started West was to convince that part of the country that there was need for a change in administration and that he was a desirable alternative to Woodrow Wilson. The Republican candidate, his biographer tells us, "threw himself into the campaign with every ounce of energy he possessed."[2] Traveling through Chicago, St. Paul, Minneapolis, and Seattle in a railroad car named the "Constitution," Hughes encountered the first overt indication of the traumatic experience he would undergo in California: ". . . the vast and bitter controversy between the Hiram Johnson Progressives and the Crocker-Keesling Republican machine in the state, in a life and death struggle for control."[3]

With Hughes on the campaign train was Frederick M. Davenport, a close friend of the candidate. Davenport had been a New York state senator during Hughes's second term as governor and was one of seven men who, from 1909 to 1911, aided him in his battle with the William Barnes machine for control of the party organization. As a Progressive, Davenport had run for governor of New York in 1912 and 1914.[4] The two men were very good friends, and during his campaign for the presidency Hughes enjoyed having Davenport nearby to talk over daily happenings and problems.

One day, as the train neared the West Coast, Hughes called Davenport into his compartment, disturbed by a problem. He asked Davenport to scan a stack of telegrams and then advise him on a course of action. The telegrams dealt with the delicate question of who was to preside at a major campaign meeting in San Francisco. Rowell had made one suggestion, and Crocker another. It seemed obvious to Rowell that the governor of the state should preside at such an important event. Willcox had not wished to interfere in a matter of "local" concern, but had wired both men that he thought it proper for a distinguished governor, supporting the presidential candidate, to preside at one of the meetings.

Crocker and Keesling opposed the idea of Johnson introducing Hughes on the alleged grounds that he was running for office. Since the primaries were so near, they deemed it unfair to give one senatorial candidate any publicity advantage. Keesling wrote Rowell on August 8 that the latter's appointment to the Republican National Committee could not by any reasonable argument be construed to sanction *any* of Hughes's meetings under the auspices of the California Progressive organization.[5] The conservatives' objection, however, was not really over a detail of publicity. As Davenport wrote many years later: ". . . It was part of the deep cleavage of economic and political lines, involving the whole life of the state at the time. It was part of a fight to the death between progress and standpatism in a powerful, expanding commonwealth." [6]

With what seems astonishing naïveté, Davenport could not comprehend why narrow-minded political jealousy should not be set aside in the broader interest of Hughes's election. He suggested that Hughes tell Willcox to summon Rowell and Crocker to a meeting in Portland. There they could explain their respective positions, in the hope that some sort of agreement could be reached to prevent Hughes from being injured in the impending collision of the two factions.

The suggestion was accepted, and Willcox subsequently wired the protagonists, asking them to meet him in Portland. On August 11, Willcox wired Crocker from New York:

HAVE TELEGRAM FROM MANAGER OF HUGHES' TRAIN WHICH SUGGESTS BOTH YOU AND ROWELL MEET TRAIN IN PORTLAND ON WEDNESDAY, AUGUST SIXTEENTH, AND TRAVEL WITH GOVERNOR HUGHES TO SAN FRANCISCO AND TO WITHHOLD FINAL ARRANGEMENTS ABOUT CHAIRMAN UNTIL THEN, UNLESS YOU HAVE COME TO AN AGREEMENT.[7]

Rowell, receiving a similar telegram, immediately wired that he would be there, but warned Willcox that he had received a letter from Crocker which stated that as members of the National Campaign Committee "we have no authority over this purely California local situation. . . ." [8] On the same day, Crocker wired Willcox *his* answer, declining to meet Hughes in Portland: "REPLYING TO YOUR TELEGRAM TODAY, ALL ARRANGEMENTS FOR CALIFORNIA HAVE BEEN COMPLETED." [9]

And so the "battle of the telegrams" continued. Willcox anticipated that the war would cease, at least for the duration of Hughes's brief tour, and remained hopeful that a compromise between Rowell and Hughes could be achieved in Portland. As he had promised, Rowell boarded the train in Portland, where he dined and talked with Hughes. Admitting that it was formally and technically correct for a presidential candidate to remain aloof from state primaries, he frankly told Hughes that in this particular instance it would be a mistake not to have Governor Johnson at the very least preside at a campaign meeting.

Realizing that Hughes should first talk with Crocker before making up his mind, Rowell tried to persuade him that the politically wise thing to do would be to recognize directly the leader of the Progressive movement in the West. "For the sake of your own candidacy," Rowell urged, "you ought to come out for Johnson. If you do, you'll be elected. If you do not, you may not carry California."

Hughes remained unconvinced. He told Rowell that he had been accused of not being a loyal Republican while governor of New York. Although this criticism had subsided, he feared any public support of Johnson would cause it to flare up. "I couldn't possibly comply with your request, even if it should mean my defeat." [10]

Rowell had done his best, but had failed to persuade the stubborn presidential candidate to throw any support to Johnson, who was fighting for his political life. It was later reported that Hughes considered Rowell "a very exaggerated person." [11] "If he did not understand the situation," Rowell wrote Roosevelt, "he was the only person on the train who did not. . . . The thing that horrified me most was the utter lack of personal initiative or decisiveness on the part of Hughes. . . ."[12]

Crocker, Keesling, and a reception committee composed mainly of Republicans (with a few "tame" Progressives thrown in for good measure) met Hughes at Gerber, near the California-Oregon border. At the first opportunity, Crocker pulled Davenport aside and insisted that Hughes be kept away from Johnson at all costs. Any contact with Johnson, he said, would appear to be a compromise of Republican principles.[13] Davenport recounted the event to Merlo Pusey many years later and stated that Crocker's arrangements were permitted to remain unchanged.[14] And Keesling states that he and Crocker refrained from "antagonizing" Hughes by mentioning the senatorial race.[15]

Hughes remained in California from August 17 through August 22. Crocker maintained this "hands-off" attitude during all of Hughes's ill-fated journey through the state. From that time until they regained control of the Republican State Central Committee in September, the Progressive leaders had little to do with the Hughes campaign.

Davenport has passed on his opinion of William Crocker: ". . . the Southern Pacific aristocrat, seemed to me then and seems to me now, as I look back upon it, to have been the archetype of the laissez-faire Bourbon of the period, without an iota of political or national sense."[16] If Davenport felt this way *at the time,* it seems tragically unfortunate that he did not take advantage of his influence to convince Hughes that he might be misjudging the situation.

The problem still remained: what to do with Hughes in a Progressive stronghold? Crocker had a solution. Put a leash on him and lead him carefully through the state so he would not be tempted to make friends with the wrong people. The first opportunity to prevent the Progressives from associating with Hughes came on Friday night, August 18, at a campaign meeting in a packed San Francisco Civic Auditorium. Keesling has explained that the reason Rowell was not chosen to introduce Hughes in San Francisco was the probability that the meeting would have turned into a Johnson gathering. He was worried that Tom Finn, sheriff of San Francisco and a local Johnson party boss, would infiltrate the audience with members of his machine. They would have "taken over like baseball fans at a game on the home lot," Keesling feared, with Hughes being subordinated to the governor.[17]

Thus, it was Crocker who rose that Friday night to introduce the Republican candidate for President. There was a feeling of tense expectancy as Hughes stepped to the podium. Would he show himself to be a Republican of the old school, or would he commend the Progressives on their past accomplishments? Or would he do both? Before the dignified candidate could speak, someone in the balcony yelled, "Three cheers for San Francisco's favorite son!" Surprised, Hughes responded affably: "I salute with you San Francisco's favorite son." In doing so he was praising Crocker and exacerbating the sensibilities of the many Progressives in the audience. Hughes had made his first blunder. He then proceeded unabashedly to his second. "I come as the spokesman of a reunited Republican party, to talk to you of national issues—with *local* conditions I have no concern." [18]

The die was cast. To every Progressive in California, the long struggle against corporation privilege and corrupt government, and for social amelioration, was a matter of supreme importance. Forgetting that Hughes himself had been an excellent reform governor, forgetting that he valued the same ideals as they, the Progressives in the audience took his comment as a personal insult.

Despite the fact that several historians, including Hughes's biographer, ask that we dismiss Hughes's comments in San Francisco on the grounds that they were innocently made, it is difficult to do so for reasons already mentioned. After all, Hughes had devoted most of July to reading newspapers and reports. Furthermore, had he paid any attention to the warnings of his friends, campaign managers, United States Senator John D. Works from California, and Rowell, he would have been completely aware of the blunders he was committing.

Many Progressives who listened to Hughes that night in San Francisco had been reserving their final decision regarding the presidential candidate until after hearing him speak; they left the Civic Auditorium extremely disappointed. Keesling thought the statement "with *local* conditions I have no concern" probably accounted for Rowell's sudden desertion of the Hughes's entourage the next morning.[19] Rowell, however, claimed he left "to be near his ailing wife." [20] Nevertheless, the Republicans were now in absolute control of the campaign.

Hughes was to make yet a few more blunders before completing his California tour. The San Francisco Chamber of Commerce, taking advantage of the "dying" liberalism in California, was determined to wage a war to the death against organized labor. On July 10, three unions of culinary crafts—cooks, helpers, and waiters—notified the San Francisco Restaurant Association that on July 15 they would put into effect an eight-hour day at the prevailing wages. A counteroffer of a nine-hour day was rejected by the unions. Convinced of the unwarranted nature of this strike, the Chamber of Commerce established a Law and Order Committee to carry out a program seeking "the end of labor's tyranny by the establishment of open shops and by the abolition of all union violence, coercion, and intimidation including all forms of picketing." [21] The committee also saw to it that "open shop" posters were displayed in the windows of San Francisco restaurants.

Keesling knew about this strike, yet he scheduled a luncheon speech for Hughes at the Commercial Club—which was conspicuously displaying its "open shop" poster. Hughes was informed of the waiters' strike the day before the luncheon. Disregarding advice to cancel his appearance, he insisted that the affair take place as planned. Charles Farnham, his personal manager, talked with the head of the striking Cooks and Waiters Union, Hugo Ernst, and asked him to delay the walkout until after Hughes had left San Francisco. Ernst had already protested in an open letter to the San Francisco *Bulletin* against forcing Hughes into the position of endorsing the open shop. Ernst suggested in the letter that other arrangements be made to prevent that occurrence. Keesling had replied that the situation was unfortunate, but that it was too late to switch the luncheon to another location.

Ernst agreed to Farnham's plea for delay of the strike, but made a stipulation: "The men will stay on their jobs during the luncheon, but there is one condition. There is to us a very offensive placard hanging in the window of the Commercial Club, declaring against our hopes and purposes. All that we ask is that the placard be taken down from the window of the club while our men are serving the luncheon." [22]

Farnham then rushed to Crocker, who belonged to the club, and asked him to see what could be done to remove the poster. Crocker shrugged his shoulders and said he could do nothing. Farnham next sought a prominent Republican on the local committee arranging the luncheon. "Take down those placards? Not on your life," the local politico replied indignantly. "We've got those labor bastards in this town where we want them at last, and we are not going to let up on them at all." [23]

No placard removal; no union waiters. Waiters from nearby scab restaurants were hired to serve the luncheon, and blunder number three had been successfully completed. Davenport's conclusion regarding this farcical event is that "the 1916 election was easily lost around the Bay of Oakland." [24] Mowry's summation is equally damning: "Charles Evans Hughes was in San Francisco for only two days. It is possible that no presidential candidate ever managed to alienate so many votes in one region within so short a time. . . ." [25]

Hughes must have been extremely relieved as he traveled on, heading for sunny southern California. The political turmoil and labor-management strife of San Francisco were now behind him. Although he could not deny that his campaign in the Bay City had been conducted with something less than political finesse, he could anticipate a more successful campaign in the southland. His relief was to be short-lived. Harrison Gray Otis was awaiting his arrival; his platoon of conservatives would protect the Republican candidate from any and all Progressive advances. W. W. Mines, vice-chairman of the Republican State Central Committee and in charge of arrangements in Los Angeles, had assured Keesling early in August that "with these men accompanying Hughes to this city there will be little chance of either Johnson or Rowell making much of a showing. . . ." [26] In other words, everything was under control—Republican control.

The Hughes "snub" of Hiram Johnson at the Hotel Virginia in Long Beach was singled out by contemporaries as a major cause of Hughes's narrow defeat in California. This "snub" has become something of a political myth. Historians and political scientists have seized it, restated it, and have passed it on without much change. Since the contemporary accounts are conflicting, the true facts concerning the event are difficult to determine. As late as 1954 the "snub" was still considered an important aspect of the election of 1916. A California congressman, Leroy Johnson (no relation of Hiram Johnson), requested Edward

Dickson (who was with Hiram Johnson in the hotel and who in 1954 was the only living participant in the famous incident) to write a historical sketch about what "really happened" in Long Beach in those bygone days.[27] From this article, which was written into the *Congressional Record,* and from the accounts of the other major participants—Hughes, Johnson, Keesling, Farnham, and Davenport—we can piece together a reasonably clear pattern of events.

Johnson had been campaigning in Bakersfield. He was met in Los Angeles by Edward Dickson on Sunday, August 20. Dickson and Johnson drove together to Long Beach, where the governor expected to get some needed rest at the Hotel Virginia. As they approached the hotel they were surprised to see a large crowd gathered outside. They entered the lobby, and after registering, were informed by the manager that Charles Evans Hughes was expected soon. They went immediately to Johnson's room, accompanied by the governor's personal secretary, Paul Herriot.

Just prior to Hughes's arrival, Katherine Edson arrived to pay the governor a visit. Johnson greeted her in his room. According to her account, Johnson was very perturbed—not that Hughes was coming to the hotel, but because some people downstairs had circulated the rumor that he had come expressly to make Hughes recognize him.[28]

Hughes had planned Sunday as a day of rest. It turned into another day of handshaking and backslapping. After being embarrassed by the pastor of a Los Angeles Baptist church, who insisted that he stand and be recognized during the services, Hughes was driven to Pasadena to meet the widow of former President Garfield. After a brief respite there, he was permitted to digest his meal while touring a movie studio. The climax to his day of rest was a drive to Long Beach. At five o'clock that afternoon Hughes and his escort party pulled up to the Hotel Virginia. Dusty and jostled, the former Justice emerged from the automobile to greet the crowd that had gathered at the news of his arrival. How he must have longed for the tranquillity of his judicial chambers.[29]

Johnson and Dickson watched from the window of Johnson's hotel room as Hughes briefly addressed the crowd. They fully expected that the hotel manager (a Republican) would let Hughes know Johnson was nearby. "Had he done so," Dickson writes, "there is not the slightest doubt but that Hughes would have sought an opportunity to pay his respects to the State's Chief Executive."[30] The governor was never invited to the impromptu rally downstairs.

Johnson later claimed that the hotel manager never informed Hughes that he, Johnson, was only four floors away, even though the manager was with Hughes most of the time.[31] Keesling insists that he knew nothing of the governor's presence.[32] And Johnson, in no mood to give the impression that he was seeking publicity and forced recognition from Hughes, made no effort to greet the presidential candidate. It must be added, however, that Johnson could not have determined whether *he* was being deliberately snubbed unless he disclosed his presence to Hughes. Perhaps Mark Sullivan's explanation is the most explicit: "Johnson did not know that Hughes did not know that he, Johnson, was in the hotel."[33] One significant aspect of the Hotel Virginia incident remains a mystery. Someone in the crowd (which included many newspaper reporters hungry for a "scoop") must have seen Johnson enter the hotel. Does it not seem odd that no one asked Hughes at the time of his arrival whether he intended to visit the governor?

Later that evening, after an exhausted Hughes had returned to Los Angeles, Farnham burst into his room with the bad news. A newspaperman had just told him that Johnson had been in the hotel the entire time! Hughes ordered Farnham to telephone Johnson and then to drive immediately to Long Beach. "Explain to Governor Johnson that I did not know he was in the hotel and that I am sorry I did not meet him and ask him to preside at my meeting in Sacramento." [34] Dickson writes:

> I thought at the time that it would have been much better had Justice Hughes taken time personally to telephone Governor Johnson, rather than entrusting that responsibility to Farnham. . . . A personal phone call from Hughes to Johnson would surely have softened the tension. I detected a tinge of bitterness in Johnson's instruction to his secretary that he was engaged for the evening and would be unable to accept Hughes' invitation to dinner.[35]

Unfortunately for Hughes, Keesling (of all people!) accompanied Farnham to Long Beach. That night as Hughes was boarding his train for San Diego, he exclaimed to Davenport: "If I had known Johnson was in that hotel, I would have seen him if I had been obliged to kick the door down." [36] That was rather strong language coming from a man who was either too tired or too busy to lift a telephone receiver.

Johnson met Farnham and Keesling in the lobby of the Hotel Virginia at ten o'clock that night. He was already peeved that Hughes did not consider the incident serious enough to warrant a personal telephone call; but he became incensed when he found that Hughes had sent Keesling as his personal representative. Johnson managed to calm himself sufficiently to permit Keesling to join the conversation.

In fact, Keesling began the ill-fated ordeal. He assured Johnson that the Republican campaign committee had always wanted him to accompany Hughes through the state and that it could easily be arranged for the two men to continue together.[37]

That did it. Johnson lashed out at Keesling, damning

him for assuming sole responsibility for Hughes's campaign in California. A worried Farnham, attempting to calm the flushed and angry governor, invited him to preside at a special Sacramento meeting. Johnson made it clear to Farnham that he "did not need to preside at any meeting of Mr. Hughes; that the people of the state of California would not wish their governor to break through any cordon surrounding him in order that he might shine in Hughes' reflected light, and even if the people did want this, I would not do it anyway. . . ." [38] Johnson further stated that Crocker and Keesling had done Hughes incalculable harm in California, and had lost him a tremendous number of votes. He emphasized that the Republicans were not interested in the success of the party, but only in the defeat of progressivism and the return of Old Guard control of California politics. Keesling and Farnham left the hotel without reaching any agreement with Johnson, but the governor *had* vented his spleen.

After the heated exchange, Farnham left for San Diego. The next morning, after conferring with Hughes, he telephoned Johnson and asked him to exchange with Hughes "letters of greeting." He did not bring up the Sacramento meeting. The governor said he would think it over and wire him back. Perhaps because Hughes had not called in person, or possibly because Johnson had already decided on a negative reply, the following message was sent to Farnham:

> IT GOES WITHOUT SAYING THAT I WISH AND HAVE WISHED TO EXTEND TO MR. HUGHES A MOST CORDIAL AND HEARTY WELCOME TO CALIFORNIA, AND THAT IN VIEW OF MY ADVOCACY OF HIM I WOULD BE VERY GLAD TO PRESENT HIM TO MY FELLOW CITIZENS AND TO STATE TO THEM THE REASONS FOR MY ADVOCACY. UNTIL NOW IT HAS BEEN RENDERED IMPOSSIBLE FOR ME TO DO EITHER. . . . AT THIS LATE DATE WHEN BOTH OUR ITINERARIES ARE FULL AND FIXED, AND UPON THE EVENT OF MR. HUGHES' DEPARTURE FROM CALIFORNIA, FOR ME, EVEN AT YOUR SUGGESTION, TO WRITE

MR. HUGHES, AND FOR HIM TO REPLY, OR FOR ME TO PRESIDE AT HIS SACRAMENTO MEETING WOULD BE MISUNDERSTOOD AND MISINTERPRETED AND MALICIOUSLY DISTORTED. . . .[39]

That message was the last communication between Johnson and the Hughes entourage in California. On the same day, the press of the entire nation carried reports of Hughes's "snub" of Governor Johnson in the Hotel Virginia. It was regarded by most as being representative of Hughes's attitude toward Johnson and California progressivism.

Marshall Stimson and Lieutenant Governor William Stephens attended the final Los Angeles campaign meeting for Hughes, who had returned from San Diego in time for the meeting on Monday evening. Nearly every foot of available space in the Shrine Auditorium was filled with enthusiastic Hughes supporters. More than 6,000 Republicans had turned out to bid their candidate farewell. Stimson and Stephens felt that a Republican lieutenant governor should be seated on the stage, regardless of his progressive leanings. Although he *was* the highest-ranking state dignitary present, Stephens was informed that there was no room for him. Evidently party regularity meant more than rank or position. Finally, conservative leaders realized that the obvious exclusion of Stephens might backfire, so he was invited to sit near the rear of the stage. He told them to "go to hell" and started to leave; but he was induced to return, and took his seat among five hundred other "vice-presidents." [40]

Shortly thereafter, Hughes entered the auditorium, accompanied by former United States Senator Cornelius Cole, and by the archconservative Harrison Gray Otis. Crocker and W. W. Mines tagged along behind. Hughes delivered a speech with no recognition of, nor appeal to, the few Progressives present. They went away even more determined than ever "not to support this tactless and deluded individual." [41]

Crocker and Keesling accompanied Hughes to Sacramento the next day, their campaign train passing through Fresno, Tracy, and Stockton. That night an "old-line regular Republican" presided over the final California meeting in the state capitol. By Wednesday morning Hughes was on his way to Reno.

Thus Charles Evans Hughes came and went and did not even shake hands with the governor of California. Harold Ickes writes in his *Autobiography* that Hughes "breakfasted with Republicans; he lunched with Republicans, he dined with Republicans, he may have slept with them for all I know." [42] Merlo Pusey concludes that Hughes "had done everything humanly possible to wipe out any offense that might have resulted from the misadventure at Long Beach, which was no fault of his in the first place." [43]

We may agree with Pusey that there is no ground for saying, as historians have repeated for more than four decades, that Hughes snubbed Johnson—at Long Beach. Perhaps we may also agree that if there was any snubbing there, it was done by Johnson himself; but when Hughes did not even bother to lift a telephone receiver and attempt to console the irascible and crotchety Johnson, he had *not* done "everything humanly possible" to remedy the situation. It was not too much to ask even of a busy presidential candidate, considering the gravity of the incident, to say nothing of common courtesy. The point of the matter is that Hughes had evidently decided to snub Johnson everywhere, and blame for the "snub" cannot be shifted entirely to Johnson merely because Hughes did not know he was in the hotel. Johnson is not without fault, and we shall see that he did not forget the incident. There is no reason to doubt the word of Keesling, who denies knowing that Johnson was present. We can only guess, judging from the Republican leader's stated intention of keeping Hughes away from Johnson at all costs, that he would have done nothing, even if the manager had told him that the governor of California was in the hotel. One factor is indisputable: even though Hughes could not have snubbed Johnson at the Hotel Virginia because he was ignorant of the latter's presence, he did purposely ignore the Progressives during his entire tour—that was the snub. "What happened in Long Beach," writes Mowry,

> was but the most dramatic of a logical sequence of events begun when Willcox refused to intervene in the arrangements for the reception of the candidate. A Hughes-Johnson meeting there might have patched up a facade of harmony, but it would have been only that. At that late date, nothing less than a complete endorsement would have mollified Johnson's Progressives. . . .[44]

It is safe to say that a good many Progressives had made up their minds about Hughes before the Long Beach incident. Mowry suggests that nothing could have changed their minds but a complete endorsement by Hughes; however, the national election was still two and one-half months away. It is reasonable to assume that many Progressives could still have been swayed by Johnson and by an effective campaign for Hughes. We must remember that Hughes lost California by less than 4,000 votes.

We will see that Johnson publicly continued to support Hughes, though the effectiveness of his support is doubtful because of the manner in which it was given. How about the campaign for Hughes? Was it effectively run at the precinct level, where most elections are won or lost? The evidence indicates that there was much to be desired in the conduct of the Republican presidential campaign in California, especially after the Progressives captured control of the Republican State Central Committee in September and assumed responsibility for that campaign.

William Allen White called on Hughes in Estes Park several days after the California tour. The tired and battle-scarred candidate was resting in the pleasant Colorado resort. During the course of a hike along the Fall River, the men talked over the California campaign. Hughes was conscious of his blunders. He asked White: "What are the Progressive issues? I have been out of politics so long that I am not familiar with them. Just how should I express my sympathy with the Progressive movement?"

White recommended that Hughes speak out for several issues, including laws limiting working hours and establishing minimum wages; that he support an eight-hour day, old-age pensions, and several other liberal programs.[45] Hughes expressed his gratitude for White's advice, and then proceeded to ignore most of it. His ignorance of the major issues of the day, or his refusal to discuss them publicly, continues to astound and baffle the student of the Hughes campaign. His tour of California had served only to send the political temperature soaring, as the chasm separating Progressives and Republicans grew even wider.

# 10

## THE INITIAL RESPONSE

On August 16 Hiram Johnson had shouted to a Progressive crowd in Sacramento's Clunie Theater that the people of California would have to choose whether their state would be represented in the national Congress by "the philosophy of Mr. De Young and Mr. Otis and Mr. Spreckels and Mr. Crocker, with his inherited Southern Pacific millions, or whether it goes there with your viewpoint and your philosophy of government." [1] After Hughes left the state, the governor stepped up his attack against the regular Republicans. If he were elected, Johnson proclaimed, he would continue to be a Progressive. "You and I must not repine the passing of the Progressive party," said Johnson in a Los Angeles speech on August 24. "I stand now right where I have stood for the past six years. When I had to choose between the candidates I chose Hughes. . . . If his policies commend themselves to me, I will support them." [2]

Meanwhile, regular Republicans kept demanding the

eviction of all Progressives from their party. Willis Booth proved to be a formidable and effective campaigner. The tall, handsome banker pictured the contest between himself and Johnson as one "between real and bogus Republicans." He was ardently supported in his charge by the Republican organization. To Republicans the paramount question was whether California would remain in the clutches of the Johnson machine. They were certain that all signs pointed to its defeat. There had never been a more crucial election in the state.

On the night before the primary, Francis Keesling was positive that a notable victory for genuine Republican candidates would be scored at the polls. "I have never felt more confident of victory in an election than tonight, and I believe that we shall elect enough regular Republicans to insure a State Central Committee that will be composed of genuine Republicans. I expect Tuesday, August 29, to be remembered as a notable day in the history of the Republican party in California." [3] After nearly six powerless years, the Old Guard scented victory in the evening breezes.

On election day the Los Angeles *Times* predicted "that Johnson will be doomed to disappointment, for the returned Progressives will vote for Booth and the unreturned ones will vote for the Democratic nominee or not vote at all, and all that will be left of Hiram W. Johnson after November will be the memory of his mephitic public career. . . ." The *Times* further advised the governor to "dig his own political grave, dig it deep and crawl into it." [4]

On August 29 the voters of California expressed their preference. Despite a handicap of 300,000 supporters being registered without major party affiliation and therefore unable to vote, Hiram Johnson won *both* the Progressive and Republican primaries—the latter by more than 15,000 votes.[5] Hiram Johnson, flouted by the leaders of the Republican party and running as a devout Progressive, became both parties' candidate for United States senator. Each side had utilized every possible advantage of its respective political position, but ultimately Progressives and progressive-Republicans absorbed like a great sponge the votes necessary for a Johnson victory.

The primary election was California's message to the nation. It was California's answer to the assertion that progressivism was dead. Rowell rubbed some salt into Hughes's wounds after the returns were counted. He wired the presidential candidate, who was still resting in Estes Park, advising him to congratulate Johnson by telegram. It would be interesting to know what went through Hughes's mind as he dictated the following congratulatory message, wishing Johnson success in the coming national election: ". . . I TRUST THERE WILL BE A COMPLETE UNION OF FORCES, INSURING A THOROUGHGOING VICTORY." [6] "I WAS VERY GLAD TO RECEIVE YOUR TELEGRAM OF CONGRATULATIONS," Johnson replied tersely, "AND I THANK YOU FOR IT." [7]

Some accounts of the Hughes campaign in California state that as soon as the primary was over and his election to the United States Senate was practically assured, Johnson "spoke ardently and enthusiastically for Hughes" [8] and that he "swallowed his resentment . . . and advocated Hughes to the limit of his ability." [9] Mowry contends that the "documents of the campaign do not justify the judgment" that Johnson gave little more than lip service to Hughes and by so doing encouraged his own supporters to vote for Wilson. "This was the charge made by California conservatives after the election," writes Mowry, "and this has been the popularly held verdict ever since." Mowry admits that Johnson campaigned for Hughes with no great personal conviction and points out that he did not attack President Wilson in his speeches. He also states that Johnson nevertheless campaigned for Hughes "in his customary energetic fashion." After referring to the fact that Johnson again and again described Hughes in terms of progressivism—"a champion of the people," "a progressive pioneer who had fought in New York for the very things we now have in California"—Mowry concludes by stating: "If that were not sufficient evidence of Johnson's good works, the request of the national campaign committee that he speak for the national ticket in the Progressive Middle West should close the question." [10] But should it? An analysis of certain campaign speeches indicates that the governor spoke highly of Hughes's progressive accomplishments, but with a "Johnsonian" slant. The following extract from an address delivered by Johnson at the Trinity Auditorium in Los Angeles on October 27 illustrates this "Johnsonian" bias:

> I watched at first with passing interest and then with great enthusiasm the record of Charles Hughes as governor of the state of New York. I saw him, while he was governor of that great state, make his valiant and fearless fight against a boss of his own party. . . . I saw him do it just as I loved to make that fight in the state of California, by going over the heads of all politicians. . . .
> I saw him . . . ever take the advice from the many and dictation from none. He was his own master. . . .[11]

Johnson was speaking as much for himself as he was for the presidential candidate. He had once confided to Katherine Edson that he had made his choice for Hughes, but would go his own way. Now he publicly confirmed what everyone already knew: that he was his own master. Nor did he seldom miss slipping in a few subtle jabs at Hughes and many obvious slams at the regular Republicans. For example, at Porterville on October 21, Johnson declared: "Whenever there is any candidacy on my part I do not ask permission of any millionaire newspaper proprietor or any great corporation or any little clique of politicians." [12] Johnson was not about to see the props knocked out from under his accomplishments as governor, and then stand idly by. If Hughes's election meant control of the state by Crocker and his kind, he would do everything to prevent it.

During the final days of the campaign, it is true, Johnson was speaking nightly for Hughes. On November 1 he advocated Hughes's election in Palo Alto. The next day he made a strong speech for him in Oakland, and on the following night in San Francisco he spoke twice for the Republican candidate. In one of the speeches he praised Hughes's record as governor of New York in much the same manner as he had elsewhere: "I saw Governor Hughes drive out of the State Capitol at Albany the black horses of privilege, the same as we drove them out at Sacramento." [13]

Thus Johnson mirrored *himself* in Hughes's past progressive accomplishments. He wanted Progressive, Republican, *and* Democratic votes; he could not afford to speak against either presidential candidate—Hughes or Wilson. Instead of employing the political maneuver normally used by state politicians—that of grabbing the coattails of a national candidate—Johnson cleverly reversed the tactic: if Hughes was going to win in California, it would be as a progressive, not as a reactionary. If voters remained unconvinced that Hughes could ever be a progressive Republican President, Johnson could not be bothered. His election came first; his machine and his own accomplishments were infinitely more important. Self-interest and justifiable pride had triumphed.

The state convention that would select the new State Central Committee, adopt the state platform, and select the presidential electors met in Sacramento on September 19. This convention was composed of individuals who had been nominated in the primaries for the state legislature;

of these the Progressives had a substantial majority. "When the Republican state convention was called to order in the Assembly chamber of the state capitol at two o'clock," the *Star* reported, "Hiram Johnson had gained complete control of the body." [14]

In an effort to neutralize the Johnson majority, Assemblyman Bartlett of Los Angeles, representing the regular Republicans, introduced an amendment before the roll call was taken. It stated that all delegates must have their proper credentials certified by the regular Republican secretary of state, Frank Jordan. The purpose of the amendment was to prevent those delegates who had won Republican nominations at the primaries, but who were not registered as Republicans, from receiving convention credentials. The amendment was rejected. This resulted in the voting of credentials to four registered Progressives and three additional candidates for the legislature whose elections were being contested by the regular Republicans. For the first time in California history, even under the direct primary, delegates registered in another party were allowed to vote in a Republican convention.

During the adjournment that followed the selection of a temporary chairman, emissaries from the pro-Johnson group informed regular Republicans that they would adopt a resolution endorsing the nomination of Hughes, provided Republicans would not oppose a resolution endorsing the Johnson administration.

When the Republicans found they could secure the endorsement of Hughes only as a concession and not as a right, they decided to remain silent throughout the convention. They would take no part either for or against any program the Johnson administration might propose. "We found ourselves placed in a position where we must take the administration program or start a row that might have endangered seriously the chances of Hughes and Fairbanks [the vice-presidential candidate] in California," complained a Republican assemblyman. "The only thing to do," he added, "was to accept our humiliation in the interests of the Republican national ticket." [15]

Control of the State Central Committee had been easily wrested from Crocker and Keesling, who watched helplessly from the sidelines. As the convention adjourned, another meeting was being planned for September 30 to organize the fall campaign.

Several days after the state convention, Lissner wrote Roosevelt and told him that the Progressives had regained control of the Republican party in California. "We are now the 'regular' Republicans of the state of California," Lissner bragged. A State Central Committee of three hundred men and women had been selected, he reported, nearly all of whom had progressive inclinations. The committee had soothed Republican feelings by making Willis Booth, the defeated Republican senatorial candidate, a presidential elector, "but the mean, nasty fellows, the irreconcilables—the stilleto men—we left off entirely." [16]

The new committee met again September 30 in San Francisco. Rowell was elected chairman and commented sarcastically that the process seemed like the Methodist church admitting a blackened sinner on probation one day and electing him bishop the next.[17] Chairmanship of the important fifty-man Executive Committee—which included Lissner, Dickson, and Stimson—was given to Raymond Benjamin, a Progressive and chief deputy of the state attorney general. This committee was divided into two parts on a geographical basis: thirty members were to handle the state north of the Tehachepi, and the rest were put in charge of southern California.

Temporarily, the Republican party in California no longer existed, so far as the management and control of the campaign were concerned. "As a result," wrote Senator John D. Works to Hughes after the national election in November, "there were members on the state central committee and members of the presidential electors . . . who were disloyal to you as a candidate of the Republican party and actively supported Wilson. . . ." [18]

How effective was the campaign waged by the new State Central Committee in behalf of the Republican presidential candidate? One significant contention emerges from the correspondence of Lissner, Rowell, and Johnson to nationally prominent figures like Roosevelt, Perkins, Ickes, Robins, and others in the East. Letter after letter states that "almost without exception, the leading members of our organization are in good faith doing everything we can for the national ticket. But Mr. Hughes left matters in a bad mess for us and we must not be blamed if the showing he makes is not what it should be. . . ." [19] These letters imply that the Progressive-controlled committee was fighting a futile battle against overwhelming odds. But was the battle diligently fought?

The papers of Francis Keesling contain some highly interesting and damning evidence. In mid-October Keesling, curious and concerned about the effectiveness of the campaign being waged against Wilson, wrote letters to many local Republicans in cities and towns throughout California. He requested that they indicate to him what was being done for Hughes, and what was planned for the next few weeks. The following excerpts, and there are many more, have been selected at random from the return letters postmarked from October 16 to October 29:

> From Alameda County: "Are Republican meetings being held in your county?—No. What meetings are being scheduled between now and the elections—None."

> From Sacramento County: "Republican meetings have not and are not being held in this city." "There has been nothing done so far as the national campaign is concerned and Republicans are disgusted."

From San Francisco County: "From all I can see around the headquarters, they don't want Hughes, but want Wilson. Up in Room 422 it is full of Hughes literature, and I think they will get it out next Christmas from the way they are working, but the Johnson stuff is moving very fast."

From Yreka: "In regard to our County, no meetings have been held whatever and I do not know that there will be any. Everything is as dead as can be. . . . In other words, our committee is somewhat disgusted."

From Los Angeles County: ". . . There is no energetic campaign being made for the national ticket in this county. . . ."[20]

These excerpts, and the many other letters Keesling saved, are a strong indictment of the new campaign organization under Progressive control. In addition, we have the written opinion of Edgar A. Luce, state senator from San Diego County, who wrote John Francis Neylan:

Aside from the general causes that produced the large Wilson vote in this state, the reasons purely local were: First, the San Diego *Sun* conducted a very able campaign for Wilson. . . . On the other hand, the San Diego *Union* conducted a very brainless campaign as usual and drove votes away from Hughes. . . . In the second place, there was practically no local work done. The committee was $300 in the hole when the campaign started and we found it almost impossible to raise money. . . . Consequently, we had no money for ordinary campaign work, including distribution of literature.
Between us, as you doubtless know, the Central Committee was not worth a damn. They were constantly kidding themselves with the idea that Hughes would carry the county by 5,000. . . .[21]

Neylan himself was extremely disappointed with the lack of effort on Hughes's behalf in southern California. In his opinion, local committees did not realize how desperate the Hughes fight was and remained "blissfully complacent," concentrating instead upon congressional races in Orange, San Bernardino, and San Diego counties.[22] "It seems humorous now to have such papers as the Los Angeles *Times* speak of our not exerting every effort in behalf of Hughes," Neylan wrote State Senator John M. Anderson of Santa Ana. "I think you will remember how annoyed the Committee in Orange County became at my insistence that the Congressional fight was not the great overshadowing struggle, and that it was unjust for them to let Mr. Hughes' fight lag. . . ."[23]

While the available evidence is not absolutely conclusive, it suggests strongly that on the grass-roots level, Hughes did not receive full-scale support. If the Republicans neglected their presidential candidate to concentrate on congressional races, the Democratic organization devoted its entire effort to Woodrow Wilson's election. Greatly outnumbered in registration, though united in leadership, the Democrats worked diligently to overcome adverse conditions. Their diligence paid dividends.[24]

"If there is anything certain in politics, it is that Governor Hiram Johnson, of California, will be elected on November 7 to the United States Senate," reported the progressive *Outlook* in late October, "yet California in the presidential election is regarded as a doubtful state."[25] Charles Evans Hughes had been convinced that he should, in his own interest, ignore Hiram Johnson and the California Progressives in August. Assuming that the regular Republicans were going to "kick the Johnson machine out of California politics," he chose to play on their team. He thereby identified his cause with their cause. Johnson surprised them all by winning the primary election. Shortly thereafter the Progressives took control of the Hughes campaign. The final drive during October and the first week of November was not conducted with any great vigor or with any sense of urgency.

With the world situation so critical, most Americans felt there ought to be some excellent reasons before making a change in Presidents. "Why are we called to make the change?" asked Walter Lippmann, then an editor of the *New Republic*. "A change of government ought to take place only if there is a sharp necessity and a real alternative. The necessity may exist, but the alternative doesn't." [26]

Would California Progressives consider Hughes a necessary alternative? Or had his obvious preference for regular Republicans and his indifference toward the Progressives and their accomplishments convinced them that he would be a negative alternative to Woodrow Wilson? In California the outcome of the election would depend ultimately upon those who had voted for Roosevelt in 1912, but had not transferred their allegiance to Wilson during his term of office. Had the drift of Progressive votes to Wilson been checked? Had Johnson, Rowell, and the new State Central Committee managed to convince the Progressives that their votes should be cast for Charles Evans Hughes? It was with a sense of growing interest that the nation turned its attention to California, where it was felt the final act would be played out on November 7.

# 11

## THE FINAL RESPONSE

As the polls closed in the East on election day, voters in the western part of the nation were still casting their ballots. The East was Hughes territory, and there was little surprise when early returns from New England and New York showed large pluralities for the Republican candidate. It became apparent by nine o'clock Tuesday night that Hughes had not only carried most, if not all, of the North Atlantic seaboard states, but had won in the midwestern states of Illinois, Michigan, and Wisconsin. Many observers considered Wilson's chances for reelection negligible. Even the New York *Times*, a reluctant supporter of Wilson, flashed from the top of its tower a red light, signaling to the people of New York City that a new President had been elected. Early returns from the Rocky Mountain states and the Pacific Coast indicated narrow pluralities for Hughes. Meanwhile, in his suite on the eighth floor of the Hotel Astor in New York City, Hughes slept the deep sleep of an exhausted presidential candidate.[1]

That night, the *Evening Post* was the only major New York newspaper that did not concede the election of Hughes.[2] The editor of the *Times* wrote his Wednesday morning editorial, which read in part: "The marvel of it is that the Republican party has been united after the disastrous division of 1912. . . . Mr. Roosevelt was the breath of life, the whole soul of the Progressive party in 1912. The bulk of his party preceded him in the march back to the Republican camp."[3]

During that night, however, the distance between the two candidates narrowed. Party managers kept their eyes glued upon returns from the West. In one western state after another, Wilson pulled up on the inside rail and moved into the lead. The race in California was neck and neck. On Tuesday night it appeared to be safely won by Hughes, but then was thrown in the doubtful list by the returns of a substantial bloc of Wilson precincts in and around San Francisco. Wilson had carried these in 1912, so they were shrugged off by Republicans as being indecisive. All eyes turned toward Los Angeles. When that county went for Hughes, Rowell predicted to reporters that the state would go Republican by a small margin. It all depended upon the rest of the state. Returns came in slowly Wednesday and Thursday, and it was not until Thursday night that they were all tallied. At eleven o'clock Chairman Rowell conceded the state to Wilson. Hughes had been defeated by less than 4,000 votes, while Hiram Johnson had been elected to the United States Senate by a margin of nearly 300,000 votes.[4]

Whether registered in their own party or as Republicans, the California Progressives had responded to the challenge presented them by the conventions in Chicago and by Hughes's presidential campaign. They had not forgotten what they believed in 1912, and for what compelling reasons they had joined a new national party. Motivation for their response is perhaps best described by William Allen White, who had explained to an irate Theodore Roosevelt why Mrs. White had voted for Wilson. White wrote that ". . . she feared the Wall Street taint upon Hughes, and she did not want to encourage by her vote anything that had any connection with the group that controlled the Republican convention of 1912 or that throttled Republican sentiment in 1916." [5] Hiram Johnson and Chester Rowell's campaign organization had failed to replace that frightening Wall Street image created in California by the Old Guard and by Hughes himself.

On Friday morning, November 10, 1916, the Los Angeles *Times* in a front-page editorial accused Johnson's political machine of treachery. On Saturday it charged that the "Governor fairly out-did his own record as a prestidigitator with the double cross." Claiming that Johnson had been a political traitor from the time he had appeared in California public life, the *Times* further denounced him for having "treacherously sacrificed friends, supporters and colleagues wherever and whenever it would give him office and emoluments." [6] Other conservative newspapers and periodicals joined in the condemnation.

There is no doubt that Johnson had been extremely disappointed by the Hughes who had toured California. Shortly after Hughes's departure, Johnson had written to the astute E. A. Van Valkenberg, publisher of the Philadelphia *North American*, a strong progressive newspaper: "I am unable to understand the man. The man I met in New York I thought was strong, alert mentally, and brave. The man who came to California was cringing and cowardly and contemptible. . . ." [7]

Soon after the election, Johnson wrote to major Progressives and Republican leaders in the East and explained to them that "it was a matter of profound regret to me that we did not carry the state for Hughes." He assured them:

"... we did the best we could to undo the harm that was done at the time Hughes visited California and we almost succeeded. ..."[8] At the same time he wrote his friend Medill McCormick, who had been vice-chairman of the Progressive National Committee in 1912 and was then publisher of the Chicago *Tribune*, that "... the time is past when the ivory-headed, adamantine, backward-looking standpatter can get by with our people. ..."[9]

As George Mowry suggests, any attempt to assign reasons for the defeat or victory of a particular candidate in such a historic election is an extremely risky undertaking. The closer the election, the more risky the attempt becomes. Minor considerations, which might be overlooked by the historian, could have in fact been decisive.

The election of 1916, however, was one of the most crucial in our history. The Progressives had contributed for the second time to the defeat of the Republican party. Had Hughes won, the course of United States history, to say nothing of the Republican party itself, might have been altered considerably. At the time, the *Manchester Guardian* argued that the Germans were fully aware Wilson would not lead the United States to war—that he was "too proud to fight." If Hughes had been elected—so the argument ran—the Germans would have known from his campaign speeches that he was no appeaser. As a result, they would not have launched their submarine attack upon American merchant-marine shipping, for fear it might prompt United States intervention. Thus, American intervention in World War I might have been avoided.[10] Another "might-have-been" is implied by Walter Johnson: a Hughes victory would have precluded the election of Harding and the subsequent terms of Coolidge. A decade of "Babylonian debauchery" and even a depression might have been avoided.[11]

The might-have-beens of history, however, are seldom

a profitable or worthwhile subject for historical inquiry. The fact is that Hughes lost the national contest by twelve electoral votes. To win he required 266 votes; he received 254. One state had the thirteen electoral votes that would have defeated Wilson—California. Granted, the attempt to determine how and why Hughes was defeated in California is most difficult owing to the closeness of the vote; yet the crucial importance of the election warrants a careful analysis of the results.

Arthur Link states that there was an almost perfect alignment of progressives and conservatives into two opposing camps during the campaign of 1916, "and that the issue of further advancement toward a dynamic social welfare democracy drew large numbers to Wilson's side." "But," Link continues, "to interpret the campaign solely within this framework would be to miss the most important phenomenon of the contest: the fusion of the peace cause with the ideal of progressive democracy that the President and his campaigners effected." [12]

The peace issue *was* significant in California, particularly among women voters. It has been suggested earlier that California Progressives resented international commitments because they threatened continued domestic reform.[13] This noninterventionist sentiment accounted in great measure for the Progressives' response in 1916, and Wilson capitalized on it. Hughes, on the other hand, was caught on the horns of a dilemma: realizing the voter appeal in the slogan "he kept us out of war," he was forced to condone Roosevelt's persistent denunciations of Wilson's cowardly weakness and timidity in foreign affairs. This permitted the Democrats to use the peace issue as one of their main themes, and to accuse Hughes of interventionist intentions.

Furthermore, Wilson received the support of labor in California, and not just because Hughes was served lunch by nonunion waiters in San Francisco. When the Adamson Act was passed on September 2, establishing an eight-hour day for railroad brotherhoods, Hughes attacked it viciously in an effort to bolster his drooping campaign, thereby alienating many union members.

The political conversion of the *New Republic*'s persuasive editors—Walter Lippmann, Walter Weyl, and Herbert Croly—must have convinced some voters. There were only 24,000 subscribers to the *New Republic* in 1916; but, as Charles Forcey suggests in his book dealing with these three political journalists of the Progressive era, "a paper that had the support of Croly, Weyl, Lippmann, Frankfurter, Beard, Dewey, Hand, and so many others might just help swing the old Bull Moose vote."[14]

Wilson's "moves to the left" during 1916 (particularly his appointment of Louis D. Brandeis to the Supreme Court in January) had pleased the *New Republic* editors. By May, when the President began speaking of a league of nations, they had become extremely enthusiastic. These events, joined with Wilson's stand for such domestic policies as child-labor regulation and a tariff commission, indicated to them that a great change had taken place in his administration.

Nevertheless, in June, Croly and his associates declared themselves to be politically "on the fence." In fact, Forcey writes: ". . . privately the editors began the campaign strongly disposed toward the Republican candidate."[15] Despite their criticism of Wilson during the summer, the editors could work up little enthusiasm for Hughes. They objected to his "mildness and tendency to temporize." They also disliked the fact that Hughes failed to include social reform in his preparedness plans. Although Forcey makes no mention of the California tour, Hughes's blunders and his failure to commend the California Progressives could have had only a negative effect on the *New Republic* editors.

Lippmann was the first of the three openly to support Wilson. Three weeks before the election he wrote that he intended to vote for the "Wilson who is evolving under experience and is remaking his philosophy in the light of it, for the Wilson who is temporarily at least creating, out of the reactionary, parochial fragments of the Democracy, the only party which at this moment is national in scope, liberal in purpose, and effective in action." [16] Readers of the *New Republic* still undecided for whom to vote in late October might have been swayed by the able and astringent Croly. With "all the tortured integrity that gave his leadership its peculiar strength," he waited until the next to last issue before the election to declare that the Republican party consisted of a fortuitous collection of warring factions united only by an intolerance of Wilson. "Toryism under Sir Robert Peel," he quipped, "was once described as organized hypocrisy; Republicanism under Charles Evans Hughes may be described as organized incompatibility." [17]

In addition to the peace issue, the labor vote, and the editorials of respected political journalists, there was another factor contributing to Hughes's defeat. By the fall of 1916, the Democratic congressional majority had enacted almost every important plank in the Progressive platform of 1912. Progressivism had found acceptance by a major party, and this caused many Progressives throughout the nation to "move en masse to the Wilson camp." [18] Arthur Link suggests that to single out the independent progressives—the social workers, sociologists, and articulate intellectuals—who voted for Wilson would be "to name practically the entire leadership of the advance wing of the progressive movement in the United States." [19] Many Progressive leaders who had voted for Roosevelt in 1912 also came out for Wilson—Francis J. Heney, John M. Parker, Bainbridge Colby, Victor Murdock, and Matthew Hale, to name a few.

## The Final Response   163

Mowry states that in addition to support from Progressive defectors and from the labor vote, the peace votes, and the women's votes, it "might also be argued that Wilson won because he appealed to the small towns and the countryside. . . ."[20] It can *also* be argued that he won in these places because of inefficient Republican campaign organization. Mowry does not emphasize the fact that the Progressives took over the State Central Committee and were then responsible for the Hughes campaign during the final important weeks. It became this committee's task to persuade undecided voters to cast their ballots for Hughes. Perhaps California Progressives registered as Republicans "were not automatons to be shoved around as Johnson pleased," as suggested by Mowry, but there were undoubtedly many others who could have been convinced by a driving campaign that Hughes, once in office, would be a progressive President.

The authors of *The People's Choice*, a study of voting behavior in the 1940 presidential election, have stated that a presidential campaign has three effects upon voters: first, it activates the indifferent; second, it reinforces the partisan; and third, it converts the doubtful.[21] The most important of these effects in the election of 1916 in California were the first and the third.

The California presidential campaign *was* successful in "activating the indifferent"—at least nonvoting for President in 1916 was not so great as in 1912 or 1920. In fact, only 24 percent of the registered voters did not cast presidential ballots, as compared with 32 percent in 1912 and 31½ percent in 1920.[22]

An even more important campaign endeavor during the final weeks was to "convert the doubtful"—to convince Progressives and others that Hughes would not be a reactionary President. In 1916 registered Republicans outnumbered registered Democrats about two to one in California. We can therefore estimate that at least half the voters were potential Hughes voters. Yet we have the written testimony of concerned Republicans who claimed the campaign was conducted without vigor and expressed their disgust at the lack of Hughes campaign meetings scheduled.

"In the last analysis," conclude the authors of *The People's Choice,*

> more than anything else people can move other people. From an ethical point of view this is a hopeful aspect in the serious social problem of propaganda. The side which has the more enthusiastic supporters and which can mobilize grass-roots support in an expert way has great chances of success.[23]

The extraordinary number of "split tickets" cast in the 1916 California election—votes for Johnson, running as a Republican, and for Wilson, a Democrat—testified to the fact that Hughes did not receive expert mobilization of grass-roots support.

If it could be determined for which presidential candidate Johnson and Rowell voted in 1916, perhaps we could then know what motivations guided their conduct in the months preceding the election. We do not know this, and probably never will, unless convincing evidence turns up in the correspondence still retained by their respective families. There are, however, two letters of extreme importance, one by Johnson and the other by Rowell.

In a handwritten letter on Hotel Virginia stationery (written on a Sunday, probably after the "snub" incident at the hotel, though otherwise undated) Johnson informed Rowell that their treatment by Hughes and the regular Republicans was "not only outrageous but positively insulting." He was uncertain of his immediate course of action, but made it very clear to Rowell that they could not permit a return to power by the old Southern Pacific machine:

*The Final Response* 165

... Here's the big thing that moves me: In 1910 we kicked the Southern Pacific out of the government of California. In 1916, through Mr. Hughes, the inherited Southern Pacific millions are again to control the State. In your analytical and wonderfully intellectual fashion, you may academically palliate the blow; but Mr. Hughes' election and Mr. Crocker's absolute control mean exactly what I say—that the Crocker millions inherited from Southern Pacific infamy again dominate California! We can get along without a United States Senator; I can afford to be beaten. Can I afford, can I supinely permit that which I've so consistently fought, the destruction of which has been my consuming thought politically, again to command my State? I'm not clear as to my duty; but my dear Rowell . . . , if I conclude my duty to California demands, at any hazard, the defeat of Mr. Crocker and the prevention of the return to power of the old regime, and that only by defeating Hughes can these sinister influences be defeated in our State, I'll throw the Senatorship aside, and devote myself exclusively to the endeavor necessary. . . .[24]

Johnson does not order Rowell to see to it that Hughes does not win, but it is obviously on his mind. Rowell must have been affected by such sentiments so forcefully expressed by Johnson.

We also have a record of a statement made by Chester Rowell more than ten years after the election of 1916. Tucked away in the Lincoln-Roosevelt Republican Club Papers at Stanford University is a copy of a letter written by Rowell in 1927. In it he told a friend that Hughes apparently understood that his defeat in 1916 was partially his own fault. "At least he made this remark to Senator Johnson within the last two years: 'If I had had as much sense for five minutes in California in 1916 as I have all the time now, I would have been President.'" Rowell continued:

The fact is that if anybody is responsible for Hughes' defeat, aside from himself and from the stupid bunglers whom he permitted to seize custody of himself in California, I am that person. I stirred up the entire disturbance, made all the fight during the period of controversy, and then when the explosion was over I was made head of the committee whose business it was to carry California for Hughes. I am conscious that I did my honest best to bring about that result, but I am also conscious that I failed in it, and one must take responsibility for his own failures. . . .[25]

The truth is that neither faction of the Republican party—progressive nor regular—worked for unity and combined effort. The truth is that Charles Evans Hughes was sacrificed between their respective ambitions and mutual antipathies. His mistake was in choosing the wrong side, for we can now see that Johnson's political power had not waned. Here we may agree with Mowry, who contends that "the vote was so close in the state that despite these potent factors [labor and noninterventionist sentiment] Hughes probably would have won had he not alienated many Progressives." [26] He would have won, however, not because Hiram Johnson and the California Progressives had any faithful allegiance to the Republican party. Had Hughes chosen to be guided on his tour by Progressives, he would have won because Johnson's pride would not have been insulted and his control of California politics would not have been jeopardized. Johnson's image, and that of his party as well, had been badly tarnished by the defeat of the nonpartisan bill in 1915 and by the failure of the United Republican movement in 1916. It was vitally necessary for him to regain this lost prestige, and to defend his reform accomplishments, by preventing a return to power by the old regime. He feared that if Hughes won, not only would his image suffer another blow, but regular Republicans would take credit for the victory and thereby feel justified in demanding at least equal representation in state politics. In other words, Hiram Johnson was not convinced that Hughes's victory was fair compensation for the risk of ultimately losing his own political control.

Thus the truth lies somewhere between the charge of betrayal made by the Los Angeles *Times* and a complete acquittal of Hiram Johnson and the California Progressives. Perhaps a conclusion that squares closest with the facts is that Hiram Johnson and the California Progressives were ultimately accountable for the defeat of Charles Evans Hughes in 1916, not by active betrayal but by inactive support. Johnson, by not lashing out at Wilson for fear of losing Democratic votes, and Rowell, by not conducting a positive and vigorous campaign, each contributed to Hughes's defeat in his own decisive way.

Assuming Johnson and Rowell gave only perfunctory support to Hughes, was their indifference justified? Can a political machine that seeks to perpetuate itself by employing questionable means be excused on the grounds that it functions for admirable ends? Is there a difference between a machine that condones corporation dominance and vested interests in government, and a machine that does not? Does the action of the Old Guard in keeping Hughes away from Johnson "at all costs" cancel out the subsequent inaction of Rowell's State Central Committee? These are questions that can only be answered by each reader. But certain facts are indisputable. In a state that for five years had been controlled by Hiram Johnson and his supporters, Charles Evans Hughes was presented to the electorate in the exclusive custody of the leaders of a deposed political machine attempting to regain power. In a state where Hiram Johnson was the most influential political figure, the absolute condition insisted upon was that Johnson and Hughes must not meet.[27]

Hughes could have been elected had he actively courted the Progressives. It is obvious that he and his advisers misjudged Hiram Johnson's political power. Perhaps Johnson himself could have changed the course of history by letting Hughes know he was present in the Hotel Virginia. While Johnson's actions are subject to rebuke—he was running on the Republican ticket and was ostensibly supporting Hughes—it was the regular Republicans who threw the first punch, and splenetic Hiram Johnson was not the kind of man to go into a clinch and not punch back. Many readers might feel that Hiram Johnson, Chester Rowell, and the California Progressives would deserve a much higher "historical rating" had they risen above their pride and the turbulence of California politics. Perhaps this study will help to explain why they could not.

# 12

## AN APPRAISAL

Hiram Johnson had so closely identified himself with progressivism in California that when the time came to turn over the reins of government to his successor, Lieutenant Governor William D. Stephens, he refused to resign. Stephens, a successful Los Angeles businessman and former United States congressman, had been appointed lieutenant governor upon John Eshleman's untimely death in February, 1916. Forced upon a reluctant Johnson by prominent Progressive leaders in southern California, the new lieutenant governor was never accorded complete acceptance or recognition by Johnson and his close friends. Fearful that Stephens would easily succumb to conservative pressures, Johnson remained in office until the very last minute. Only a summons from President Wilson to attend a special congressional session in April, 1917, convinced Johnson that the time had come to leave California. Had that summons not arrived, he might well have stayed on for the remainder of his legal term.

Johnson's almost pathological distrust of Stephens did not wane after he had settled in Washington, D.C. The fires of this distrust were fanned by John Francis Neylan, who sent periodic reports of Stephens' alleged ineptitude and vacillation. On one occasion Johnson acknowledged such a report by referring to Stephens as a "mere swine with his head in the trough," and issued Neylan this warning: ". . . Be ever on your guard. Be as cautious and as wily and as clever as they are. Don't permit any act of yours to be distorted to your disadvantage. . . ."[1] Thus the transfer of power in California was made very difficult by Johnson himself, who continually failed to heed Chester Rowell's friendly advice: "You can not win loyalty by suspicion or confirm support by ungenerousness. Neither can you teach the people to trust your successor by doubting him yourself. . . ."[2]

Johnson's conduct during that transitional period was most unfortunate. His pessimistic appraisal of his successor was not only ungracious, it was unfounded. William Stephens worked diligently to preserve the reforms of the Johnson administration, and even managed to achieve progressive tax legislation in the later years of his own term.[3] Nevertheless, in political matters, Hiram Johnson was a very suspicious and ungenerous individual. Several actions during his governorship testify to his selfishness and to his willingness to place his own political survival above that of any organization or party: the waging of a campaign independent of the Lincoln-Roosevelt League in 1910; his fight with Francis Heney and the formation of nonpartisan Johnson-Eshleman clubs independent of the California Progressive party in 1914; and his conduct during the Hughes campaign of 1916. These various maneuvers, and others, were conceived and executed by a skillful tactician who fully comprehended the realities of political life. Hiram Johnson played the game of politics to win, and win he did; and because he won, California benefited from

*An Appraisal* 171

strong, vigorous leadership during the years 1911 to 1917. We must judge the administration of Hiram Johnson not alone by the governor's own political machinations, but chiefly by the way it devised machinery to meet the pressing political, social, and economic problems of the day.

Emancipation of California from railroad rule—this is the most publicized and perhaps most significant contribution of the Johnson administration; for the liberation *was* accomplished, and without damaging the economic position of the railroads. In fact, those corporate enterprises enjoyed continued and increased prosperity. The Southern Pacific, for example, suffered no antitrust barrage from the Johnson administration. Instead, while declaring that the Southern Pacific should be preserved as a great corporate entity, the railroad commissioners announced the economic ideal that governed their work: "monopoly with potential competition." [4]

Indeed, the advent of effective public regulation of California's railways was praised even by William Herrin, chief counsel and political manager of the Southern Pacific. Addressing the California Bar Association in November, 1913, Herrin made this remarkable statement:

> No principle is more vital in railway administration than that there shall be no unjust discrimination between shippers as to service rendered or the rates charged therefore. . . . There could be no more insidious or vicious practice than to favor one shipper or class of shippers at the expense of others. . . . Yet these vicious discriminations were frequent before they were abolished by the force of government regulation. . . . I think no railroad manager would agree to dispense with government regulation at the cost of returning to the old conditions. . . .[5]

Because of his railroad background, Herrin's statement had special significance. Yet it was clear that he voiced the opinion of most Californians, particularly the farmers and shippers, who flourished under the new conditions. The jurisdiction of the reorganized and revitalized Railroad Commission was not restricted to railroads, however. Of equal importance was control over the rate charges of utility companies, previously outside the purview of public supervision. Under the provisions of the Public Utilities Act of 1911, such control was taken from municipalities and county boards of supervisors and was given to the state.

Effective railroad and public-utility regulation thus required a drastic modification of the doctrine of laissez-faire. In repudiating the Jeffersonian concept of the limited state, the Johnson administration placed itself squarely in line with the growing tendency of the time to centralize state government and to create some sort of state control over business locally operated. Richard Hofstadter has pointed out that in attempting to remedy the most pressing ills of industrial society, Progressives "quickly learned that they could not achieve their ends without using the power of the administrative state. . . ." [6] In this sense, they laid the foundation of the welfare state.

In a book entitled *Efficiency and Uplift,* Samuel Haber discusses the application of Frederick Taylor's principle of scientific management in industry to the conduct of governmental affairs. Haber contends that the reform movement of the early twentieth century "was less a matter of rooting up and destroying than of management, control, and regulation. . . . [Reform] became a technical question in which considerations of efficiency were important." [7] Haber does not specifically mention California's experience with reform, but his general theme is applicable there also.

Californians during the governorship of Hiram Johnson displayed a growing interest in the "scientific" management of governmental affairs. Reliance upon commissions of experts, and upon boards of laymen who hired experts, characterized the Progressives' efforts to solve social and economic problems. These experts collected data on wages and working conditions, published statistics relating to industrial accidents, made field surveys of housing conditions, and so forth, in an attempt to construct some factual bases for further legislative action.

The Johnson administration's devotion to efficiency and economy in government reached its apogee in John Francis Neylan's Board of Control. Created to provide close supervision of the state's finances, the Board of Control also investigated state agencies, audited state accounts, submitted budgets, exposed and prevented graft, and generally acted as a financial watchdog. Such activities, however, were merely incidental objectives of the board. As Neylan stated in a summary report to Governor Johnson, the major work of the Board of Control "was to systematize the business of the State of California in such a way that after a reasonable time it could challenge comparison of the State's system with the system in vogue in those great corporations that are models of modern commercial enterprise." Although state expenditures in 1917 were nearly double what they had been when Johnson took office, Neylan was proud to announce that an inherited deficit of more than $250,000 had been converted into a surplus of more than $4,500,000 by the end of 1916.[8]

In addition to their demand for administrative efficiency and scientific management, progressives favored more direct participation in governmental affairs by California's citizens. Disgusted by a succession of corrupt legislatures dominated by railroad interests, the reformers adopted certain "panaceas"—direct primary, initiative, referendum, and recall—which they believed would permit the incorrupt "people" to purify political activity and raise the level of political leadership in the state. California progressives may have been overly optimistic about the consequences of direct legislation, for "the people" often proved to be exceedingly cautious and conservative in their use of such tools.[9]

More important, the simplistic division of "the people" versus "the interests" ignored the crucial fact that society is composed of many groups, each seeking some special goal. "It has been shown clearly that initiative measures do not originate with any mythical group, 'the People,'" writes Winston Crouch, an authority on California politics. "The moving forces in politics are relatively small groups of men animated by some 'interest.' . . ."[10] In short, "the people" are diverse, not monolithic.

California progressives, however, did not accept the desirability of competition among self-interest groups for control of the state. In their eyes, the individual voter was virtuous and interest groups were self-seeking. According to these reformers, such groups should not attempt to control the state for their own selfish purposes. Instead, legislation should result from careful deliberation by honest men who convene as impartial arbiters to seek the public good, and who always maintain the strictest neutrality with respect to competing organizations.

Accompanying their democratic faith in the wisdom of the individual voter was a distrust of formal party organizations, which were viewed as the media of special-interest power. A perceptive political scientist, Grant McConnell, has pointed out that the most effective way for progressives to lash out at special interests was to alter the party system by means of nonpartisan devices, including the cross-filing provision. "The logic of this approach," writes McConnell, "was carried further in California than perhaps anywhere else the Progressives came to power."[11] Furthermore, it was argued by progressives that science and efficient management would solve the problems of government; parties were irrelevant and unnecessary.

The political legacy of the Progressive movement is still

very apparent in California; but many thoughtful observers have expressed doubts about the effectiveness and the expense of direct-legislation measures in a complex, industrial age, and have also called for a strengthening of the party system.[12]

California progressives have been criticized for failing to make a special appeal to workingmen. After acknowledging the fact that labor won numerous victories during Hiram Johnson's first administration, Mowry writes: ". . . progressivism might well have broadened its appeal and cemented labor to its cause by caring for the unfortunates. . . ." He accuses Johnson of silence and inaction in the face of hunger and unemployment, and of acquiescing in the "use of the firehose and the club." Mowry also contends that progressives were more concerned with "bread and butter" issues than with "social and industrial justice." [13]

Several points can be made in rebuttal to these charges. In the first place, California progressives did not think in terms of organized groups such as "business" and "labor" battling for political favors and recognition. Their principal desire was to achieve a balance among many powerful interests without arousing feelings of class consciousness, and to advance the whole of society while at the same time advancing its individual parts. They conceived of the good society as a classless society in which the conduct of individuals would be governed by such moral qualities as honesty, frugality, and high character. It would therefore have been inconsistent with their vision of society for progressives to have made special appeals to organized labor.

Second, enactments such as eight-hour laws for women, a workmen's compensation law, mandatory periodic payment of wages, and child-labor restrictions, plus the activities and accomplishments of the Industrial Welfare Commission, the Industrial Accident Commission, and the Commission of Immigration and Housing, belie the accusation that the Johnson administration lacked concern for "the unfortunates." Third, Hiram Johnson never acquiesced in the use of the "firehouse and the club," but responded to instances of labor unrest—particularly in San Diego and in the Wheatland hop fields—with alacrity, assurance, and understanding. And finally, although organized labor was sometimes skeptical of progressives in general, especially those from southern California, it was immensely grateful to Hiram Johnson for his support of the workingman's cause. If the Johnson administration was not prolabor in the modern sense, it can at least be concluded that labor was pro-Johnson.[14]

The high tide of reform in the areas of economics, politics, and social welfare was not matched by similar advances in conservation and agriculture. Some progress was made in both areas, but important factors intervened to preclude effective action.

Not a crusading conservationist of the Pinchot variety, Hiram Johnson nonetheless utilized the symbols of the conservation controversy during his 1910 campaign. Despite the fact that the political implications of conservation in the early years of the twentieth century were subordinate to the scientific, Johnson managed to cast the issue of natural resources in terms of "the people" versus "the interests." In this manner, he clearly identified himself as an insurgent Republican in sympathy with the policies of Roosevelt and Pinchot and opposed to those of Taft. During the remainder of his administration, however, conflicts among conservationists themselves prevented the passage of much significant legislation. The greatest advances were made in the areas of water control and use, fire protection, and reforestation of cutover lands.

It was not until Johnson's second term that action was

taken to solve the state's land and agricultural problems. In February, 1915, a committee appointed by the governor began a thorough study of land colonization and rural credits. Owing to budgetary limitations, little was accomplished for many months. Finally, in September, 1915, the State Colonization and Rural Credits Commission was established, but it received only lukewarm support from Johnson. Shortly thereafter the commission members concluded that the loan provisions of the Federal Farm Loan Act were comprehensive enough to cover California farmers, and action on the state level was temporarily abandoned.

More substantial progress was made in efforts to achieve statewide marketing of agricultural produce. Successes in local cooperative marketing led some to believe that the activities of growers and shippers could be combined on a statewide basis in order to regulate fresh-fruit shipments to the East. When Harris Weinstock was appointed state market director in 1915, their hopes rose; but Weinstock received little support for his program from the state's growers, and was vigorously opposed by groups of retail grocers, packers, manufacturers, and canners. The spirit of individualism among farmers and growers, and the local rivalries among various citrus industries, precluded extensive cooperation. Regardless of these failures and disappointments, Hiram Johnson, Harris Weinstock, Simon Lubin, and others had recognized the existence of acute land and agricultural problems and had attempted remedial action.[15]

Of course, not everything done in the name of reform from 1911 to 1917 was desirable. Local option and anti-Oriental legislation, for example, were later considered wrongheaded by most people. In fact, the Alien Land Act of 1913 is the major blot on the otherwise admirable record of the Johnson administration. California Progressives were practically unanimous in their support of the measure, however, and all shared responsibility for its passage.

Nor was reform necessarily synonymous with liberalism. Reform in the early twentieth century often had only a remote relationship to the "liberal" reform battles of the 1960's, for example. The most important public issues of that day were not civil rights and anti-Communism, but corporate power, finance capitalism, popular democracy, and the role of the state and federal governments as shapers of public policy.

It is therefore very difficult to generalize about the "liberalism" or "conservatism" of California Progressives. If "liberalism" refers broadly to substantive goals—for example, government intervention in the economy for welfare purposes; a concern for minority rights, civil rights, and civil liberties; and an internationalist approach to foreign policy—then they were both "liberal" and "conservative." Some historians would stress their conservatism, pointing out that they desired change within established institutions. Others might remark that in a political sense Hiram Johnson and his followers were extraordinarily radical. After all, it was they who first bolted the Republican party in 1912—the "established institution"—and would have done so again in 1916 had Theodore Roosevelt chosen to run as a Progressive.

Even among prominent Progressives there were spokesmen for both ideological positions. Conservative Philip Bancroft, a retired grower of pears and walnuts from the San Francisco Bay area, reminisced in an interview:

> [As Lincoln-Roosevelt Leaguers] we weren't in there to try to upset the world or anything of that kind, and the great fight we were making was to try to get control of the government back into the hands of the people instead of being in the hands of the Southern Pacific machine. . . .
> We weren't radicals and yet we were progressives. We

wanted to have progress. We weren't against any *proper* [emphasis added] reforms, but on the other hand we weren't for tearing down our whole economic system or turning it into a socialistic drive or anything of that kind.[16]

Marshall Stimson also viewed the accomplishments of the Johnson administration from a conservative point of view, later repudiating the "bureaucratic" results of social and economic legislation of the Progressive era, which he felt endangered the American ideal of self-reliance and "hampered business and sapped individual initiative."[17] Meyer Lissner, on the other hand, remained ultraliberal even in his later years, and wrote to Will H. Hays after World War I:

> I don't think there is much difference between a radical Progressive and an evolutionary Socialist. The world eventually will adopt most of the Socialist program. I am in favor of taking it in assimilable doses. Before the war of course I would not have been in favor of taking as big a "gob" as I now am; but the war has made all the difference in the world. It has accelerated public ownership and the Socialist program at least a hundred years and we may as well recognize that first as last. . . .[18]

Actually, the term "Progressive" may correctly be applied to a number of notions, ranging from a belief in efficient government by honest businessmen to a desire for radical alterations in the economic and social system. However, the major interpretation of the Progressive movement, which emerged during the 1950's and remains the most widely accepted, is that of a judicious, upper middle-class movement, moral in attitude, unsophisticated in approach, and cautiously reformist in nature. Richard Hofstadter, the most prominent spokesman for this interpretation, feels that Progressives were lost in the complexities of the twentieth century, and is distressed by their lack of intellectual sophistication and excess of moral absolutism.

For Hofstadter, then, Progressivism was a very mild reform movement.[19]

After examining the careers of 47 of 100 early Progressive leaders in California, George Mowry found that most of them came from the professions, business, and the clergy. Most were college-educated and Protestant in their religious affiliations. According to Mowry, who also subscribes to the "mild, middle-class" interpretation, these men reacted politically when their position in society was threatened by the growth of large corporate enterprise on one side and a strong labor movement on the other.[20]

While correct in many essentials, these interpretations require substantial qualification. Several historians have recently challenged the assumptions of Hofstadter and Mowry, especially those regarding the Progressive movement's alleged conservative, middle-class nature, and the provocative concept of "status revolution." [21] Some of these critics deny that Progressive leaders were more concerned about their own status in society than they were genuinely troubled by the exploitation of women and children, municipal corruption, and other social and economic problems. (Most California Progressives, for example, *were* genuinely concerned and troubled about such matters.)

While these historians may agree with Mowry's conclusion that California Progressives were predominantly middle-class Protestants, they then ask, "So what?" Old Guard Republican leaders had essentially the same class characteristics. A more important distinction than that of class was the degree of political experience—Progressives tended to be amateurs in politics. Samuel P. Hays states the case most succinctly: "If its opponents were also middle class, then one cannot describe Progressive reform as a phenomenon, the special nature of which can be explained in terms of middle-class characteristics. One cannot explain the distinctive behavior of people in terms of characteristics which are not distinctive to them." [22] In other words, the status-revolution thesis fails to make middle-class Progressives distinctive or different from their contemporary opponents.

Samuel Hays has also inquired: "Can one describe an entire movement by the characteristics of its top-level leaders?" [23] Obviously not, for such aspects as local leadership and the voting base must also be taken into consideration. There is certainly a great need for analysis of the California Progressive movement on the local, municipal level. Yet the fact remains that even when writing of the leaders of the California Progressive movement, Mowry neglected a very important element—Jews like Harris Weinstock, Simon Lubin, Meyer Lissner, Aaron Sapiro. This element was perhaps the most liberal of all, and especially after 1912 provided much of the major impetus for meaningful reform.

Nor can we fail to recognize the entrepreneurial aspects of Progressive reform in California. A perceptive student of this era, Arthur Mann, has written: ". . . Unlike the New Deal, which helped those who could not help themselves, the Populists and Progressives labored to sweep away impediments in the economy that prevented the man on the make from getting ahead. . . ." [24] Many California Progressives were "men-on-the-make," and this feature of the movement has not been sufficiently examined. These entrepreneurs wished to challenge the dominance of established businessmen; their desire was to increase their own profits by means of expanded business opportunities. Yet California Progressivism was much more than a struggle of little capitalists against big capitalists, of small business against monopoly, of entrepreneurial versus vested interests. It was also an impressive effort to improve the living conditions and to increase the wages of urban and rural workers, as well as to assimilate immigrants into American society. At both the state and national levels the Progressive movement was an attempt, in the words of one historian, "to make Americans worthy of their history." [25]

The key figure in California, of course, was Hiram Johnson. His detractors have argued that Progressivism owed little to him, that he reaped what others had sown. There is some truth in this. Yet without him the Progressive movement would have lost much of its dynamism and impact. Hiram Johnson, without ever really acknowledging the fact, built up a powerful political machine, more powerful in many ways than the Southern Pacific's. He did not, however, use it for corrupt ends; and, with one or two exceptions, he did not use it to enact laws contrary to the general welfare.

Did Johnson do all this from a disinterested regard for the welfare of the people, or with an eye to his own political advancement? Without a doubt Johnson nursed strong political ambitions; but so did other leading Progressives of his day. Hiram Johnson was first and foremost a politician, but it is impossible to believe that he would have endured six years of bitter public abuse from his enemies unless he sincerely believed in the measures and causes for which he fought.

# APPENDIX I

## An Apologia for Theodore Roosevelt

There are generally extenuating circumstances for every political act in which the element of betrayal seems present. It is true that Roosevelt used the Progressive party in 1916 as a weapon to frighten the Republicans into nominating him. When he failed in this he discarded the weapon with an alacrity that was nothing less than cruel. It is true, I believe, that at no time in 1916 did he intend to run on the Bull Moose ticket unless nominated also by the Republicans. It is true that notwithstanding this, he allowed the Progressives to believe that he would carry their flag through thick and thin. It is true that, though he never directly promised the Progressives he would run, he promised by the implication of his actions and used the Progressives as pawns in a maneuver they did not understand till too late. All this was bad; at the time it seemed unforgiveable. And yet, in the light cast on these events by Roosevelt's own peculiar philosophy, there was a certain justification. As described in his own letters, Roosevelt's position was as follows: he believed that the most important thing in the world was for America to enter the war on the side of the Allies. Comparatively speaking, domestic issues did not exist for him. He was wrapped up in the war. Even the good and bad trust issue was subordinated to the international situation. In 1916 Wilson was a pacifist. He had skillfully encouraged antiwar feeling and was running on the slogan, "He kept us out of war." Roosevelt felt—and how much his personal animosity toward Wilson warped his judgment cannot be told—that the essential thing was to get rid of Wilson. For him to run as a Progressive would have meant to re-elect Wilson. Therefore he refused the nomination.

SOURCE: Amos R. E. Pinchot, *History of the Progressive Party, 1912–1916* (New York: New York University Press, 1958), p. 223.

## APPENDIX II

### LETTERS TO FRANCIS KEESLING FROM LOCAL REPUBLICANS

From San Francisco County:

". . . so far as the county committee is concerned, I do not hear of their doing anything."

"It is perfectly easy to understand the situation in California and that the Hughes campaign is not going with anywhere near the force and vigor that should be put into it. . . ."

"Each committeeman was called upon to report conditions in his district, and the answer invariably was 'no literature,' 'no meetings,' 'decided apathy,' 'Wilson stronger.' "

"Do not consider that an energetic campaign is being made."

"If it were not for the *Chronicle* and some of our splendid Republican papers, the public would not be enlightened at all to the real issues and arguments for Hughes and the Republican ticket."

". . . the prevailing Wilson sentiment which exists could be offset if the Republican County and State Central Committee would act in the matter. Up to this late date, they have not done one single thing to further the candidacy of Hughes. . . ."

From Ventura County:
"... The Progressive paper, the Ventura *Free Press,* seems to be supporting Hughes but its principle interest is in Johnson's candidacy."

From Grass Valley:
"... there is a pronounced spirit of indifference."

From Petaluma:
"Governor Johnson spoke to three hundred people here the other morning. It was a Johnson meeting, just a few words being spoken for Hughes.... The press stuff they are sending us makes me sick. I have not used a line of it and shall not unless they put a punch in it."

From Los Angeles County:
"Republican meetings are being held in the county but national issues are being discussed incidently through individual campaigns of district nominees.... There is no energetic campaign being made for the national ticket in this county.... So far as the outlook is concerned, Los Angeles County will probably go for Hughes, but not anywhere near as strong a majority as we had a right to expect two months ago."

"The State Central Committee so far has ignored the Central Committee of this County."

On October 25, 1916, W. W. Mines wrote Keesling: "The State Committee, whose Vice-Chairman is A. F. Naftzger, has been doing all in his power along lines of co-operation, but you know that oil and water don't mix and it is mighty hard to get any of our fellows that will mix with Lissner, Bill Stephens and that bunch.... As a matter of fact, the Progressives are not for Hughes.... As a fatter of fact, Marshall Stimson told Phil Wilson yesterday that he didn't care very much whether Hughes won or not as long as Johnson did."

SOURCE: Francis V. Keesling Papers, Borel Collection, Stanford University.

# APPENDIX III

## 1916 CALIFORNIA PARTY VOTE FOR ELECTORS
### (BY STATE AND BY COUNTY)

STATE:

DEMOCRATIC ... 466,289
REPUBLICAN .... 462,516
OTHER ........ 70,976

| County | Democratic | Republican | Other | Total |
|---|---|---|---|---|
| Alameda | 43,748 | 51,417 | 6,983 | 102,148 |
| Alpine | 23 | 60 | 0 | 83 |
| Amador | 1,766 | 1,209 | 174 | 3,149 |
| Butte | 4,888 | 3,956 | 834 | 9,678 |
| Calaveras | 1,524 | 1,175 | 174 | 2,873 |
| Colusa | 1,998 | 1,011 | 174 | 3,183 |
| Contra Costa | 6,092 | 5,731 | 1,214 | 13,037 |
| Del Norte | 471 | 499 | 166 | 1,136 |
| Eldorado | 1,755 | 1,068 | 219 | 3,042 |
| Fresno | 14,241 | 11,707 | 2,587 | 28,535 |
| Glenn | 1,797 | 1,342 | 203 | 3,342 |
| Humboldt | 4,103 | 5,786 | 1,431 | 11,320 |
| Imperial | 3,273 | 2,694 | 697 | 6,664 |
| Inyo | 966 | 846 | 205 | 2,017 |

## California's Prodigal Sons

| | | | | |
|---|---:|---:|---:|---:|
| Kern | 9,566 | 5,611 | 818 | 15,995 |
| Kings | 2,905 | 2,221 | 479 | 5,605 |
| Lake | 1,164 | 791 | 278 | 2,233 |
| Lassen | 1,323 | 877 | 176 | 2,376 |
| Los Angeles | 114,070 | 135,554 | 18,158 | 267,782 |
| Madera | 1,880 | 1,323 | 276 | 3,479 |
| Marin | 3,789 | 4,328 | 531 | 8,648 |
| Mariposa | 802 | 451 | 122 | 1,375 |
| Mendocino | 3,371 | 3,494 | 606 | 7,471 |
| Merced | 2,637 | 2,132 | 475 | 5,244 |
| Modoc | 1,222 | 768 | 113 | 2,103 |
| Mono | 158 | 137 | 32 | 327 |
| Monterey | 3,878 | 3,499 | 562 | 8,039 |
| Napa | 3,088 | 3,914 | 463 | 7,465 |
| Nevada | 2,548 | 1,586 | 376 | 4,510 |
| Orange | 6,474 | 10,609 | 1,668 | 18,751 |
| Placer | 3,375 | 1,954 | 470 | 5,799 |
| Plumas | 1,025 | 663 | 130 | 1,818 |
| Riverside | 4,561 | 7,452 | 1,621 | 13,634 |
| Sacramento | 14,538 | 10,696 | 1,399 | 26,633 |
| San Benito | 1,688 | 1,440 | 134 | 3,262 |
| San Bernardino | 9,398 | 11,932 | 2,219 | 23,549 |
| San Diego | 16,815 | 16,978 | 2,759 | 36,552 |
| San Francisco | 78,225 | 63,093 | 7,762 | 149,080 |
| San Joaquin | 11,454 | 7,861 | 1,358 | 20,673 |
| San Luis Obispo | 3,539 | 2,854 | 724 | 7,117 |
| San Mateo | 4,485 | 5,207 | 733 | 10,425 |
| Santa Barbara | 5,198 | 4,453 | 826 | 10,477 |
| Santa Clara | 14,185 | 16,592 | 1,910 | 32,687 |
| Santa Cruz | 4,511 | 4,228 | 710 | 9,449 |
| Shasta | 2,828 | 2,008 | 565 | 5,401 |
| Sierra | 594 | 360 | 65 | 1,019 |
| Siskiyou | 3,447 | 2,059 | 541 | 6,047 |
| Solano | 5,678 | 3,536 | 522 | 9,736 |
| Sonoma | 8,377 | 9,733 | 1,230 | 19,340 |
| Stanislaus | 5,490 | 4,401 | 1,810 | 11,701 |
| Sutter | 1,543 | 1,211 | 130 | 2,884 |
| Tehama | 2,534 | 1,739 | 526 | 4,799 |
| Trinity | 661 | 424 | 121 | 1,206 |

| | | | | |
|---|---|---|---|---|
| Tulare | 7,299 | 6,845 | 1,446 | 15,590 |
| Tuolumne | 1,584 | 1,057 | 286 | 2,927 |
| Ventura | 2,835 | 3,980 | 404 | 7,219 |
| Yolo | 2,922 | 2,334 | 248 | 5,504 |
| Yuba | 1,980 | 1,530 | 133 | 3,643 |
| | 466,289 | 462,516 | 70,976 | 999,781 |

SOURCE: Edgar Eugene Robinson, *The Presidential Vote, 1896–1932* (Palo Alto: Stanford University Press; London: Humphrey Milford Oxford University Press, 1934), Table IX, pp. 145–150.

# NOTES

1: THE GENESIS OF REFORM

[1] Frank Norris, *The Octopus* (New York: Doubleday, 1901), p. 100.

[2] In one of his many articles Gerald D. Nash has reacted against the Populistic-Frank Norris view of "The Octopus," suggesting that the Southern Pacific Railroad's political control was not so pervasive as is commonly asserted and that "valid generalizations concerning the railroad's influence on state government cannot yet be made. . . ." "Bureaucracy and Economic Reform: The Experience of California, 1899–1911," *Western Political Quarterly*, 13 (Sept., 1960), 680. Until such time, however, as the common assertion is successfully refuted, scholars can only repeat it with caution. The standard interpretation of the Southern Pacific's power is substantiated in a recent account, Ward McAfee's "Local Interests and Railroad Regulation in Nineteenth Century California" (unpublished Ph.D. dissertation, Stanford University, 1965). See also Stuart Daggett, *Chapters in the History of the Southern Pacific* (New York: Ronald Press, 1922), and Hans C. Palmer, "The Valley Road: The San Francisco and San Joaquin Valley Railway, 1895–1900" (unpublished M.A. thesis, University of California, Berkeley, 1959), esp. chaps. 1–3.

[3] There had been several unsuccessful attempts prior to 1900 to curb the power of the railroad. In 1878, for example, the Workingmen's party, led by a fiery young Irishman named Denis Kearney, managed to elect fifty-one delegates out of a total of 152 to the state constitutional convention. This powerful minority helped to secure the creation of a railroad commission with the sole power to regulate rates; but as I have already suggested, effective rate regulation was not forthcoming. See John W. Caughey, *California* (Englewood Cliffs: Prentice-Hall, 1960), pp. 386–389.

[4] Margaret Gordon estimates that 87.1 percent of the net increase in

California's population during the period 1900–1910 came from in-migration, as opposed to only 12.9 percent increase from native-born. This pattern has always held true for California: net in-migration has always been greater than natural increase per decade. See Margaret Gordon, *Employment Expansion and Population Growth: The California Experience, 1900–1950* (Berkeley and Los Angeles: University of California Press, 1954), p. 6, esp. table 2. See also Frank L. Beach, "The Transformation of California, 1900–1920: The Effects of the Westward Movement on California's Growth and Development in the Progressive Period" (unpublished Ph.D. dissertation, University of California, Berkeley, 1963), pp. 4–13, and Warren S. Thompson, *Growth and Changes in California's Population* (Los Angeles: Haynes Foundation, 1955), pp. 25, 67.

[5] Caughey, *California*, p. 381.

[6] See Franklin K. Hichborn, "The Party, the Machine, and the Vote—The Story of Cross-filing in California Politics," pt. 1, *California Historical Society Quarterly*, 38 (Dec., 1959), 353.

[7] William F. Herrin, chief counsel and political manager for the Southern Pacific, directed the Political Bureau from the company's headquarters in San Francisco. For further information about Herrin see Abraham Ruef, "The Road I Traveled," San Francisco *Bulletin*, July 13, 1912, and Edward F. Staniford, "Governor in the Middle: The Administration of George C. Pardee, Governor of California, 1903–1907" (unpublished Ph.D. dissertation, University of California, Berkeley, 1955), pp. 13–15.

[8] See C. P. Connolly, "Big Business and the Bench," *Everybody's Magazine*, 26 (March, 1912), 300. See also the revelations of James W. Rea, published in the San Francisco *Call*, July 4, 1908. Rea, a former railroad commissioner, was threatening to sue Herrin for defrauding him of $90,000 worth of bonds in a San Jose railroad company. In the *Call*, Rea described in detail Southern Pacific influence on the jury system in California. As county boss for the machine in Santa Clara, he had provided Herrin with lists of prospective jurors who would be sympathetic to the company in railroad cases. For additional information see John Randolph Haynes, "The Birth of Democracy in California" (typed MSS in Haynes Collection, Government and Public Affairs Reading Room, University of California, Los Angeles), pp. 3–6.

[9] George E. Mowry, *The California Progressives* (Berkeley and Los Angeles: University of California Press, 1951), p. 21.

[10] W. H. Hutchinson, "Prologue to Reform: The California Anti-Railroad Republicans, 1899–1905," *Southern California Quarterly*, 44 (Sept., 1962), 175–183. Hutchinson has subsequently written a two-volume study, *Oil, Land and Politics: The California Career of Thomas Robert Bard* (Norman: University of Oklahoma Press, 1965). See especially Vol. II, chaps. 18–19. See also Alice Rose's account of Bard's "crashing" of the railroad machine in her exhaustively researched "Rise of California Insurgency" (unpublished Ph.D. dissertation, Stanford University, 1942), pp. 34–41.

[11] See Franklin Hoyt, "Influence of the Railroads in the Development

of Los Angeles Harbor," *Historical Society Quarterly of Southern California* (later changed to *Southern California Quarterly*), 35 (Sept., 1953), 195–210, and Richard W. Barsness, "Railroads and Los Angeles: The Quest for a Deep-Water Port," *Southern California Quarterly*, 47 (Dec., 1965), 379–394.

[12] See W. W. Robinson, *Land in California* (Berkeley and Los Angeles: University of California Press, 1948), pp. 159–160.

[13] Mowry, *The California Progressives*, p. 22.

[14] Frank Beach, "The Transformation of California," p. 251, stresses the impact heavy migration into the cities had on California's political growth, a migration that "set loose constructive forces of urban development that motivated the cities to adopt realistic, utilitarian policies that aimed at reform and civic progress. . . ."

[15] For an excellent analysis of the Los Angeles reform movement see Albert H. Clodius, "The Quest for Good Government in Los Angeles, 1890–1910" (unpublished Ph.D. dissertation, Claremont Graduate School, 1953), *passim*.

[16] Grace Heilman Stimson has an account of the 1904 recall in her *Rise of the Labor Movement in Los Angeles* (Berkeley and Los Angeles: University of California Press, 1955), pp. 281–286.

[17] Mowry, *The California Progressives*, pp. 44–56; Clodius, "The Quest for Good Government in Los Angeles," chaps. ii and iii; and Hutchinson, *Oil, Land and Politics*, II, 286. Samuel P. Hays has noted the paradoxical nature of municipal reform in the early twentieth century: ". . . the ideology of an extension of political control and the practice of its concentration. . . ." He suggests that reformers, despite their "democratic" public pronouncements, were in reality constructing municipal government so as to increase their own political power. See "The Politics of Reform in Municipal Government in the Progressive Era," *Pacific Northwest Quarterly*, 55 (Oct., 1964), 157–169. Future studies of municipal reform in Los Angeles and San Francisco will profit from Hays's suggestions; but it does seem that in Los Angeles, particularly, the broadening of the political base by means of direct-democracy measures was a genuine concern of political reformers and not merely a device to camouflage their own selfish machinations.

[18] Walton E. Bean, "Boss Ruef, the Union Labor Party, and the Graft Prosecution in San Francisco, 1901–1911," *Pacific Historical Review*, 17 (Nov., 1948), 444–445. See also Edward Joseph Rowell, "The Union Labor Party of San Francisco, 1901–1911" (unpublished Ph.D. dissertation, University of California, Berkeley, 1938), *passim*, and Alexander Saxton, "San Francisco Labor and the Populist and Progressive Insurgencies," *Pacific Historical Review*, 34 (Nov., 1965), 429.

[19] Bean, "Boss Ruef, the Union Labor Party, and the Graft Prosecution in San Francisco," pp. 446–447. See also Bean's book, *Boss Ruef's San Francisco* (Berkeley and Los Angeles: University of California Press, 1952), pp. 89–90, 101–102. George Mowry has an account of the Ruef-Schmitz machine in *The California Progressives*, pp. 25–30.

[20] Bean, "Boss Ruef, the Union Labor Party, and the Graft Prosecution in San Francisco," p. 448. Herrin was chief counsel of the railroad until 1910, when he became vice-president.

[21] Fremont Older, *My Own Story* (San Francisco: Call Publishing Co., 1919), pp. 65–67; Bean's article, p. 449; and Bean, *Boss Ruef's San Francisco*, p. 76. See also Robert E. Hennings, "James D. Phelan and the Wilson Progressives of California" (unpublished Ph.D. dissertation, University of California, Berkeley, 1961), p. 49. For additional biographical material on Heney see Helene Hooker Brewer, "A Man and Two Books," *Pacific Historical Review*, 32 (Aug., 1963), 221–234, and John Messing, "Public Lands, Politics, and Progressives: The Oregon Land Fraud Trials, 1903–1910," *Pacific Historical Review*, 35 (Feb., 1966), 35–66.

[22] Bean, *Boss Ruef's San Francisco*, pp. 260–261.

[23] See drafts of Hiram Johnson, Jr.'s biography of his father in the recently opened Part VI of the Johnson Papers (Bancroft Library, University of California, Berkeley). Also, Andrew Rolle, *California: A History* (New York: Thomas Y. Crowell, 1963), p. 454.

[24] See Irving McKee, "The Background and Early Career of Hiram Warren Johnson, 1866–1910," *Pacific Historical Review*, 19 (Feb., 1950), 25–26. Father John B. McGloin has pointed out in a review of Rolle's *California: A History* that three appellate judges and seven state Supreme Court justices agreed that Schmitz had not received a fair trial and that no direct proof of his guilt had been presented. *Southern California Quarterly*, 46 (June, 1964), 180–181.

[25] Mowry, *The California Progressives*, pp. 36–37.

[26] For a thorough discussion of municipal reform in Fresno see Miles C. Everett, "Chester Harvey Rowell, Pragmatic Humanist and California Progressive" (unpublished Ph.D. dissertation, University of California, Berkeley, 1965), chap. 8.

[27] See Dickson's historical sketch of the Lincoln-Roosevelt League in Box 11 of his Papers (Special Collections Library, University of California, Los Angeles). See also Rowell to Mark Sullivan, May 27, 1910, Rowell Papers (Bancroft Library, University of California, Berkeley), in which he discusses the meeting at length. For excellent biographical material on Rowell see Miles Everett, "Chester Harvey Rowell," *passim*, and Victor Bogart, "Chester H. Rowell and the Lincoln-Roosevelt League, 1907–1910" (unpublished M.A. thesis, University of California, Berkeley, 1962), pp. 2–12.

[28] See Caughey, *California*, pp. 461–462. Parts of the remainder of chap. 1 of the present study and parts of chap. 2 have appeared in my article, "Hiram Johnson, the Lincoln-Roosevelt League, and the Election of 1910," *California Historical Society Quarterly*, 45 (Sept., 1966), 225–240.

[29] *California Weekly*, Jan. 29, 1909, p. 145.

[30] Franklin Hichborn, *Story of the Session of the California Legislature of 1909* (San Francisco: James H. Barry, 1909), p. 7. Hichborn's detailed reports of the various sessions of the state legislatures beginning in 1909 were very important, for as Chester Rowell wrote to Hiram Johnson:

"... There is no intimidation on the legislator stronger than the fear that the people will read Hichborn's tables of how he voted and find out that he did not vote the way they sent him to vote. ..." Sept. 15, 1913, Rowell Papers.

[81] Under the district advisory plan, legislators could vote either for the candidate receiving the most votes in the senatorial or congressional districts of the state, or for the candidate receiving the endorsement of their party in the greatest number of districts electing members of that party to the legislature. It was not until 1911 that the Oregon plan was adopted. Under this plan the electorate was given a statewide nominating vote and each candidate for the legislature was given an opportunity to pledge himself to abide by that vote.

[82] Franklin Hichborn, "The Party, the Machine, and the Vote," pt. 2, *California Historical Society Quarterly*, 39 (March, 1960), 21. See also Hichborn, *Story of the Session of the California Legislature, 1909*, chaps. viii–xi.

[83] D. F. Pegrum, *Rate Theories and the California Railroad Commission* (Berkeley: University of California Press, 1932), p. 4.

[84] Mowry, *The California Progressives*, p. 142. For a contemporary opinion see the *California Outlook*, March, 1912, p. 11: "The California railroad commission . . . went its serene, subservient, salaryful way for thirty-one slap-him-on-the-back-boys years of somnolent placidity and good fellowship. . . ."

[85] Gerald D. Nash, "The California Railroad Commission, 1876–1911," *Southern California Quarterly*, 44 (Dec., 1962), 287. For a discussion of the modification of a reformer's ideas about railroad regulation in the face of the complexity of the task, see Nash's "The Reformer Reformed: John H. Reagan and Railroad Regulation," *Business History Review*, 29 (June, 1955), 189–196.

[86] Nash, "The California Railroad Commission," p. 298.

[87] Nash, "The Role of the State Government in the Economy of California, 1849–1911" (unpublished Ph.D. dissertation, University of California, Berkeley, 1957), p. 362.

[88] For the legislative history of the Hepburn bill see John Morton Blum, *The Republican Roosevelt* (New York: Atheneum, 1962), pp. 87–105. A different interpretation, emphasizing the railroads' role in the passage of the legislation, may be found in Gabriel Kolko, *Railroads and Regulation, 1877–1916* (Princeton: Princeton University Press, 1965), chap. 7. See also George Mowry, *The Era of Theodore Roosevelt, 1900–1912* (New York: Harper and Bros., 1958), pp. 198–206.

[89] See Gerald Nash, *State Government and Economic Development: A History of Administrative Policies in California, 1849–1933* (Berkeley: Institute of Governmental Studies, 1964), p. 252, drawing upon the San Francisco *Call*, Oct. 3, 4, 5, 1907, and Feb. 16, 1908. See also Anne Wintermute Lane and Louise Herrick Wall, eds., *The Letters of Franklin K. Lane: Personal and Political* (Boston and New York: Houghton Mifflin, 1922), pp. 63–64.

[40] Railroads in California consumed nearly 25 million barrels of fuel

oil in 1910. By that year California was the largest oil producer in the United States, its output being more than twice that of Pennsylvania and greater than that of any foreign country. The Geological Survey estimated that California in 1900 possessed two-thirds of the oil supply in all public lands of the United States and one-third of the national supply in its private lands. San Francisco *Bulletin,* Dec. 9, 1911, and J. Leonard Bates, *The Origins of Teapot Dome: Progressives, Parties, and Petroleum, 1909-1921* (Urbana: University of Illinois Press, 1963), p. 18.

[41] For a discussion of the connection between the railroads and the major oil companies, see Hichborn's article in the Sacramento *Bee,* March 25, 1913.

[42] See *Report on the Transportation of Petroleum,* U.S. Bureau of Corporations (Washington, 1906), pp. 395-396, 402, 407-442, 464-488, as cited in Nash, *State Government and Economic Development,* p. 253. See also Gerald T. White, *Formative Years in the Far West: A History of Standard Oil Company in California and Predecessors Through 1919* (New York: Appleton-Century-Crofts, 1962), esp. pp. 233-235, 366-371.

[43] White, *Formative Years in the Far West,* pp. 373-374.

[44] When the Union Oil Company was finally purchased by General Petroleum, the independent oil producers no longer had a selling agent. Moreover, in late 1912 Standard Oil sharply cut back its purchases from the independent producers. To aid the independents, the legislature of 1913 passed, and Governor Johnson signed, a bill that made all pipelines common carriers. This permitted the independents to use the numerous pipelines running out of the central California oil fields. By 1913, their organization contained 175 members and produced 22 percent of California's oil. See Hichborn's article in the Sacramento *Bee,* March 25, 1913, and J. Leonard Bates, *The Origins of Teapot Dome,* p. 105.

[45] Arthur J. Pillsbury, "Wright Law and Webb Bill Compared," *California Weekly,* March 4, 1910, pp. 235-237. The Webb bill was introduced in the Senate by State Senator William Stetson and was commonly referred to by his name.

[46] Mowry, *The California Progressives,* p. 81. For a detailed analysis of the fight over the Wright and Stetson bills see chaps. xii-xiv of Hichborn's *Story of the Session of the California Legislature, 1909.*

[47] *Los Angeles Express,* Dec. 8, 1909.

[48] Lissner to La Follette, Dec. 15, 1909, Lissner Papers (Borel Collection, Stanford University).

2: "A FIGHT AGAINST THE INTERESTS"

[1] Rowell to Hiram Johnson, Jan. 26, 1910, Rowell Papers (Bancroft Library, University of California, Berkeley).

[2] Lissner to Rowell, Jan. 29, 1910, Rowell Papers.

[3] *California Weekly,* Feb. 11, 1910, p. 186. Marshall Stimson, in a letter to Irving McKee on April 6, 1949, explained how Heney withdrew in favor of Hiram Johnson: "There was intense opposition in San Francisco, even among the so-called Progressives, to Heney—not so much against

him personally, but it was thought inexpedient to nominate him on account of the strong opposition he had stirred up by reason of his courageous course. . . . He told me he felt Johnson was the proper one and the way to do was for the committee to name him and then inform him afterwards. He was confident if that were done, Johnson would accept." See Irving McKee, "The Background and Early Career of Hiram Warren Johnson, 1866–1910," *Pacific Historical Review*, 19 (Feb., 1950), 30n. Heney's support of the recall of judges further discredited him in the eyes of many progressives. See Helen Hooker Brewer, "A Man and Two Books," *Pacific Historical Review*, 32 (Aug., 1963), 223–226.

[4] For a biographical sketch of Weinstock see Grace Larsen, "A Progressive in Agriculture: Harris Weinstock," *Agricultural History*, 32 (July, 1958), 187–188.

[5] Franklin Hichborn, "California Politics, 1891–1939" (copy in the University of California School of Law, Berkeley), II, 913.

[6] Rowell to Lissner, Jan. 31, 1910, Rowell Papers.

[7] George E. Mowry, *The California Progressives* (Berkeley and Los Angeles: University of California Press, 1951), p. 109; Marshall Stimson to Viola May Knoche, July 8, 1947, as cited in her "The Gubernatorial Nomination of Hiram W. Johnson, 1910" (unpublished M.A. thesis, Stanford University, 1947), p. 49. See also Miles Everett, "Chester Harvey Rowell, Pragmatic Humanist and California Progressive" (unpublished Ph.D. dissertation, 1965), for a somewhat different account that stresses Rowell's successful efforts to secure Johnson's acceptance to run.

[8] Weinstock to Johnson, Feb. 13, 1910, Johnson Papers (Bancroft Library).

[9] Johnson to Rowell, Feb. 23, 1910, Johnson Papers.

[10] Irving McKee, "The Background and Early Career of Hiram Warren Johnson," pp. 17–19. After his son's selection as the league's candidate for governor, Grove Johnson let it be known that he would fight him in every precinct in the state. "I had no such information at the time of my nomination," Hiram Johnson wrote C. K. McClatchy, "but I doubt if it would have altered my course anyway. . . . [It] would be quite heartbreaking to me if father should personally assail me during the campaign. . . ." Feb. 26, 1910, Johnson Papers. Grove Johnson was defeated for renomination at the primaries, as he later was at the general election, when he ran for the Assembly as a Prohibitionist. He resigned from office on December 1, 1910, a month before his term expired. Sacramento *Bee*, Dec. 2, 1910.

[11] See Robert E. L. Knight, *Industrial Relations in the San Francisco Bay Area, 1900–1918* (Berkeley and Los Angeles: University of California Press, 1960), p. 241.

[12] Rowell to J. O. Haynes, March 14, 1910, Rowell Papers.

[13] *California Weekly*, March 18, 1910, p. 264. Gilman Ostrander writes that at the time of the election of 1910, Wallace was the "closest link between the [Anti-Saloon] League and the Progressive movement." *The Prohibition Movement in California, 1848–1933* (Berkeley and Los Angeles: University of California Press, 1957), p. 106.

[14] *California Weekly,* March 25, 1910, p. 281.
[15] Los Angeles *Times,* March 6, 1910; San Francisco *Argonaut,* Feb. 19, 1910, p. 115, and Feb. 26, 1910, p. 129.
[16] Rowell to Mark Sullivan, May 27, 1910, Rowell Papers. See also W. H. Hutchinson, *Oil, Land and Politics: The California Career of Thomas Robert Bard* (Norman: University of Oklahoma Press, 1965), II, 311.
[17] Rowell to Johnson, Feb. 22, 1910, Johnson Papers.
[18] Johnson to C. K. McClatchy, Feb. 26, 1910; Johnson to Lissner, to Stimson, and to A. A. De Ligne, March 1, 1910, Johnson Papers. See also Johnson to Rowell, Feb. 20, 1910, Rowell Papers. For a list of the California newspapers supporting Johnson, see Hiram Johnson, Jr. to Edward Dickson, March 31, 1910, Johnson Papers. In a letter to Norman Hapgood on April 19, 1910, Hiram Johnson, Jr. claimed that eighty or ninety of the country newspapers, in addition to several major newspapers, were supporting his father's candidacy.
[19] Johnson to C. K. McClatchy, April 19, 1910, Johnson Papers.
[20] Johnson to Rowell, April 19, 1910, Johnson Papers. See also Johnson to Lissner (undated, 1910) in recently opened Part VI of Johnson Papers. After the August primaries, the Republican nominee for lieutenant governor, Albert Wallace, complained about the lack of support he received from Johnson, contending that Johnson had conducted a "selfish campaign." Johnson wrote Lissner, Stimson, and Dickson: ". . . I felt more or less contrite and told him that perhaps his criticism was just. . . ." Aug. 20, 1910, Johnson Papers. Johnson had earlier written Rowell that Wallace "got on his nerves." Rowell to Lissner, April 20, 1910, Rowell Papers. Nor was Johnson's bias against Works alleviated in years to come, as he wrote to Lieutenant Governor Wallace on July 24, 1912: ". . . I wish he [Works] were in any other place than the United States Senate." Johnson Papers. John D. Works also complained about lack of support from the league and from Lissner, Stimson, and Lee Gates. See Works to Johnson, June 6 and Aug. 22, 1910, Johnson Papers. Years later, Works wrote Chester Rowell: ". . . I never had the sympathetic or earnest support of the Lincoln-Roosevelt League at Los Angeles from the very first. . . ." April 29, 1914, Works Papers (Bancroft Library).
[21] Rowell to Lissner, April 20, 1910, Rowell Papers.
[22] Rowell to Johnson, April 22, 1910, Rowell Papers.
[23] For example, see Johnson to Bert A. Towne, March 1; to C. H. Bentley and to James H. Haynes, March 2; and to F. L. Platt, March 3, 1910, Johnson Papers.
[24] Johnson to Mr. Brown, March 30, 1910, Johnson Papers.
[25] The most complete account of Johnson's itinerary and speeches is George Wallace Milias, "Hiram Johnson's Campaign for the Governorship of California in 1910" (unpublished M.A. thesis, Stanford University, 1949). Of less value is Viola May Knoche, "The Gubernatorial Nomination of Hiram W. Johnson, 1910" (unpublished M.A. thesis, Stanford University, 1947).
[26] Johnson to McCabe, May 29, 1910, Johnson Papers.

[27] Carey McWilliams, *California: The Great Exception* (New York: Current Books, 1949), p. 100. See also Gilbert C. Fite, *The Farmers' Frontier, 1865–1900* (New York: Holt, Rinehart and Winston, 1966), pp. 162–164, and Clarke A. Chambers, *California Farm Organizations* (Berkeley and Los Angeles: University of California Press, 1952), chap. 1.

[28] See Paul W. Gates, "The Homestead Law in an Incongruous Land System," *American Historical Review*, 41 (July, 1936), 668. For general land policy see W. W. Robinson's *Land in California* (Berkeley and Los Angeles: University of California Press, 1948), *passim*.

[29] Charles A. Barker, "Henry George and the California Background of *Progress and Poverty*," *California Historical Society Quarterly*, 24 (June, 1945), 109, and Barker, *Henry George* (New York: Oxford University Press, 1955), pp. 146–154. Also Fite, *The Farmers' Frontier*, pp. 164–166, 174, and Gerald D. Nash, "The California State Land Office, 1858–1898," *Huntington Library Quarterly*, 27 (Aug., 1964), 355–356.

[30] McWilliams, *California: The Great Exception*, p. 101.

[31] See chap. 3 of Robert J. Pitchell's "Twentieth Century California Voting Behavior" (unpublished Ph.D. dissertation, University of California, Berkeley, 1955). A bulletin issued in 1912 by the Bureau of Census, Department of Commerce and Labor, revealed that the number of farms in California in 1910 was 88,197. Of the 88,197 farm operators, 66,632 were classified as owners, 3,417 as managers, and 18,148 (or 20.6 percent) as tenants. See the San Francisco *Bulletin*, March 5, 1912.

[32] Commission on Land Colonization and Rural Credits, *Report* (Sacramento, 1916), pp. 7–8, as quoted in Samuel E. Wood, "The California State Commission of Immigration and Housing: A Study of Administrative Organization and the Growth of Function" (unpublished Ph.D. dissertation, University of California, Berkeley, 1942), p. 13. Wood states that in 1916 "over four million acres of land suitable to intensive cultivation and capable of supporting a dense population were owned by 310 landed proprietors. . . ." *Ibid.*, p. 14.

[33] I am indebted to Professor Roger Daniels for pointing out this literacy requirement, a requirement that still exists. The most complete data regarding agricultural employment in California during this period relate to 1909, when surveys were made by both the United States Immigration Commission and the State Bureau of Labor Statistics. On 2,369 farms the bureau found the proportion of labor by race and nationality to be as follows:

| | | |
|---|---:|---:|
| Whites | 25,826 | 47.4% |
| Japanese | 22,811 | 41.9 |
| Chinese | 2,091 | 3.8 |
| Mexicans | 1,847 | 3.4 |
| Indians | 1,033 | 1.9 |
| Hindus | 733 | 1.4 |
| Others | 82 | 0.2 |
| | 54,463 | 100.0% |

From the Bureau of Labor Statistics' *Fourteenth Biennial Report, 1909–1910*, p. 268, as cited in Levi Varden Fuller, "The Supply of Agricultural Labor as a Factor in the Evolution of Farm Organization in California" (unpublished Ph.D. dissertation, University of California, Berkeley, 1939), p. 158. Fuller's study was printed as Exhibit A in U.S. Senate, Committee on Education and Labor, *Agricultural Labor in California*, Hearings, 76th Cong., 3d sess., on S. Res. 266, Jan. 13, 1940, pt. 54 (Washington: Government Printing Office, 1940), pp. 19777–19898.

[34] For an incisive discussion of agrarian entrepreneurialism in California during the Progressive era, see Robert Kelley, "Taming the Sacramento: Hamiltonianism in Action," *Pacific Historical Review*, 34 (Feb., 1965), 45–47, 49.

[35] *Statement of the Vote of California, Direct Primary Election, August 16, 1910*, California Secretary of State (Sacramento, 1910), p. 3. The votes of the other candidates were as follows: Curry—55,390; Anderson—38,295; Stanton—18,226; and Ellery—2,028. Lieutenant Governor Wallace won 66,762 votes, while the "regular" Republican candidate, Francis V. Keesling, received 61,037.

[36] Gilman Ostrander writes that by "1910, 68 per cent of the population of San Francisco was foreign born or children of foreign born, while in Los Angeles County the foreign born and first-generation Americans made up but 35 per cent of the population. . . . In 1906 the population of Los Angeles was 56 per cent Protestant, of San Francisco, 15 per cent Protestant. . . ." *The Prohibition Movement in California*, p. 65. Also, George W. Bemis, "Sectionalism and Representation in the California State Legislature, 1911–1931" (unpublished Ph.D. dissertation, University of California, Berkeley, 1935), p. 32.

[37] Ostrander, *The Prohibition Movement in California*, p. 115.

[38] Robert E. Hennings, "James D. Phelan and the Wilson Progressives of California" (unpublished Ph.D. dissertation, University of California, Berkeley, 1961), p. ii.

[39] *Ibid.*, pp. 44, 47.

[40] *San Francisco Chronicle*, Sept. 8, 1910.

[41] *San Francisco Bulletin*, Oct. 6, 1910. See also the reports of speeches in Fresno and San Luis Obispo in the *Bulletin*, Oct. 1 and 7, 1910.

[42] *Ibid.*, Oct. 31, 1910.

[43] James Crawford, "The Democratic Party of California and Political Reform, 1902–1910" (unpublished M.A. thesis, University of California, Berkeley, 1959), pp. 135–136. Bell's "following," however, caused him some harm among California Democrats, for as James D. Phelan wrote Henry Morgenthau of New York: ". . . Bell has affiliated with the . . . United Railroad 'machine.' . . . For these reasons, Bell has lost the confidence of the right thinking Democrats and independent men of California." Aug. 29, 1910, Phelan Papers (Bancroft Library).

[44] Porterfield to Johnson, Aug. 24, 1910, Johnson Papers. Earlier in the year, Francis Heney had praised Johnson to E. W. Scripps as "by far the best man of the entire bunch of candidates of both parties . . ."

and suggested that the Scripps newspapers endorse Johnson's candidacy. Heney to Johnson, March 9, 1910, quoting letter to Scripps of March 2, 1910, Johnson Papers. The attention of California voters was momentarily diverted from the campaign by news of the dynamiting of the Los Angeles *Times'* building on October 1, 1910. Hiram Johnson's "out" letters from October 1, 1910, through December, 1911, contain no mention of this event, nor of the McNamara trial that followed. The October 2, 1910, issue of the Los Angeles *Times* does quote Johnson as follows: "No punishment is great enough for the criminal who planned it or for the loathsome miscreant who carried it into execution." A complete account of the "Crime of the Century" appears in Grace H. Stimson, *Rise of the Labor Movement in Los Angeles* (Berkeley and Los Angeles: University of California Press, 1955), chap. 21.

[45] The gubernatorial returns were as follows: Johnson—177,191; Bell—154,835; J. Stitt Wilson (Socialist)—47,819; and Simon Pease Meads (Prohibitionist)—5,807. *California Blue Book, 1911*, California Secretary of State (Sacramento, 1913), p. 432.

[46] Gerald Nash, "Bureaucracy and Economic Reform: The Experience of California, 1899–1911," *Western Political Quarterly*, 13 (Sept., 1960), 680–691; Nash, "The Role of the State Government in the Economy of California" (unpublished Ph.D. dissertation, University of California, Berkeley, 1957), p. 362; and Ira B. Cross, *Financing an Empire: History of Banking in California* (Chicago, San Francisco, Los Angeles: S. J. Clarke, 1927), II, 724.

[47] See Mowry, *The California Progressives*, pp. 135–136, and Franklin Hichborn, *Story of the Session of the California Legislature of 1911* (San Francisco: James H. Barry, 1911), pp. 18–23.

3: ONWARD CHRISTIAN CAPITALISTS

[1] For the importance of "efficiency" and "scientific management" on the national level during the Progressive era, see Samuel Haber, *Efficiency and Uplift: Scientific Management in the Progressive Era, 1900–1920* (Chicago: University of Chicago Press, 1964), and Dwight Waldo, *The Administrative State—A Study of the Political Theory of American Public Administration* (New York: Ronald Press, 1948), esp. chap. 3. Also see Robert H. Wiebe's excellent new book, *The Search for Order, 1877–1920* (New York: Hill and Wang, 1967). On page 166 Wiebe states: ". . . The heart of progressivism was the ambition of the new middle class to fulfill its destiny through bureaucratic means."

[2] See Franklin Hichborn, *Story of the Session of the California Legislature of 1911* (San Francisco: James H. Barry, 1911), pp. i–xvi, for the entire inaugural address.

[3] See the *Pacific Outlook*, Jan. 14, 1911, p. 6. This weekly journal was the unofficial organ of the progressives in southern California and of the nonpartisan movement in Los Angeles. In February, 1911, it merged with the northern *California Weekly* to form the *California Outlook*. The *California Outlook* continued as a weekly voice for progressives until Septem-

ber, 1915, when it became a monthly. It resisted mounting deficits until 1918 and then discontinued publication.

⁴ See D. F. Pegrum, *Rate Theories and the California Railroad Commission* (Berkeley: University of California Press, 1932), pp. 5–6. The "long-and-short haul" principle simply meant that no greater compensation could be charged for the transportation of passengers or freight for a shorter than for a longer distance over the same line in the same direction.

⁵ See Max Thelen, "The Public Utilities Act and Its Relation to the Public," in Eugene R. Hallet, ed., *Public Utilities Act of California* (San Francisco, 1912), p. 17.

⁶ Gerald Nash, "The California Railroad Commission, 1876–1911," *Southern California Quarterly*, 44 (Dec., 1962), 302.

⁷ "Max Thelen: California Progressive, Railroad Commissioner, and Attorney" (oral history interview conducted by Willa Klug Baum, University of California, Berkeley, 1962), p. 23.

⁸ Thelen's *Report on Leading Railroad and Public Service Commissions* is reprinted in Hallet, ed., *Public Utilities Act of California*, pp. 35–154.

⁹ Nash, "The California Railroad Commission," pp. 300–301; Pegrum, *Rate Theories and the California Railroad Commission*, pp. 7–8.

¹⁰ Thelen, "The Public Utilities Act and Its Relation to the Public," pp. 18–19. Also Gerald Nash, *State Government and Economic Development: A History of Administrative Policies in California, 1849–1933* (Berkeley: Institute of Governmental Studies, 1964), pp. 256–263.

¹¹ See "The Supreme Court and the Railroad Commission," *California Outlook*, Oct. 17, 1914, p. 9. For the legal aspect of the new commission see Carl I. Wheat, "Practice and Procedure before the Railroad Commission of California," *California Law Review*, 15 (Sept., 1927), 450–483.

¹² Los Angeles *Express* and San Francisco *Bulletin*, Sept. 11, 1912. See also the Sacramento *Star*, Nov. 28, 1911, which reported that $800,000 was saved by the Railroad Commission during the first year of the Johnson administration.

¹³ *California Outlook*, June 22, 1912, p. 8.

¹⁴ Another illustration of the Johnson administration's effort to ensure equality of competition is provided by a 1913 law that made all pipelines in California common carriers. This law enabled the independent oil producers, who were battling against an economic squeeze being administered by Standard Oil and other large companies, to use the numerous pipelines running out of the central California oil fields and thereby to compete more equitably in the oil market.

¹⁵ The John Francis Neylan Papers, recently opened at the Bancroft Library, University of California, Berkeley, are an extremely important source for this period. Neylan was a close friend of Johnson, and their letters are most informative. For biographical information on Neylan see *Time*, April 29, 1935, pp. 50–51, and *The Coast*, Oct., 1938, pp. 9–12 and Dec., 1938, pp. 28–31.

¹⁶ For the confession and resignation of the superintendent of the state

hospital at Napa, see the *California Outlook,* Feb. 3, 1912, p. 11, and the San Francisco *Bulletin,* Jan. 27, 1912.

[17] See the Los Angeles *Express,* May 27, 1913. Also Neylan to Katherine Edson, Sept. 25, 1913, Neylan Papers.

[18] After Hiram Johnson went to Washington in 1917 as United States senator, Neylan entered private law practice in San Francisco. By 1925 he was general counsel for the Hearst enterprises and reputedly the only man whom Hearst would trust. See W. A. Swanberg's *Citizen Hearst* (New York: Charles Scribner's Sons, 1961), p. 365.

[19] For a more complete discussion of these contrasting ideas about direct democracy, see Richard Hofstadter's *The Age of Reform* (New York: Alfred A. Knopf, 1955), pp. 259-265. See also James Q. Wilson, *The Amateur Democrat: Club Politics in Three Cities* (Chicago: University of Chicago Press, 1962), pp. 26-27, as well as Dwight Waldo, *The Administrative State,* pp. 17, 36, 133, 135-136. Croly's views may be found in *The Promise of American Life* (New York: Macmillan, 1909), esp. chaps. 6, 11-12.

[20] Franklin Hichborn, "The Party, the Machine, and the Vote—The Story of Cross-filing in California Politics," pt. 2, *California Historical Society Quarterly,* 39 (March, 1960), 22. Also Dean R. Cresap, *Party Politics in the Golden State* (Los Angeles: Haynes Foundation, 1954), pp. 15-16; Eugene C. Lee, *The Politics of Nonpartisanship—A Study of California City Elections* (Berkeley and Los Angeles: University of California Press, 1960), pp. 23, 28-31; and William Buchanan, *Legislative Partisanship: The Deviant Case of California* (Berkeley and Los Angeles: University of California Press, 1963), pp. 12-13.

[21] For the problems that soon arose from this unique election law, see H. Brett Melendy, "California's Cross-Filing Nightmare: The 1918 Gubernatorial Election," *Pacific Historical Review,* 33 (Aug., 1964), 317-330. Cross-filing was finally abolished in 1959, during Governor Edmund "Pat" Brown's administration. On cross-filing, in addition to the other works cited, see Dean E. McHenry, "Cross-Filing of Political Candidates in California," *Annals of the American Academy of Political and Social Science,* 248 (Nov., 1946), 226-231, and "The Pattern of California Politics," *Western Political Quarterly,* 1 (March, 1948), 53; Robert J. Pitchell, "The Electoral System and Voting Behavior: The Case of California's Cross-Filing," *Western Political Quarterly,* 12 (June, 1959), 459-484; James C. Findley, "Cross-Filing and the Progressive Movement in California Politics," *Western Political Quarterly,* 12 (Sept., 1959), 699-711; Grant McConnell, "California Conundrum—Why It Votes G.O.P.," *Nation,* 179 (Dec. 4, 1954), 477-478, and his recent *Private Power and American Democracy* (New York: Alfred A. Knopf, 1966), chap. 2.

[22] Hichborn, "California Politics, 1891-1939" (copy in the University of California School of Law, Berkeley), II, 1026.

[23] *California Blue Book, 1913-1915,* California Secretary of State (Sacramento, 1915), p. 373.

[24] Hichborn, "California Politics," II, 1028. See also Thomas W. Casstevens, "Reflections on the Initiative Process," in Eugene C. Lee, ed.,

The California Governmental Process (Boston and Toronto: Little, Brown, 1966), p. 89.

[25] See the San Francisco Chronicle, Oct. 9, 1911; San Diego Union, Oct. 8, 1911; and Los Angeles Times, Oct. 11, 1911, as cited in George Mowry, The California Progressives (Berkeley and Los Angeles: University of California Press, 1951), p. 317.

[26] Earl C. Crockett, "The History of California Labor Legislation, 1910–1930" (unpublished Ph.D. dissertation, University of California, Berkeley, 1931), pp. 119–120.

[27] Ibid., p. 120, referring to California Statutes, 1907, pp. 119–120.

[28] Quoted in Gerald D. Nash, "The Influence of Labor on State Policy, 1860–1920: The Experience of California," California Historical Society Quarterly, 42 (Sept., 1963), 250. For a more complete discussion of the Roseberry law see A. J. Pillsbury, "An Adventure in State Insurance," American Economic Review, 9 (Dec., 1919), 681–682. See also Labor Clarion, March 15, 1912, p. 13.

[29] See Nash, "The Influence of Labor on State Policy," p. 243.

[30] Grace Stimson, Rise of the Labor Movement in Los Angeles (Berkeley and Los Angeles: University of California Press, 1955), pp. 356–357.

[31] Crockett, "The History of California Labor Legislation," pp. 5–11. On May 27, 1912, the California Supreme Court unanimously upheld the constitutionality of the eight-hour law for women employed in hotels (Ex parte Miller, 162 Cal. 687). See the Labor Clarion, May 31, 1912, p. 8, and the Bureau of Labor Statistics' Fifteenth Biennial Report, 1911–1912 (Sacramento, 1912), p. 62. And in 1915 California's eight-hour law for women was upheld by the United States Supreme Court. See Sacramento Bee, Feb. 23, 1915.

[32] See the Bureau of Labor Statistics' Fifteenth Biennial Report, 1911–1912, p. 29.

[33] See George W. Bemis, "Sectionalism and Representation in the California State Legislature, 1911–1931" (unpublished Ph.D. dissertation, University of California, Berkeley, 1935), pp. 88–92, for an analysis of the failure of these two bills due to sectional differences.

[34] Labor Clarion, April 7, 1911, p. 3. According to Alexander Saxton, San Francisco working-class voters did show their appreciation by voting heavily for Johnson in 1914. "San Francisco Labor and the Populist and Progressive Insurgencies," Pacific Historical Review, 34 (Nov., 1965), 433–435.

[35] Samuel P. Hays, Conservation and the Gospel of Efficiency: The Progressive Conservation Movement, 1890–1920 (Cambridge: Harvard University Press, 1959), esp. pp. 1–4. For a valuable discussion of research opportunities in the field of conservation, see Gordon B. Dodds, "The Historiography of American Conservation—Past and Prospects," Pacific Northwest Quarterly, 56 (April, 1965), 75–81.

[36] Elmo R. Richardson, "Conservation as a Political Issue: The Western Progressives' Dilemma, 1909–1912," Pacific Northwest Quarterly, 49 (April, 1958), 49.

[37] Ibid., p. 52.

[38] For a concise discussion of the Ballinger-Pinchot-Glavis affair see George Mowry, *The Era of Theodore Roosevelt, 1900–1912* (New York: Harper and Bros., 1958), pp. 250–259. A fresh appraisal may be found in Samuel P. Hays, *Conservation and the Gospel of Efficiency*, pp. 165–174. See also James Lal Penick, Jr., "A Postscript to the Ballinger-Pinchot Controversy," *Pacific Northwest Quarterly*, 55 (April, 1964), 67–75.

[39] Johnson to Lissner, Jan. 25, 1913, Johnson Papers (Bancroft Library). See also "Hearing before the Governor of California into the Activities of Louis Glavis," Dec. 20, 1912, MSS in W. H. Taft Papers, Library of Congress, and cited in Penick, "A Postscript to the Ballinger-Pinchot Controversy," p. 69.

[40] Elmo R. Richardson, *The Politics of Conservation: Crusades and Controversies, 1897–1913* (Berkeley and Los Angeles: University of California Press, 1962), p. 126. This study is based on his Ph.D. dissertation, "The Politics of the Conservation Issue in the Far West, 1896–1913" (University of California, Los Angeles, 1958). See also C. Raymond Clar, *California Government and Forestry* (Sacramento: California Department of Natural Resources, Division of Forestry, 1959), pp. 331–334.

[41] Clar, *California Government and Forestry*, p. 335.

[42] George Pardee conducted a long fight against State Forester Homans after Louis Glavis was dismissed. In 1915 a bill to remove the governor's appointive power of the state forester and to place it with the Conservation Commission was rigorously opposed by Homans. Sacramento *Bee*, March 23, 1915. See also Gerald D. Nash, "The California State Board of Forestry, 1883–1960," *Southern California Quarterly*, 47 (Sept., 1965), 295.

[43] Clar, *California Government and Forestry*, p. 404. See also Franklin Hichborn, *Story of the Session of the California Legislature of 1913* (San Francisco: James H. Barry, 1913), chaps. ix–xii.

[44] See Elmo R. Richardson, "The Struggle for the Valley: California's Hetch Hetchy Controversy, 1905–1913," *California Historical Society Quarterly*, 38 (Sept., 1959), 249–252. The most thorough discussion of the battle over Hetch Hetchy is Holway R. Jones, *John Muir and the Sierra Club: The Battle for Yosemite* (San Francisco: Sierra Club, 1965), chaps. 4–6. For a discussion of one of Muir's earlier conflicts over the question of whether forest reserves were reserved *for* use or *from* use, see Lawrence Rakestraw, "Sheep Grazing in the Cascade Range, John Minto vs. John Muir," *Pacific Historical Review*, 27 (Nov., 1958), 371–382. Also see Roderick Nash, "The American Cult of the Primitive," *American Quarterly*, 18 (Fall, 1966), 533–537.

[45] Correspondence between Muir and Johnson is in Box 7 of the Robert Underwood Johnson Collection, deposited in the Bancroft Library.

[46] Hays, *Conservation and the Gospel of Efficiency*, p. 127. See also Richardson, "The Struggle for the Valley," p. 256.

[47] Gilman Ostrander, *The Prohibition Movement in California, 1848–1933* (Berkeley and Los Angeles: University of California Press, 1957), p. 102.

⁴⁸ See James H. Timberlake, *Prohibition and the Progressive Movement, 1900–1920* (Cambridge: Harvard University Press, 1963), p. 110. For further analysis from a sociological point of view, see Joseph R. Gusfield, *Symbolic Crusade: Status Politics and the American Temperance Movement* (Urbana: University of Illinois Press, 1963), pp. 99–100, 104–106. Gusfield's thesis supports the middle-class, "status revolution" concepts of Mowry and Hofstadter. For a good discussion of the Timberlake and Gusfield books, see Norman H. Clark, *The Dry Years—Prohibition and Social Change in Washington* (Seattle: University of Washington Press, 1965), pp. 118–126.

⁴⁹ Daniel Gandier to Rowell, Nov. 22, 1910; Rowell to Gandier, Nov. 26, 1910, Rowell Papers, as cited in Ostrander, *The Prohibition Movement in California*, p. 115. In 1916 Hichborn became a prohibitionist, heading Gandier's prohibition campaign. According to Hichborn, this was the one serious difference of opinion between himself and C. K. McClatchy. See chap. lxix of his "California Politics, 1891–1939," II, 1445–1490.

⁵⁰ Ostrander, *The Prohibition Movement in California*, p. 117, drawing upon the *Anti-Saloon League Year Book, 1914*, pp. 104–105.

## 4: THE "BULL MOOSE" CAMPAIGN

¹ See Arthur S. Link, *Woodrow Wilson and the Progressive Era, 1910–1917* (New York: Harper and Bros., 1954), p. 3.

² San Francisco *Bulletin*, Oct. 18, 1911. For an account of Taft's attitude toward the tariff issue see Stanley D. Solvick, "William Howard Taft and the Payne-Aldrich Tariff," *Mississippi Valley Historical Review*, 50 (Dec., 1963), 424–442.

³ Johnson to Theodore Roosevelt, Oct. 20, 1911, Roosevelt Papers (Library of Congress, Washington, D.C.).

⁴ San Francisco *Bulletin*, Nov. 27, 1911.

⁵ George E. Mowry, *Theodore Roosevelt and the Progressive Movement* (Madison: University of Wisconsin Press, 1946), p. 197.

⁶ John Blum, *The Republican Roosevelt* (New York: Atheneum Press, 1962), p. 146.

⁷ See A. Lincoln, "Theodore Roosevelt, Hiram Johnson, and the Vice-presidential Nomination of 1912," *Pacific Historical Review*, 28 (Aug., 1959), 267, 283. Roosevelt had visited California in March, 1911, just after the progressives' reform program had been enacted by the state legislature. At that time he had declared: "California has come mighty near to realizing my governmental ideals." See A. Lincoln, "My Dear Governor—Letters Exchanged by Theodore Roosevelt and Hiram Johnson," *California Historical Society Quarterly*, 38 (Sept., 1959), 232.

⁸ Roosevelt to Johnson, Jan. 12, 1912, Roosevelt Papers; Johnson to Lissner, Jan. 16, 1912, Lissner Papers (Borel Collection, Stanford University).

⁹ See Robert Marion La Follette, *La Follette's Autobiography* (Madison: Robert M. La Follette, 1913), pp. 608–609; Belle Case and Fola La Follette,

Robert M. *La Follette* (New York: Macmillan, 1953), Vol. I, chap. 33; Amos R. E. Pinchot, *History of the Progressive Party, 1912–1916* (Washington Square: New York University Press, 1958), pp. 135–137; and Robert S. Maxwell, *La Follette and the Rise of the Progressives in Wisconsin* (State Historical Society of Wisconsin, 1956), pp. 182–183.

[10] Edwin Earl to Roosevelt, July 5, 1912, Roosevelt Papers.

[11] For newspaper coverage within California and activities elsewhere, see A. Lincoln, "Theodore Roosevelt, Hiram Johnson, and the Vice-presidential Nomination of 1912," pp. 273–276.

[12] San Francisco *Bulletin*, March 11, 1912.

[13] As quoted in *ibid.*, May 18, 1912.

[14] Johnson to Lissner, June 9, 1912, Lissner Papers; Johnson to Hiram Johnson, Jr., of the same date, Johnson Papers (Bancroft Library, University of California, Berkeley).

[15] See *The Autobiography of William Allen White* (New York: Macmillan, 1946), p. 464.

[16] San Francisco *Bulletin*, June 17, 1912.

[17] See George E. Mowry, *The California Progressives* (Berkeley and Los Angeles: University of California Press, 1951), p. 184.

[18] San Francisco *Examiner* and New York *Times*, both for June 23, 1912, as quoted by A. Lincoln, "Theodore Roosevelt, Hiram Johnson, and the Vice-presidential Nomination of 1912," pp. 279–280.

[19] William Henry Harbaugh, *Power and Responsibility: The Life and Times of Theodore Roosevelt* (New York: Farrar, Straus, 1961), p. 437.

[20] For a more complete discussion of the Progressive party convention of 1912 see Mowry, *Theodore Roosevelt and the Progressive Movement*, p. 273.

[21] As quoted in the San Francisco *Bulletin*, Aug. 8, 1912.

[22] Johnson to Lissner, July 29, 1912, Lissner Papers. This problem was later solved with the famous cross-filing provision of 1913. See chap. 3, p. 44.

[23] As quoted in Alfred Holman, "The Case of Hiram Johnson—Guilty," *North American Review*, Feb., 1917, p. 190.

[24] Mowry, *The California Progressives*, p. 189.

[25] San Francisco *Bulletin*, Sept. 16, 1912.

[26] Roosevelt to Alfred W. Cooley, Aug. 29, 1911, Roosevelt Papers, as quoted by George E. Mowry in *The Era of Theodore Roosevelt, 1900–1912* (New York: Harper and Bros., 1958), p. 55. See also the perceptive article by John Braeman, "Seven Progressives," *Business History Review*, 35 (Winter, 1961), 581–592. Braeman labels the representatives of the two ideological wings of progressivism as "moderns" and "traditionalists."

[27] *California Outlook*, Feb. 10, 1912, p. 9. Works also delivered a couple of speeches in the United States Senate on this subject: one on May 5, 1913, "Trusts and Combinations"; another on July 17, 1914, "Trust Legislation." Copies in the Haynes Papers (Government and Public Affairs Reading Room, University of California, Los Angeles).

[28] San Francisco *Bulletin*, April 19, Dec. 8 and 22, 1913.

[29] *California Outlook*, April 19, 1913, p. 2.
[30] Mowry, *Theodore Roosevelt and the Progressive Movement*, p. 280.
[31] Blum, *The Republican Roosevelt*, p. 150. For a discussion of the role of social reformers, see Allen F. Davis, "The Social Workers and the Progressive Party, 1912-1916," *American Historical Review*, 69 (April, 1964), 671-688.
[32] As quoted in Clifford B. Liljevist, "Senator Hiram Johnson: His Career in California and National Politics" (unpublished Ph.D. dissertation, University of Southern California, 1953), pp. 98-99.

5: ACCEPTANCE AND REJECTION IN 1913

[1] Parts of this chapter have appeared in my article "European Immigrant and Oriental Alien—Acceptance and Rejection by the California Legislature of 1913," *Pacific Historical Review*, 35 (Aug., 1966), 303-315.
[2] *California Outlook*, Feb. 18, 1911, p. 4.
[3] *Fresno Republican*, Dec. 26, 1911.
[4] See Peter Clark Macfarlane, "A California 'Stateslady': An Early American of Tomorrow," *Collier's*, 52 (Nov. 1, 1913), 5-6, 29-31. See also Norris C. Hundley, Jr., "Katherine Philips Edson and the Fight for the California Minimum Wage, 1912-1913," *Pacific Historical Review*, 30 (Aug., 1960), 271-273.
[5] See Robert V. Ohlson, "The History of the San Francisco Labor Council, 1892-1939" (unpublished M.A. thesis, University of California, Berkeley, 1941), pp. 174-175. Ohlson cites the *Labor Clarion*, official weekly journal of the San Francisco Labor Council, Dec. 27, 1912, Jan. 24, Feb. 21, and April 4, 1913.
[6] For further information see Milton W. Dobrzensky, "A Digest of Child Labor Laws and Regulations Applicable in California," *California Law Review*, 8 (Sept., 1920), 404-418, and Barbara N. Armstrong, "Persons and Industrial Law," *California Law Review*, 18 (March, 1930), 274-278.
[7] To complete the membership Johnson chose Walter G. Mathewson, a San Jose labor leader; two businessmen, A. Bonnheim and A. B. Dohrmann; and Frank J. Murasky, a San Francisco Superior Court judge.
[8] Industrial Welfare Commission, *First Biennial Report, 1913-1914* (Sacramento, 1915), p. 12.
[9] Hundley, "Katherine Philips Edson and the Fight for the California Minimum Wage," pp. 278-279. See also the Industrial Welfare Commission's *First Biennial Report*, pp. 49-50, and Edson to Mary White, May 26, 1915, Edson Papers (Special Collections Library, University of California, Los Angeles). Even by 1917, 44 percent of women employees in California were still earning less than $9.00 per week. See Proceedings of the *Eighteenth Annual Convention of the California State Federation of Labor* (held at Sacramento, Oct., 1917), p. 52.
[10] Industrial Welfare Commission, *Second Biennial Report, 1915-1916* (Sacramento, 1917), pp. 271-275.

[11] Industrial Welfare Commission, *Third Biennial Report, 1917–1918* (Sacramento, 1919), p. 11.

[12] Hundley, "Katherine Philips Edson and the Fight for the California Minimum Wage," p. 283. The constitutionality of the delegation of power from the legislature to a commission to fix minimum wages for women and minors was confirmed by the United States Supreme Court in April, 1917. See Industrial Welfare Commission, *Third Biennial Report*, p. 8.

[13] See chap. 3, p. 47.

[14] *Labor Clarion*, June 27, 1913, p. 4.

[15] *Ibid.*, May 16, 1913, p. 4.

[16] Crockett, "The History of California Labor Legislation, 1910–1930" (unpublished Ph.D. dissertation, University of California, Berkeley, 1931), p. 302. The Industrial Accident Commission's General Safety Orders may be found in the Bancroft Library, University of California, Berkeley. They include such diverse activities as woodworking, trench construction, mines, petroleum, and electricity.

[17] See Gerald D. Nash, "The Influence of Labor on State Policy, 1860–1920: The Experience of California," *California Historical Society Quarterly*, 42 (Sept., 1963), 251.

[18] For the financial aspects of the program, see Arthur J. Pillsbury, "An Adventure in State Insurance," *American Economic Review*, 9 (Dec., 1919), 687–692. See also Industrial Accident Commission, *Report for July 1, 1917–June 30, 1918* (Sacramento, 1918), pp. 27–32, and *Labor Clarion*, 14 (Aug. 13, 1915), 5.

[19] See Carleton H. Parker's report to Hiram Johnson on the causes of the Wheatland riot, reprinted in his *The Casual Laborer and Other Essays* (New York: Harcourt, Brace and Howe, 1920), pp. 171–199. His account of the Wheatland episode in chap. ii of that book is most informative. Parker was executive secretary of the Commission of Immigration and Housing. For a study of more current problems caused by California's reliance upon foreign agricultural labor, see N. Ray Gilmore and Gladys W. Gilmore, "The Bracero in California," *Pacific Historical Review*, 32 (Aug., 1963), 265–282.

[20] See the excellent and neglected work by Samuel Edgerton Wood, "The California State Commission of Immigration and Housing: A Study of Administrative Organization and the Growth of Function" (unpublished Ph.D. dissertation, University of California, Berkeley, 1942), p. 82.

[21] For a biography of David Lubin see Olivia Rossetti Agresti, *David Lubin: A Study in Practical Idealism* (Berkeley and Los Angeles: University of California Press, 1941). Lubin and his stepbrother, Weinstock, opened a dry-goods store in Sacramento in 1874. Within ten years it was the largest department store and mail-order house on the Pacific Coast. Lubin was also a founder of the International Institute of Agriculture in Rome and devoted much of his life after 1885 to agricultural matters.

[22] Samuel E. Wood, "The California State Commission of Immigration and Housing: A Study of Administrative Organization and the Growth of Function," pp. 83–85. All Lubin letters mentioned hereafter are cited in

this dissertation. The Lubin Papers are housed in the Bancroft Library, University of California, Berkeley, but certain sections are restricted.

[23] Johnson to Simon Lubin, Aug. 15, 1912, Lubin Papers.

[24] Johnson to Simon Lubin, Aug. 20, 1912, Lubin Papers. Other appointees included Robert Watchorn and Reverend Dana W. Bartlett of Los Angeles, and Katherine Felton and Robert N. Lynch of San Francisco. See also Franklin Hichborn's article in the Sacramento *Bee*, March 8, 1913.

[25] Lubin to commissioners, Nov. 2, 1912, Lubin Papers.

[26] Lubin to Robert Lynch, Nov. 23, 1912, Lubin Papers. See also Wood, "The California State Commission of Immigration and Housing," p. 95.

[27] Wood, "The California State Commission of Immigration and Housing," p. 102.

[28] By September, Johnson had announced his appointments to the new commission: Simon Lubin as chairman, Reverend Edward J. Hanna, Paul Scharrenberg, Mrs. Frank A. Gibson, and Arthur J. Fleming.

[29] Austin Lewis to Inez Haynes Gillmore, as quoted in *Harper's Weekly*, March 13, 1915, p. 247. Also see Carleton H. Parker, "State Commission of Immigration and Housing," *Labor Clarion*, 13 (Sept. 4, 1914), 56–57. For a thorough discussion of the commission's remarkable activities with respect to labor camp inspection, immigrant education, and housing, see Commission of Immigration and Housing, *Second Annual Report, January 2, 1916* (Sacramento, 1916), *passim*.

[30] Wood cites the *Report on Unemployment to His Excellency, Governor Hiram Johnson* (Sacramento, 1914), which includes two studies: "Life-History Statistics" and "Employment Agency Situation in California." The third published report was "The Wheatland Hop Field Riot," which may be found in U.S. Congress, Senate, Subcommittee of the Commission on Education and Labor, *Agricultural Labor in California*, Hearings, 76th Cong., 3d sess., pt. 54, pp. 20069-20072. Summaries of all the surveys are found in the annual reports of the Commission of Immigration and Housing for 1915 and 1916.

[31] Lubin to Mrs. Frank Gibson (undated) 1915, Commission File, cited in Wood, "The California State Commission of Immigration and Housing," p. 258n.

[32] See Earl Crockett, "The History of California Labor Legislation," p. 240, and Wood, "The California State Commission of Immigration and Housing," pp. 188–189. For the early activities of the free employment bureaus see the *Labor Clarion*, Sept. 1, 1916, pp. 8–10.

[33] Much of my account of antiorientalism during the Johnson administration has been drawn from Roger Daniels, *The Politics of Prejudice: The Anti-Japanese Movement in California and the Struggle for Japanese Exclusion* (Berkeley and Los Angeles: University of California Press, 1962), esp. pp. 16–64. For a provocative general account see Daniels, "Westerners from the East: Oriental Immigration Reappraised," *Pacific Historical Review*, 35 (Nov., 1966), 373–383.

[34] Daniels, *The Politics of Prejudice*, p. 21, quotes Phelan's remarks from

the San Francisco *Examiner* and *Chronicle*, both for May 8, 1900. See also Fred H. Matthews, "White Community and 'Yellow Peril,'" *Mississippi Valley Historical Review*, 50 (March, 1964), 613–614.

[35] For Phelan's use of antiorientalism in the 1912 presidential campaign, see Robert E. Hennings, "James D. Phelan and the Woodrow Wilson Anti-Oriental Statement of May 3, 1912," *California Historical Society Quarterly*, 42 (Dec., 1963), 291–296. Additional information regarding Phelan may be found in Hennings, "California Democratic Politics in the Period of Republican Ascendancy," *Pacific Historical Review*, 31 (Aug., 1962), 267–280.

[36] Fresno *Republican*, April 28, 1900. In April, 1913, Rowell wrote David Starr Jordan: ". . . Aliens of the German race are not objectionable. Natives of the Chinese race are objectionable. . . . A permanent separation of the main bodies of the two peoples on the two sides of the Pacific is absolutely imperative to the peaceful relation and the racial integrity of both. . . ." Rowell to Jordan, April 26, 1913, Rowell Papers (Bancroft Library). For a thorough analysis of Rowell's racial views, see Miles Everett, "Chester Harvey Rowell, Pragmatic Humanist and California Progressive" (unpublished Ph.D. dissertation, University of California, Berkeley, 1965), chap. 14.

[37] See Herbert B. Johnson, *Discrimination against Japanese in California* (Berkeley: Courier Publishing Co., 1907), p. 42, quoting from the San Francisco *Chronicle*, Jan. 2, 1907.

[38] Carey McWilliams, *Factories in the Field* (Boston: Little, Brown, 1939), p. 111. See also Ralph F. Burnight, "The Japanese in Rural Los Angeles County," *Studies in Sociology*, 4 (June, 1920), 5; Fred Matthews, "White Community and 'Yellow Peril,'" p. 618; and Earl Pomeroy, *The Pacific Slope—A History of California, Oregon, Washington, Idaho, Utah, and Nevada* (New York: Alfred A. Knopf, 1965), pp. 271–272.

[39] California Fruit Growers' Convention, *Proceedings, 1907*, p. 69, as quoted in the California State Relief Administration study, *Migratory Labor in California* (Sacramento: Division of Special Surveys and Studies, 1936), p. 22. Chester Rowell repeated this charge in 1909: ". . . the one overshadowing contrast is this: The Chinese will keep a contract; the Japanese will not. . . ." See Rowell, "Chinese and Japanese in America," *Annals of the American Academy of Political and Social Sciences*, 34 (Sept., 1909), 5. For a different point of view see Masakazu Iwata, "The Japanese Immigrants in California Agriculture," *Agricultural History*, 36 (Jan., 1962), 28.

[40] *Journal of the Assembly, 1909* (Sacramento, 1909), p. 317.

[41] *Journal of the Senate, 1909* (Sacramento, 1909), p. 279.

[42] Johnson to A. E. Yoell, May 18 and July 29, 1910, Johnson Papers (Bancroft Library).

[43] Johnson to Philander C. Knox, Jan. 6, 1911, Johnson Papers.

[44] Rowell to Johnson, Jan. 6, 1913, Rowell Papers.

[45] Rowell to Johnson, March 16, 1913, Rowell Papers.

[46] Johnson to Roosevelt, June 21, 1913, Johnson Papers. As Robert

Kelley points out in a recent article, V. S. McClatchy, president of the Sacramento *Bee* and owner of 1,200 acres of land in the Sutter Basin, was an avid opponent of Japanese immigration: ". . . If he was creating a farm empire for the purpose of preserving what agrarians always regarded as the bedrock of American society, the family farm, the families on them had also to be traditionally American, not Japanese." See "Taming the Sacramento: Hamiltonianism in Action," *Pacific Historical Review*, 34 (Feb., 1965), 46–47.

⁴⁷ Johnson to Roosevelt, June 21, 1913, Johnson Papers.
⁴⁸ Johnson to Rowell, March 17, 1913, Rowell Papers.
⁴⁹ Wilson to Phelan, April 9, 1913, Wilson Papers, as quoted in Arthur S. Link, *Wilson: The New Freedom* (Princeton: Princeton University Press, 1956), p. 290.
⁵⁰ See William Kent, "Some Reminiscences of Hiram Johnson," MS in the Kent Papers, Yale University; Kent to Johnson, April 7, 1913, Wilson Papers, Library of Congress; and Johnson to Kent, April 8, 1913, Wilson Papers, all cited in Link, *Wilson: The New Freedom*, pp. 290–291. Wilson did communicate directly with Johnson on April 22, 1913; see Johnson Papers.
⁵¹ Thomas A. Bailey, "California, Japan, and the Alien Land Legislation of 1913," *Pacific Historical Review*, 1 (March, 1932), 40.
⁵² Link, *Wilson: The New Freedom*, p. 293.
⁵³ *Journal of the Senate, 1913*, p. 2324; *Journal of the Assembly, 1913*, p. 2495. Recently opened Part VI of the Johnson Papers contains a 113-page transcript of the closed executive session in which Bryan met with California legislators—"Conference in re Anti-Land Law of California," in Assembly Chamber, April 28–29, 1913. For Bryan's role, see Roger Daniels, "William Jennings Bryan and the Japanese," *Southern California Quarterly*, 48 (Sept., 1966), 227–240, and Paolo E. Coletta, " 'The Most Thankless Task': Bryan and the California Alien Land Legislation," *Pacific Historical Review*, 36 (May, 1967), 163–187.
⁵⁴ See Johnson's reply to Bryan of May 14, 1913, Johnson Papers. Also Bailey, "California, Japan, and the Alien Land Legislation of 1913," p. 47. The Naturalization Act of 1906 restricted naturalization to white persons and persons of African descent, and by a special act of Congress Chinese were specifically barred. There was no direct provision relating to Japanese, but West Coast exclusionists assumed that the Japanese, being neither white nor of African descent, were not entitled to naturalization.
⁵⁵ See Johnson to Lissner and to Theodore Roosevelt, Jan. 23, 1915, Johnson Papers.
⁵⁶ Daniels, *The Politics of Prejudice*, p. 59.
⁵⁷ *Ibid.*, p. 135 n. 66.
⁵⁸ Johnson to Lissner, May 7, 1913, Johnson Papers.
⁵⁹ Johnson to Roosevelt, June 21, 1913, Johnson Papers.
⁶⁰ Johnson to Lissner, June 9, 1913, Johnson Papers.
⁶¹ Daniels, *The Politics of Prejudice*, p. 63. Miles Everett is not so critical of Johnson's motives for support of the alien land bill, arguing

that the governor worked diligently to play down the importance of such legislation. Everett suggests that although Johnson favored Oriental exclusion, his most important consideration "was quieting the agitation which stirred anti-Japanese feelings in California and embittered relations between the United States and Japan." Everett also points out, however, that Johnson recognized the political implications of the passage of the bill. See "Chester Harvey Rowell," pp. 417, 421, 424–425, 427.

[62] Daniels, *The Politics of Prejudice*, p. 63. See also the State Board of Control report, *California and the Oriental* (Sacramento, 1920), p. 135; U.S. Congress, House of Representatives, Committee on Immigration and Naturalization, *Japanese Immigration, 1920*, Hearings, 66th Cong., 2d sess., pp. 98–99; and T. Iyenaga and Kenoske Sato, *Japan and the California Problem* (New York: G. P. Putnam's Sons, 1921), pp. 139–140. The 1913 Alien Land Act is reprinted in its entirety on pp. 204–206 of the latter work; the 1920 law on pp. 207–215.

[63] See T. Scott Miyakawa's review of *The Politics of Prejudice* in the *Southern California Quarterly*, 46 (March, 1964), 107–108. Roger Daniels believes that Miyakawa's argument has some validity, but suspects "that it will develop upon investigation that most of these Japanese farmers who left their land were relatively late entrants into agricultural ownership who had little capital and were hurt by the post-war slump in much of agriculture." Letter to author, Oct. 19, 1966.

[64] Reliance upon commissions of experts to solve industrial and urban problems was also characteristic of Wisconsin Progressives during Robert La Follette's administration. See Robert S. Maxwell, *La Follette and the Rise of the Progressives in Wisconsin* (State Historical Society of Wisconsin, 1956), p. 196.

## 6: MUTINY AND PARTY DISCORD

[1] Lissner to Dickson, Dec. 21, 1913, Lissner Papers (Borel Collection, Stanford University).

[2] Johnson to Lissner, Dec. 12, 1912, Lissner Papers. See also Johnson to Roosevelt, Jan. 21, 1913, Johnson Papers (Bancroft Library, University of California, Berkeley).

[3] *Ibid.*

[4] Works to A. M. Drew, Jan. 16, 1914, Works Papers (Bancroft Library).

[5] Works to Spreckels, Feb. 9, 1914, Works Papers (Bancroft Library).

[6] See the San Francisco *Chronicle*, Nov. 20 and Dec. 19, 1913. See also Mildred E. Dickson, "Third Party Technique, 1912–1916" (unpublished M.A. thesis, University of California, Berkeley, 1937), p. 27.

[7] Robert Knight, *Industrial Relations in the San Francisco Bay Area, 1900–1918* (Berkeley and Los Angeles: University of California Press, 1960), p. 285.

[8] McLaughlin to Johnson, Jan. 23, 1914, Johnson Papers.

[9] See Robert Hennings, "James D. Phelan and the Wilson Progressives

*Notes to pages 95–100* 213

of California" (unpublished Ph.D. dissertation, University of California, Berkeley, 1961), p. 168.

[10] Johnson to Eustace Cullinan, April 23, 1914, Johnson Papers. Also, Rudolph Spreckels was still miffed at Johnson's refusal to support La Follette in 1912.

[11] Johnson to Roosevelt, Aug. 19, 1914, Johnson Papers. See also Johnson to Matt Sullivan, July 25, 1914.

[12] Los Angeles *Express*, March 29, 1913, and Sacramento *Bee*, March 31, 1913. See also E. T. Earl to Johnson, March 29, 1913, Johnson Papers; Rowell to Earl, April 11, 1913, copy in Lissner Papers; and Johnson to John Eshleman, July 23 and 31, 1914, Johnson Papers. For the decline of the Los Angeles reform movement after 1913, see Albert H. Clodius, "The Quest for Good Government in Los Angeles, 1890–1910" (unpublished Ph.D. dissertation, Claremont Graduate School, 1953), pp. 530–536.

[13] Lissner to Katherine Edson, Nov. 18, 1916, Edson Papers (Special Collections, University of California, Los Angeles).

[14] George E. Mowry, *The California Progressives* (Berkeley and Los Angeles: University of California Press, 1951), p. 211.

[15] Anonymous, *The Mirrors of Washington* (New York and London: Knickerbocker Press, 1921), p. 191. Mention is also made of Borah's statement in Robert Glass Cleland, *California in Our Time: 1900–1940* (New York: Alfred A. Knopf, 1947), p. 40.

[16] Rowell to Edson, Nov. 25, 1914, Edson Papers.

[17] Cleland, *California in Our Time*, p. 40.

[18] A copy of Luce's letter to Mowry, written Feb. 7, 1953, may be found in Box 46 of the Neylan Papers (Bancroft Library).

[19] See the following University of California oral history interviews: "Herbert C. Jones on California Government and Public Issues" (conducted by Corinne L. Gilb, 1957); "The Memoirs of William Jarvis Carr" (conducted by Doyce B. Nunis, 1959); "Philip Bancroft: Politics, Farming, and the Progressive Party in California" and "Max Thelen: California Progressive, Railroad Commissioner, and Attorney" (both conducted by Willa Klug Baum, 1962).

[20] On January 6, 1914, Johnson wrote Lissner: ". . . It was a very hard struggle with myself to keep from elbowing Heney out of the United States Senatorship and then having Eshleman meet him for Governor. . . ." Lissner Papers.

[21] Rowell to Lissner, Dec. 19 and 26, 1913, Lissner Papers.

[22] The vote was 78,359 to 33,575. See California Secretary of State, *Statement of the Vote at Primary Election held on August 25, 1914 in the State of California* (Sacramento, 1914), p. 21. Johnson was very disappointed with his friend's performance. After the primary election Rowell received a letter from Martin Madsen, Johnson's executive secretary, who wrote: "I have been told that yours was a 'sick' candidacy. . . . I am not alone in wishing that there was more effort on your part." (undated) 1914, Rowell Papers (Bancroft Library). Just prior to Johnson's de-

parture for the United States Senate in late March, 1917, Rowell confessed that he had not been much interested in his own senatorial candidacy in 1914, and did not care whether he was elected or not. Rowell to Johnson, March 24, 1917, Johnson Papers.

[23] Johnson to Heney, Aug. 31, 1914, Johnson Papers.

[24] Johnson to Lissner, Aug. 31, 1914, Lissner Papers. See also Johnson to Dickson on the same day, Johnson Papers.

[25] See Alfred Holman, "The Case of Hiram Johnson—Guilty," *North American Review*, Feb., 1917, p. 191. See also Heney to Johnson, Oct. 28, 1914, Johnson Papers.

[26] Hennings, "James D. Phelan and the Wilson Progressives of California," p. 218. The two letters referred to are a memorandum attached to a Phelan letter to A. P. Bettersworth, Sept. 1, 1914, and J. S. Irby to Phelan, Sept. 8, 1914, Phelan Papers (Bancroft Library). See also Mowry, *The California Progressives*, p. 219.

[27] Rowell to Johnson, Dec. 18, 1913, Johnson Papers.

7: THE DECLINING YEARS

[1] *California Outlook*, Jan. 16, 1915, p. 12. In mid-December, 1914, Johnson had written Dickson that he hoped the session of 1915 "would make a record for brevity, both in the number of bills and in the length of the session. . . ." Dec. 12, 1914, Johnson Papers (Bancroft Library, University of California, Berkeley). On March 2, 1915, Johnson wrote Dickson: ". . . I hope we can impress upon our legislators the necessity for a quick, snappy session, and the lack of necessity for passing many bills." Dickson Papers (Special Collections, University of California, Los Angeles).

[2] *Sacramento Bee*, Jan. 4, 1915.

[3] Grace Larsen, "A Progressive in Agriculture: Harris Weinstock," *Agricultural History*, 32 (July, 1958), 190. A valuable source for Weinstock's activities is his "Scrapbooks" in the Bancroft Library.

[4] Johnson to Rowell, Barrows, and Weinstock, Feb. 15, 1915, Rowell Papers (Bancroft Library).

[5] See the article from *Orchard and Farm*, May, 1916, in Weinstock's Scrapbook no. 16. See also Elwood Mead, *How California Is Helping People Own Farms and Rural Homes*, University of California College of Agriculture, Agricultural Experiment Station, Circular no. 221 (Berkeley, 1920), pp. 1–5.

[6] Rowell to Johnson, Feb. 17, 1915, Johnson Papers.

[7] E. J. Wickson, *Rural California* (New York: Macmillan, 1923), p. 84. Also *Report of the Commission on Land Colonization and Rural Credits of the State of California* (Sacramento: Nov., 1916), pp. 5–7.

[8] Johnson to Rowell, March 11, 1915, Johnson Papers.

[9] For the early history of cooperative marketing see Erich Kraemer and Henry E. Erdman, *History of Cooperation in the Marketing of Cali-*

fornia Fresh Deciduous Fruits (Berkeley: Giannini Foundation of Agricultural Economics, 1933). See also Henry E. Erdman, "The Development and Significance of California Co-operatives, 1900–1915," *Agricultural History*, 32 (July, 1958), 179–181.

[10] Kraemer and Erdman, *History of Cooperation in the Marketing of California Fresh Deciduous Fruits*, p. 27.

[11] As quoted in Grace Larsen, "A Progressive in Agriculture: Harris Weinstock," p. 191.

[12] Weinstock to Johnson, Feb. 15, 1916, Johnson Papers.

[13] Larsen, "A Progressive in Agriculture: Harris Weinstock," p. 192.

[14] See Grace Larsen and Henry E. Erdman, "Aaron Sapiro: Genius of Farm Co-operative Promotion," *Mississippi Valley Historical Review*, 49 (Sept., 1962), 242–245.

[15] *Ibid.*, p. 246.

[16] In 1919 Weinstock broke with his dynamic assistant, after questioning the fees Sapiro was asking of his cooperative association clients. Sapiro then turned his attention to farm problems outside California, becoming "one of the most controversial figures ever to appear in the nation's agricultural movement. . . ." *Ibid.*, p. 242. See pp. 251–268 for a thorough discussion of Sapiro's work in the cooperative movement during the 1920's.

[17] Kraemer and Erdman, *History of Cooperation in the Marketing of California Fresh Deciduous Fruits*, p. 94.

[18] *California Outlook*, May 1, 1915, p. 10.

[19] *Labor Clarion*, May 14, 1915, p. 3.

[20] *Ibid.*, June 4, 1915, p. 3.

[21] The legislature's action was defeated by the voters 156,967 to 112,681. See Eugene C. Lee, *The Politics of Nonpartisanship—A Study of California City Elections* (Berkeley and Los Angeles: University of California Press, 1960), p. 23.

[22] *California Outlook*, Dec., 1915, p. 162. See also "California Clings to Her Parties," *Literary Digest*, Nov. 13, 1915, p. 1069.

[23] As quoted in "California Clings to Her Parties," p. 1069.

[24] George E. Mowry, *The California Progressives* (Berkeley and Los Angeles: University of California Press, 1951), p. 228.

[25] Grove Johnson to Francis Keesling, May 8, 1916, Keesling Papers (Borel Collection, Stanford University).

[26] Rowell to Lissner, March 27, 1916, Rowell Papers.

[27] Rowell to Johnson, April 8, 1916, Rowell Papers.

[28] Johnson to Gilson Gardner, May 4, 1916, Johnson Papers.

[29] William D. Stephens, United States congressman from California and the man picked by Johnson as his successor for the governorship, had often written Edward Dickson of the same Republican confidence in the national Congress: "The standpat Republicans are the most confident politicians you ever knew. There seems to be no question whatever in the minds of any of them but what a Republican candidate is sure to

be elected in 1916. . . ." Stephens to Dickson, Feb. 26, 1915, Dickson Papers.

³⁰ Johnson to Irving Martin, May 11, 1916, Johnson Papers. See also Johnson to C. K. McClatchy, May 12; to Gilson Gardner, Lissner, and McClatchy, May 15; and to Stanley Washburn, May 26, 1916—all in the Johnson Papers.

³¹ Johnson to Older, May 26, 1916, Johnson Papers.

## 8: DISINTEGRATION AND DEADLOCK

[1] "His methods were so relentless and his disclosure so startling that at once he was catapulted into leadership of the progressive wing of the Republican party in New York." Arthur S. Link, *Woodrow Wilson and the Progressive Era, 1910–1917* (New York: Harper and Bros., 1954), p. 231. See also Merlo J. Pusey, *Charles Evans Hughes* (New York: Macmillan, 1951), Vol. I, chap. 15.

[2] For a transcript of Roosevelt's conversations with party leaders, see John A. Garraty, "T. R. on the Telephone," *American Heritage*, 9 (Dec., 1957), 99–108. For a complete account of George Perkins' role in both the 1912 and the 1916 conventions, see Garraty, *Right-Hand Man: The Life of George W. Perkins* (New York: Harper and Bros., 1957). See also Harold Ickes, "Who Killed the Progressive Party?" *American Historical Review*, 46 (Jan., 1941), 306–307.

[3] Representing the Republicans were Reed Smoot of Utah; Murray Crane from Massachusetts; Idaho's former Senator William F. Borah; Nicholas Murray Butler, president of Columbia University; and A. R. Johnson from Ohio. The Progressive members were George Perkins, Hiram Johnson, Horace Wilkinson from New York, Charles J. Bonaparte of Maryland, and John W. Parker.

[4] Roosevelt frequently spoke to Gilson Gardner of the Scripps newspapers and John Leary of the *World* about his distrust of Hughes. At the end of the 1916 campaign, he referred in a conversation with Leary to the "self-respect I lost supporting Hughes." Shortly after Hughes's nomination, according to Leary, Roosevelt said to him: "Close contact with [Hughes] does not make him more attractive for he is a selfish, self-centered man. . . . What these men [newspaper reporters] hate is his cowardice—his refusal to say anything, however right, that might jeopardize his chances. . . ." See John L. Leary, Jr., *Talks with T. R.* (Boston and New York: Houghton Mifflin, 1920), pp. 53–54.

[5] Amos Pinchot had attended this Progressive convention as an onlooker and described this extraordinary scene in his *History of the Progressive Party, 1912–1916* (Washington Square: New York University Press, 1958), pp. 220–221.

[6] William Allen White in his *Autobiography* (New York: Macmillan, 1946), p. 526, describes the scene in these words: ". . . Such a burst of cheering, so full of joy, so charged with exultation, I never had heard. I had been attending conventions and had heard the claque of candidates

roar on sometimes for an hour, but that ten minute outburst for Roosevelt there in the Auditorium was a cry that I had never heard before. . . ."

[7] As quoted in Harold Howland, "The Conventions at Chicago," *The Independent*, June 19, 1916, p. 480. See also George E. Mowry, *Theodore Roosevelt and the Progressive Movement* (Madison: University of Wisconsin Press, 1946), p. 354.

[8] White, *Autobiography*, pp. 526–527.

[9] See Appendix I for Amos Pinchot's apologia for Roosevelt's refusal to accept the Progressive nomination.

[10] *Sacramento Star*, June 12, 1916.

[11] *New York Times*, June 12, 1916.

[12] See Chester Rowell to Mrs. Rowell, June 14, 1916, Rowell Papers (Bancroft Library, University of California, Berkeley).

[13] Merlo Pusey interview with Hughes, April 9, 1946, cited in *Charles Evans Hughes*, I, 340.

[14] Johnson to Arthur Brisbane, July 25, 1916, Johnson Papers (Bancroft Library).

[15] Mowry, *Theodore Roosevelt and the Progressive Movement*, p. 363n, suggests that this promise may not have included support in the primary, but only in the election in the event Johnson won the primary.

[16] Harold Ickes lists the members in *The Autobiography of a Curmudgeon* (New York: Reynal and Hitchcock, 1943), p. 180: Republicans— William Crocker, John T. Adams, F. W. Estabrook, James Hemenway, Alvin Hert, Robert Howell, Alvah Martin, Herbert Parsons, Albert Perkins, Charles Warren, and Ralph Williams; Progressives—Chester Rowell, Oscar Strauss, James Garfield, Everett Colby, George Perkins, and Ickes.

[17] Pusey, *Charles Evans Hughes*, I, 335.

[18] Much of the remainder of this account is based upon my article, "Hiram Johnson, the California Progressives, and the Hughes Campaign of 1916," *Pacific Historical Review*, 31 (Nov., 1962), 403–412.

[19] *Sacramento Star*, June 28, 1916.

[20] Edson to Johnson, June 28, 1916, Edson Papers (Special Collections, University of California, Los Angeles).

[21] Johnson to Edson, June 30, 1916, Edson Papers.

[22] Johnson to James Garfield, July 5, 1916, Johnson Papers.

[23] Mowry, *Theodore Roosevelt and the Progressive Movement*, p. 364.

[24] John Randolph Haynes to Johnson, Dec. 17, 1916, Haynes Papers (Government and Public Affairs Reading Room, University of California, Los Angeles).

[25] Lissner to Edson, July 13, 1916, Edson Papers.

[26] *Sacramento Star*, July 15, 1916.

[27] As quoted in Frederick M. Davenport, "The Case of Hiram Johnson— Not Guilty," *North American Review*, Feb., 1917, p. 205. The alleged blacklisting of Johnson was by Crocker, Keesling, Mike De Young (editor of the San Francisco *Chronicle*), Harrison Gray Otis, John Spreckels of San Diego, and other men of the old Republican machine.

[28] Keesling to Willcox and Keesling to Crocker, July 15, 1916, Keesling Papers (Borel Collection, Stanford University).
[29] Rowell to Perkins, July 24, 1916, Rowell Papers.
[30] Mowry, *The California Progressives* (Berkeley and Los Angeles: University of California Press, 1951), p. 255.
[31] Report on the California campaign by Hughes's train manager, Charles W. Farnham, in Hughes Papers, cited in Pusey, *Charles Evans Hughes*, I, 341.
[32] *Ibid.*
[33] John D. Works had advised Hughes immediately after his nomination for President that he should avoid giving himself exclusively to the reactionary element of the Republican party in California. See Works to Hughes, Nov. 13, 1916, Works Papers (Borel Collection, Stanford University, copy in Works Papers, Bancroft Library). See also Works to Willcox, Sept. 18, 1916, Works Papers (Bancroft Library) and Perkins to Rowell, July 27, 1916, Rowell Papers.
[34] Rowell to Willcox, July 29, 1916, Rowell Papers.
[35] Rowell to Willcox, copy to Hughes, Aug. 8, 1916, Rowell Papers.
[36] Johnson to J. C. O'Laughlin, July 26, 1916, Johnson Papers.

## 9: BLUNDER BEGETS BLUNDER

[1] Frederick Davenport, "Across the Continent with Hughes," *Outlook*, Sept. 13, 1916, p. 89; Merlo J. Pusey, *Charles Evans Hughes* (New York: Macmillan, 1951), I, 336.
[2] Pusey, *Charles Evans Hughes*, I, 338.
[3] Davenport, "Did Hughes Snub Johnson?—An Inside Story. How and Why Charles Evans Hughes Lost California and the Presidency in 1916," *American Political Science Review*, 43 (April, 1949), 323.
[4] *Outlook*, Aug. 16, 1916, p. 879.
[5] Keesling to Rowell, Aug. 8, 1916, folder entitled "Charles Hughes' California Trip," Lincoln-Roosevelt Republican Club Papers, collected by Alice Rose, 1937–1943, and housed in the Borel Collection, Stanford University.
[6] Davenport, "Did Hughes Snub Johnson?" p. 323. In this respect the struggle in California was a microcosm of that being waged nationally.
[7] As quoted in *ibid.*
[8] Rowell to Willcox, Aug. 11, 1916, Rowell Papers (Bancroft Library, University of California, Berkeley).
[9] As quoted in Davenport, "Did Hughes Snub Johnson?" p. 324. See also Malcolm Moos, *The Republicans* (New York: Random House, 1956), p. 298.
[10] The Rowell-Hughes conversation can be found in Pusey, *Charles Evans Hughes*, I, 342. Pusey interviewed Hughes about the Portland meeting on April 9, 1946. See also Davenport, "The Case of Hiram Johnson—Not Guilty," *North American Review*, Feb., 1917, pp. 208–209.

## Notes to pages 131–136

[11] Katherine Edson to Mrs. Lyndsay Van Rensselaer, Dec. 2, 1916, Edson Papers (Special Collections, University of California, Los Angeles).
[12] Rowell to Roosevelt, Aug. 23, 1916, Rowell Papers.
[13] Davenport, "Did Hughes Snub Johnson?" p. 324.
[14] Pusey, *Charles Evans Hughes*, I, 342, from an interview with Davenport on Dec. 20, 1948.
[15] Francis Keesling's unpublished monograph, "Hiram Johnson and the Hughes Campaign in California," July 27, 1949, p. 36, Keesling Papers (Borel Collection, Stanford University). This monograph was prompted by Davenport's article, "Did Hughes Snub Johnson."
[16] Davenport, "Did Hughes Snub Johnson?" p. 325.
[17] Keesling monograph, "Hiram Johnson and the Hughes Campaign," p. 34. In another unpublished monograph, "The Hughes Campaign, 1916 —The Hotel Virginia Incident," written in 1944, Keesling states on page 48: ". . . If there had been any confidence that Governor Johnson would have been fair to the Republican candidate for president and that the audience would not have been packed with his followers and heelers who would have affronted Hughes, he might have been given that recognition as governor of the state, despite the fact that he was a Progressive candidate for a Republican nomination." Keesling Papers (Borel Collection).
[18] Davenport, "Did Hughes Snub Johnson?" p. 325; Malcolm Moos, *The Republicans*, pp. 298–299. The Los Angeles *Times* reported the next morning: "In a single sentence, Charles Evans Hughes set at doubt tonight all questions as to his attitude towards the Republican leaders of California. . . ." The wiseacre in the balcony was an employee in Crocker's bank. See Keesling to Paul Edwards, Aug. 9, 1945, in Pusey, *Charles Evans Hughes*, I, 343.
[19] Keesling's monograph, "Hiram Johnson and the Hughes Campaign," p. 37.
[20] See George E. Mowry, *The California Progressives* (Berkeley and Los Angeles: University of California Press, 1951), p. 261.
[21] *Ibid.*, p. 262. For the strike itself see *Law and Order in San Francisco —A Beginning* (San Francisco Chamber of Commerce, 1916). The strike did not end until December 16, 1916, when the Culinary Crafts Union, finally convinced of the hopelessness of their plight, called off the strike.
[22] Davenport, "Did Hughes Snub Johnson?" p. 326.
[23] *Ibid.*
[24] *Ibid.* See also Mowry, *The California Progressives*, pp. 261–265, for the Commercial Club incident and management-labor strife in general. I have not been able to find the conservatives' side of the case explained by any participant. My account is therefore one-sided.
[25] Mowry, *The California Progressives*, p. 261. Robert V. Ohlson has written: ". . . It is quite conceivable that had Hughes refused the banquet served by the 'scab' waiters and thus avoided antagonizing union labor as represented in the Labor Council, enough votes from organized labor in San Francisco would have gone to Hughes to have elected him. . . . As it was the Labor Council rejoiced at Wilson's re-election." See

"The History of the San Francisco Labor Council, 1892–1939" (unpublished M.A. thesis, University of California, Berkeley, 1941), p. 155.

[26] W. W. Mines to Keesling, Aug. 8, 1916, Keesling Papers.

[27] The correspondence between Congressman Johnson and Dickson is in Box 23 of the Dickson Papers (Special Collections, University of California, Los Angeles). On Aug. 18, 1954, Dickson complied with Johnson's solicitation, sending him a letter and the historical sketch. Johnson presented the sketch to Congress on Aug. 19, 1954. This article on "one of the most notable and costly political feuds in American history" was then written into the *Congressional Record*, for posterity to read and to judge. It can be found in U.S., *Congressional Record*, 83d Cong., 2d sess., 1954, vol. 100, A6226.

[28] Edson to Mrs. Lyndsay Van Rensselaer, Dec. 2, 1916, Edson Papers.

[29] This account, "spruced-up" a bit, is from Pusey, *Charles Evans Hughes*, I, 344–345.

[30] Dickson, "How Hughes Lost California in 1916," p. 6, unpublished MS, Dickson Papers.

[31] Johnson to Rowell, Nov. 28, 1916, Johnson Papers (Bancroft Library). This letter was to be used by Rowell on a trip to the East after the November election to explain what had happened in California.

[32] Keesling monographs, "Hiram Johnson and the Hughes Campaign," p. 43, and "The Hughes Campaign," p. 51.

[33] Mark Sullivan, *Our Times: The United States, 1900–1925* (New York: Charles Scribner's Sons, 1933), V, 242.

[34] Pusey interview with Hughes, Oct. 24, 1945, cited in *Charles Evans Hughes*, I, 346.

[35] Dickson, "How Hughes Lost California in 1916," p. 7.

[36] Pusey interview with Davenport, Dec. 20, 1948, cited in *Charles Evans Hughes*, I, 346.

[37] Keesling, "The Hughes Campaign," p. 50. In "Hiram Johnson and the Hughes Campaign," p. 35, Keesling states that he was caught off guard because when he extended the alleged invitation for Johnson to accompany the presidential party he was dealing with the governor's representative. *"We should have transmitted an appropriate written message to the Governor direct,"* writes Keesling, underlining the words himself. "In due course, conforming to the ethical, it should have been released to the press of the State. . . . That would have forestalled Mr. Rowell, clarified the situation in the minds of the public, and prevented misuse of the fateful call of Mr. Hughes at the Hotel Virginia." Keesling Papers. Dickson claims in "How Hughes Lost California," p. 7, that he attempted to arrange a speaking itinerary for Johnson which "would have enabled him at least to have an afternoon in conference with Hughes"; but Johnson refused, saying that he would not disrupt his schedule.

[38] From the explanatory letter prepared by Johnson and mailed to Rowell on Nov. 28, 1916, copy in Johnson Papers. See also Johnson to Rowell, Nov. 25 and 28, 1916, suggesting that Rowell "prepare four or five statements with a good punch in them in advance so that you may readily respond. . . ." Johnson Papers.

[39] Johnson to Farnham, Aug 21, 1916, copy in Johnson Papers.
[40] Lissner to Roosevelt, Sept. 1, 1916, Lissner Papers (Borel Collection).
[41] Marshall Stimson, "Fun, Fights, and Fiestas in Old Los Angeles," unpublished autobiography, quoted by Clifford Liljevist, "Senator Hiram Johnson: His Career in California and National Politics" (unpublished Ph.D. dissertation, University of Southern California, 1953), p. 126.
[42] Harold Ickes, *Autobiography of a Curmudgeon* (New York: Reynal and Hitchcock, 1943), p. 182.
[43] Pusey, *Charles Evans Hughes*, I, 349.
[44] Mowry, *The California Progressives*, p. 269.
[45] *The Autobiography of William Allen White* (New York: Macmillan, 1946), pp. 529-530.

## 10: THE INITIAL RESPONSE

[1] Sacramento *Star*, Aug. 16, 1916.
[2] Los Angeles *Times*, Aug. 25, 1916.
[3] *Ibid.*, Aug. 29, 1916.
[4] *Ibid.*
[5] On Sept. 17, 1916, the Los Angeles *Times* printed the final senatorial primary results: Johnson's total vote was 186,548 (Republican: 161,404; Progressive: 16,227; others: 8,917). Booth received a total of 148,167 (Republican: 146,339; Democrat: 1,277; others: 551). Patton received 69,071 votes, 68,871 of which were Democrat.
[6] Quoted in Sacramento *Star*, Aug. 31, 1916.
[7] Quoted in *ibid.*, Sept. 1, 1916.
[8] E. Ray Nichols, Jr., "An Investigation of the Contribution of the Public Speaking of Hiram Johnson to his Political Career" (unpublished M.A. thesis, University of Southern California, 1948), p. 118.
[9] Clifford Liljevist, "Senator Hiram Johnson: His Career in California and National Politics" (unpublished Ph.D. dissertation, University of Southern California, 1953), p. 140.
[10] George E. Mowry, *The California Progressives* (Berkeley and Los Angeles: University of California Press, 1951), p. 271.
[11] From a clipping of the speech, Oct. 27, 1916, Edson Papers (Special Collections, University of California, Los Angeles).
[12] Sacramento *Star*, Oct. 21, 1916.
[13] As quoted in E. Ray Nichols, "An Investigation of the Contribution of the Public Speaking of Hiram Johnson to his Political Career," p. 118.
[14] Sacramento *Star*, Sept. 19, 1916. The San Francisco *Chronicle* reported on the same day that not less than 80 of the 160 delegates backed Johnson's program.
[15] Los Angeles *Times*, Sept. 20, 1916.
[16] Lissner to Roosevelt, Sept. 23, 1916, Lissner Papers (Borel Collection, Stanford University).
[17] See "Political Miracles in California," *Outlook*, Oct. 25, 1916, p. 413.
[18] Works to Hughes, Nov. 13, 1916, Works Papers (Borel Collection, Stanford University).

[19] For example, see Johnson's letters of Sept. 12 to James Garfield, W. B. Howard, Medill McCormick, Alexander Moore, J. C. O'Laughlin, George Perkins, Raymond Robins, Frederick Davenport, and Roosevelt, thanking them for their congratulatory telegrams on his primary victory. In each letter Johnson wrote that he could not understand Hughes but would try to surmount the obstacles. See also Rowell to Perkins, Sept. 27, 1916, Rowell Papers (Bancroft Library, University of California, Berkeley).

[20] From letters returned to Keesling, Keesling Papers (Borel Collection). For further excerpts see Appendix II.

[21] Luce to Neylan, Nov. 16, Neylan Papers (Bancroft Library).

[22] Neylan to R. W. Burnham, Nov. 16, 1916, Neylan Papers.

[23] Neylan to Anderson, Nov. 14, 1916, Neylan Papers. In October, Neylan complained to T. E. Stephenson of Santa Ana that he had passed through four towns in Orange County without observing the slightest effort to arrange Hughes meetings. Oct. (?), 1916, Neylan Papers.

[24] For a discussion of the 1916 Democratic campaign effort in California, see Robert Hennings, "James D. Phelan and the Wilson Progressives of California" (unpublished Ph.D. dissertation, University of California, Berkeley, 1961), pp. 299–301.

[25] "Political Miracles in California," *Outlook*, Oct. 25, 1916, p. 412.

[26] Walter Lippmann, "The Case for Wilson," *New Republic*, Oct. 14, 1916, p. 264.

## 11: THE FINAL RESPONSE

[1] Malcolm Moos states that "contrary to the embroidered accounts of motion pictures and reckless raconteurs, Hughes was not unprepared for defeat. The story that he retired on election night thinking he was the next President does not square with the facts." See *The Republicans* (New York: Random House, 1956), pp. 303–304. See also Merlo J. Pusey, *Charles Evans Hughes* (New York: Macmillan, 1951), I, 361.

[2] See Oswald Garrison Villard, *Fighting Years* (New York: Harcourt, Brace, 1939), p. 318.

[3] New York *Times*, Nov. 8, 1916.

[4] Edgar Eugene Robinson, *The Presidential Vote, 1896–1932* (Palo Alto: Stanford University Press; London: Humphrey Milford Oxford University Press, 1934), p. 145. The final presidential tabulation showed: Democrats—466,289; Republicans—462,516; and others—70,976. See Appendix III. Johnson defeated George Patton, the Democratic candidate, 574,667 to 277,852.

[5] William Allen White to Roosevelt, Dec. 27, 1916, in Walter Johnson's *Selected Letters of William Allen White* (New York: Henry Holt, 1945), p. 174.

[6] Los Angeles *Times*, Nov. 11, 1916.

[7] Johnson to Van Valkenberg, Sept. 5, 1916, Johnson Papers (Bancroft Library, University of California, Berkeley). Johnson later refused the editor's request to publish his letter, writing: ". . . While my letter to

you relates accurately the events and with equal accuracy gives my conclusions and opinions, it is a harsh arraignment of Mr. Hughes and certainly not complimentary to him. At this particular time, when Mr. Hughes has met with a heartbreaking defeat and when he must be suffering the mental torture, I thought it inappropriate to publish drastic criticisms of his actions here." Johnson had sent a hasty telegram on Nov. 12, and this follow-up letter was written Nov. 15. Johnson Papers.

[8] Johnson to Ickes, Nov. 15, 1916. See also Johnson to Roosevelt, Nov. 20, 1916. Johnson Papers.

[9] Johnson to McCormick, Nov. 15, 1916, Johnson Papers.

[10] See Armin Rappaport, *The British Press and Wilsonian Neutrality* (Palo Alto: Stanford University Press; London: Geoffrey Cumberlege Oxford University Press, 1951), p. 99. The issue of the *Manchester Guardian* referred to was that of Nov. 9, 1916. (Most of the British press, however, agreed with Roosevelt that "only a set of whiskers" differentiated the two candidates.) As a matter of fact, Wilson planned to transfer executive authority to Hughes right after the election if Hughes won. Hughes would have been appointed secretary of state, and as soon as he took office, Wilson and Vice-President Marshall would have resigned. See the *War Memoirs of Robert Lansing* (Indianapolis and New York: Bobbs-Merrill, 1935), p. 165.

[11] Walter Johnson, *William Allen White's America* (New York: Henry Holt, 1947), p. 268.

[12] Arthur Link, *Woodrow Wilson and the Progressive Era, 1910–1917* (New York: Harper and Bros., 1954), p. 241.

[13] See chap. 7, p. 113. The seeds of the intense isolationism Hiram Johnson would display in the United States Senate prior to both World Wars had already been sown.

[14] Charles Forcey, *The Crossroads of Liberalism: Croly, Weyl, Lippmann and the Progressive Era, 1900–1925* (New York: Oxford University Press, 1961), p. 253.

[15] *Ibid.*, p. 251. The three editors were initially for Hughes, mainly because of Wilson's foreign policy. They objected to Wilson's "extreme emphasis upon abstract rights in diplomacy." They argued that "Wilson used the wrong methods to uphold world law and order. . . ." Their most serious charge was that "Wilson has failed most grievously in his role as a democratic leader. . . ." See pp. 251–252.

[16] Walter Lippmann, "The Case for Wilson," *New Republic*, Oct. 14, 1916, pp. 263–264.

[17] Herbert Croly, "The Two Parties in 1916," *New Republic*, Oct. 21, 1916, p. 287.

[18] For amplification of this election factor, see Arthur Link, *Woodrow Wilson and the Progressive Era*, pp. 229–230.

[19] *Ibid.*, p. 239. Katherine Edson came to a similar conclusion about Californians: "It was the more intellectual liberal elements of this State that thinks for itself that carried the election of Wilson. I have been told that two-thirds of the professors at the University of California voted for Wilson. I know that is true of the University of Southern California

and Los Angeles high schools." Edson to Mrs. Van Rensselaer, Dec. 2, 1916, Edson Papers (Special Collections, University of California, Los Angeles).

[20] George E. Mowry, *The California Progressives* (Berkeley and Los Angeles: University of California Press, 1951), p. 276. See Appendix III for a complete list of the 1916 presidential returns in California, county by county. This appendix is from Table IX in Edgar Eugene Robinson, *The Presidential Vote, 1896-1932*, pp. 145-150.

[21] Paul F. Lazarsfeld, Bernard Berelson, and Hazel Gaudet, *The People's Choice: How the Voter Makes Up His Mind in a Presidential Campaign* (New York: Duell, Sloan and Pearce, 1944), p. 101.

[22] These figures are derived from statistics offered by Charles H. Titus, "Voting in California, 1900-1926," *Southwestern Political and Social Science Quarterly*, 10 (June, 1929), 82, 86.

[23] Lazarsfeld, Berelson, and Gaudet, *The People's Choice*, p. 158.

[24] Johnson to Rowell, Aug. 20 (?), 1916, Rowell Papers (Bancroft Library).

[25] Rowell to C. K. McClatchy, Jan. 18, 1927, in the folder marked "Charles Hughes Campaign Trip," Lincoln-Roosevelt Republican Club Papers, collected by Alice Rose and deposited in the Borel Collection, Stanford University.

[26] George E. Mowry, *Theodore Roosevelt and the Progressive Movement* (Madison: University of Wisconsin Press, 1946), p. 366n.

[27] The result of the election did not alter Francis Keesling's attitude, for in 1949 he wrote: "Were a campaign to be waged under similar circumstances I would unhesitatingly follow the pattern of the 1916 campaign, but with the advantage of experience." See "Hiram Johnson and the Hughes Campaign," p. 45, Keesling Papers (Borel Collection).

## 12: AN APPRAISAL

[1] Johnson to Neylan, April 18, 1917, Neylan Papers (Bancroft Library, University of California, Berkeley). Also Neylan to Johnson, April 16, 1917, *ibid.*, and Johnson to Arthur Arlett, June 23, 1917, Arlett Papers (Bancroft Library).

[2] Rowell to Johnson, Feb. 28, 1917, Rowell Papers (Bancroft Library).

[3] See George E. Mowry, *The California Progressives* (Berkeley and Los Angeles: University of California Press, 1951), p. 290. For a good account of how California progressives were able, in the 1920's, "to retain and expand their program of humanitarianism and social service and at the same time promote the business virtues of economy and efficiency in government," see Jackson K. Putnam, "The Persistence of Progressivism in the 1920's: The Case of California," *Pacific Historical Review*, 35 (Nov., 1966), 395-411.

[4] "Report of the Work of the Railroad Commission, January 1911 to December 1916" (Dec. 24, 1916), pp. 49-50, prepared by Paul A. Sinheimer, Pt. VI, Johnson Papers (Bancroft Library).

⁵ William F. Herrin, "Government Regulation of Railways," *California Law Review*, 2 (Jan., 1914), 88-89. According to Gabriel Kolko, *Railroads and Regulations, 1877-1916* (Princeton: Princeton University Press, 1965), p. 232, the "federal regulation of railroads from 1887 until 1916 did not disappoint the American railroad industry. . . ." It appears that a similar conclusion could be reached about state regulation of the Southern Pacific. In saying this, however, I do not intend to subscribe to Kolko's limited definition of progressivism: ". . . a political capitalism whereby important economic interests utilize the power of the federal government to solve internal economic problems which could not otherwise be solved by voluntary or non-political means. . . ." *Ibid.*, p. 239.

⁶ Richard Hofstadter, ed., *The Progressive Movement, 1900-1915* (Englewood Cliffs: Prentice-Hall, 1963), p. 15. See also David P. Barrows, "Reorganization of State Administration in California," *California Law Review*, 3 (Jan., 1915), 94.

⁷ Samuel Haber, *Efficiency and Uplift: Scientific Management in the Progressive Era, 1890-1920* (Chicago: University of Chicago Press, 1964), pp. 54-55. See also Dwight Waldo, *The Administrative State—A Study of the Political Theory of American Public Administration* (New York: Ronald Press, 1948), chap. 3.

⁸ "Report of the State Board of Control" (Dec. 28, 1916), pp. 3, 25, prepared by John Francis Neylan, Pt. VI, Johnson Papers. See also two publications of the California Taxpayers' Association: "Income and Expenditures of Government in California, 1900 to 1940," *Tax Digest*, 19 (Jan., 1941), 5, 7, 17, 19, and same title, *Tax Digest*, 21 (Feb., 1943), 54, 60.

⁹ Between 1911 and 1920, only six of twenty-two proposed constitutional amendments were adopted, five of eighteen proposed statutes were passed, and thirty of fifty-seven referendum issues. Winston W. Crouch, *The Initiative and Referendum in California* (Los Angeles: Haynes Foundation, 1950), pp. 23-28. This pamphlet is based upon Crouch's and V. O. Key's book of the same title.

¹⁰ *Ibid.*, p. 26. See also Crouch, "The Initiative and Referendum in Cities," *American Political Science Review*, 37 (June, 1943), 491-504; and Joseph G. Lapalombara and Charles B. Hagan, "Direct Legislation: An Appraisal and a Suggestion," *American Political Science Review*, 45 (June, 1951), 400-421.

¹¹ Grant McConnell, *Private Power and American Democracy* (New York: Alfred A. Knopf, 1966), p. 43.

¹² Among others, see McConnell, *Private Power and American Democracy*, chap. 2; Eugene C. Lee, *The Politics of Nonpartisanship—A Study of California City Elections* (Berkeley and Los Angeles, University of California Press, 1960), pp. 34-38; John A. Vieg, "A New Design for California Politics," *Western Political Quarterly*, 13 (Sept., 1960), 692-701; Oscar Gass, "The Literature of American Government," *Commentary*, 41 (June, 1966), 70; Winston W. Crouch, Dean E. McHenry, John C. Bollens, and Stanley Scott, *California Government and Politics*

(Englewood Cliffs: Prentice-Hall, 1964), pp. 108–110; and Thomas W. Casstevens, "Reflections on the Initiative Process," in Eugene C. Lee, ed., *The California Governmental Process* (Boston and Toronto: Little, Brown, 1966), pp. 90–91.

[13] Mowry, *The California Progressives*, p. 296. Albert Clodius, "The Quest for Good Government in Los Angeles, 1890–1910" (unpublished Ph.D. dissertation, Claremont Graduate School, 1953), p. 484, states: "One of the most serious weaknesses of the political reform effort [in Los Angeles] was therefore its failure to make a successful appeal to the workingmen of the city. . . ."

[14] For concurring opinions, see Alexander Saxton, "San Francisco Labor and the Populist and Progressive Insurgencies," *Pacific Historical Review*, 34 (Nov., 1965), 431–438; and Miles Everett, "Chester Harvey Rowell, Pragmatic Humanist and California Progressive" (unpublished Ph.D. dissertation, University of California, Berkeley, 1965), pp. 381–383. John L. Shover of San Francisco State College has conducted important quantitative investigations of voting statistics in San Francisco and Los Angeles during the Progressive period. While his findings have not yet been published, they reveal remarkable support for Johnson among rank-and-file urban voters from working-class areas. As reported in "The Progressives and the Working Class Vote in California" (unpublished manuscript in the possession of Professor Shover).

[15] Despite the opposition Weinstock faced, no less than twelve marketing organizations were created during his first year as market director—the Associated Milk Producers, Inc., the California Hop Growers Association, Inc., and the State Bureau of Distribution for Citrus Fruits, to name a few. See "Report of State Market Commission" (Dec. 15, 1916), pp. 2–5, prepared by Weinstock, Pt. VI, Johnson Papers.

[16] See "Philip Bancroft: Politics, Farming, and the Progressive Party in California" (oral history interview conducted by Willa Klug Baum, University of California, Berkeley, 1962), pp. 90–91.

[17] See Stimson's address of April, 1921, before the Glendora Women's Club for Saner and Better Government, cited in Clodius, "The Quest for Good Government in Los Angeles," p. 543. On Stimson's post-Progressive years, also see Otis L. Graham, Jr., *An Encore for Reform: The Old Progressives and the New Deal* (New York: Oxford University Press, 1967), pp. 38, 99–100.

[18] Lissner to Hays, Aug. 19, 1918, cited in Clodius, "The Quest for Good Government in Los Angeles," p. 511.

[19] See Richard Hofstadter, *The Age of Reform—From Bryan to FDR* (New York: Alfred A. Knopf, 1955), particularly chap. iv, "The Status Revolution and Progressive Leaders." Carl Degler writes in *Out of Our Past: The Forces that Shaped Modern America* (New York: Harper Colophon, 1962), p. 338: ". . . Like the political Revolution of 1776, the Progressive movement of the early twentieth century was distinguished almost as much by what it conserved as by what it introduced." And on page 368 he states: ". . . Like so much else in the American experience, the Progressives were more a conservative than an innovating force. . . ."

[20] See Mowry, *The California Progressives*, chap. 4, "What Manner of Men: The Progressive Mind." Also his "The California Progressive and His Rationale: A Study in Middle Class Politics," *Mississippi Valley Historical Review*, 36 (Sept., 1949), 240–250.

[21] For example, see Andrew M. Scott, "The Progressive Era in Perspective," *Journal of Politics*, 21 (Nov., 1959), 685–701; J. Joseph Huthmacher, "Urban Liberalism and the Age of Reform," *Mississippi Valley Historical Review*, 49 (Sept., 1962), 231–241; Richard B. Sherman, "The Status Revolution and Massachusetts Progressive Leadership," *Political Science Quarterly*, 78 (March, 1963), 59–65; Samuel P. Hays, "The Politics of Reform in Municipal Government in the Progressive Era," *Pacific Northwest Quarterly*, 55 (Oct., 1964), 157; Hays, "The Social Analysis of American Political History, 1880–1920," *Political Science Quarterly*, 80 (Sept., 1965), 373–394; Frank Beach, "The Transformation of California, 1900–1920: The Effects of the Westward Movement on California's Growth and Development in the Progressive Period" (unpublished Ph.D. dissertation, University of California, Berkeley, 1963), chap. 8; and Miles Everett, "Chester Harvey Rowell," pp. 357-360. A recent article that makes specific reference to California is Jack Tager, "Progressives, Conservatives and the Theory of Status Revolution," *Mid-America*, 48 (July, 1966), 162–175. The most provocative recent reevaluation of progressivism is Robert H. Wiebe, *The Search for Order, 1877–1920* (New York: Hill and Wang, 1967). For an enlightening evaluation of the middle-class, reformist-progressive tradition which stresses its more radical side, see Daniel Aaron, *Men of Good Hope: A Story of American Progressives* (New York: Oxford University Press, 1951), pp. 303–308.

[22] Hays, "The Politics of Reform in Municipal Government in the Progressive Era," p. 157. Also his "The Social Analysis of American Political History," p. 378. See also William Anderson Vest, "A Comparative Study of the Republican Factions in California, 1906–1912" (unpublished M.A. thesis, San Francisco State College, 1967). Vest's important findings strongly support Samuel Hays's broader contentions about the status-revolution thesis. After comparing statistically the social characteristics of 100 leaders from each of the progressive and standpat wings of the California Republican party, Vest concluded that ". . . in the matter of age, there was not really a significant difference between the two factions." The only significant difference between the two groups was the amount of political experience. "In short," writes Vest, "both factions were representative of the upper middle class, who were educated, 'well fixed' Protestants of west-European background and/or having a north-European name." Pp. 47–48.

[23] Samuel Hays, "The Social Analysis of American Political History," p. 379.

[24] Arthur Mann, "The Progressive Tradition," in John Higham, ed., *The Reconstruction of American History* (New York: Harper Torchbooks, 1962), p. 163.

[25] Carl Degler, *Out of Our Past*, p. 370.

# BIBLIOGRAPHY

## PRIMARY MATERIAL

### MANUSCRIPTS

Arlett, Arthur. Arlett Papers. Bancroft Library, University of California, Berkeley.
Bard, Thomas Robert. Bard Papers. Huntington Library, San Marino, California.
Dickson, Edward A. Dickson Papers. Special Collections Library, University of California, Los Angeles.
———. "The Lincoln-Roosevelt League," Dickson Papers.
———. "How Hughes Lost California in 1916," Dickson Papers.
Edson, Katherine Philips. Edson Papers. Special Collections Library, University of California, Los Angeles.
Haynes, John Randolph. Haynes Papers. Government and Public Affairs Reading Room, University of California, Los Angeles.
———. "The Birth of Democracy in California," Haynes Papers.
Heney, Francis J. Heney Papers. Bancroft Library.
Hichborn, Franklin K. Hichborn Papers. Government and Public Affairs Reading Room, University of California, Los Angeles.
———. "California Politics, 1891–1939," Vol. II. Copy in University of California School of Law, Boalt Hall, Berkeley.
Irish, John Powell. Irish Papers. Borel Collection, Stanford University.
Johnson, Hiram W. Johnson Papers. Bancroft Library.
Johnson, Robert Underwood. Johnson Papers. Bancroft Library.
Jones, Herbert C. Jones Papers. Borel Collection.
Keesling, Francis V. Keesling Papers. Borel Collection.
———. "The Hughes Campaign, 1916—The Hotel Virginia Incident," Keesling Papers.
———. "Hiram Johnson and the Hughes Campaign in California," Keesling Papers.
Lincoln-Roosevelt Republican Club Papers collected by Alice Rose, 1937–1943. Borel Collection.
Lissner, Meyer. Lissner Papers. Borel Collection.
Lubin, Simon. Lubin Papers. Bancroft Library.
Lukens, Theodore P. Lukens Papers. Huntington Library.
Neylan, John Francis. Neylan Papers. Bancroft Library.

———. "Report of the State Board of Control." Johnson Papers.
Older, Fremont. Older Papers. Bancroft Library.
Pardee, George C. Pardee Papers. Bancroft Library.
Phelan, James D. Phelan Papers. Bancroft Library.
Roosevelt, Theodore. Roosevelt Papers. Library of Congress, Washington, D.C.
Rowell, Chester H. Rowell Papers. Bancroft Library.
Stimson, Marshall. Stimson Papers. Huntington Library.
Weinstock, Harris. Scrapbooks. Bancroft Library.
———. "Report of the State Market Commission." Johnson Papers.
Willard, Charles Dwight. Willard Papers. Huntington Library.
Works, John D. Works Papers. Bancroft Library and Borel Collection.
———. "Some of My Experiences in Political and Official Life." Works Papers. Borel Collection.

NEWSPAPERS

Fresno *Republican.*
Los Angeles *Express.*
Los Angeles *Times.*
New York *Times.*
Sacramento *Bee.*
Sacramento *Star.*
San Francisco *Bulletin*
San Francisco *Chronicle.*

PERIODICALS

*California Weekly.* November, 1908—December, 1910.
*California Outlook.* 1911-1917.
*Labor Clarion.* 1910-1917.
*Pacific Outlook.* January-February, 1911.
*San Francisco Argonaut.* 1910-1917.

AUTOBIOGRAPHIES, MEMOIRS, AND
PUBLISHED COLLECTIONS OF LETTERS

Ickes, Harold. *The Autobiography of a Curmudgeon.* New York: Reynal and Hitchcock, 1943.
Johnson, Walter. *Selected Letters of William Allen White.* New York: Henry Holt, 1945.
———. *William Allen White's America.* New York: Henry Holt, 1947.
La Follette, Robert Marion. *La Follette's Autobiography.* Madison: Robert M. La Follette, 1913.
Lane, Anne Wintermute, and Louise Herrick Wall. *The Letters of Franklin K. Lane: Personal and Political.* Boston and New York: Houghton Mifflin, 1922.
Older, Fremont. *My Own Story.* San Francisco: Call Publishing, 1919.
*The Autobiography of William Allen White.* New York. Macmillan, 1946.
*War Memoirs of Robert Lansing.* Indianapolis and New York: Bobbs-Merrill, 1935.

ORAL HISTORY INTERVIEWS

"Herbert C. Jones on California Government and Public Issues." Interviewed by Corinne L. Gilb, University of California, Berkeley, 1957.
"Max Thelen: California Progressive, Railroad Commissioner, and Attorney." Interviewed by Willa Klug Baum, University of California, Berkeley, 1962.
"Philip Bancroft: Politics, Farming, and the Progressive Party in California." Interviewed by Willa Klug Baum, University of California, Berkeley, 1962.
"The Memoirs of William Jarvis Carr." Interviewed by Doyce B. Nunis, University of California, Los Angeles, 1959.

STATE AND FEDERAL DOCUMENTS

Bureau of Labor Statistics. *Fourteenth Biennial Report, 1909-1910.* Sacramento, 1910.
———. *Fifteenth Biennial Report, 1911-1912.* Sacramento, 1912.
California Secretary of State. *California Blue Book, 1911.* Sacramento: State Printing Office, 1913.
———. *California Blue Book, 1913-1915.* Sacramento: State Printing Office, 1915.
———. *Statement of the Vote of California, Direct Primary Election, August 16, 1910.* Sacramento, 1910.
———. *Statement of the Vote at Primary Election held on August 25, 1914 in the State of California.* Sacramento, 1914.
California State Board of Agriculture. *Statistical Report, 1917.* Sacramento, 1917.
California State Board of Control. *California and the Oriental.* Sacramento, 1920.
California State Federation of Labor. *Proceedings of the . . . Annual Convention of the California State Federation of Labor . . . 1910-1917.*
California State Relief Administration. *Migratory Labor in California.* Sacramento: Division of Special Surveys and Studies, 1936.
Commission of Immigration and Housing. *Second Annual Report, January 2, 1916.* Sacramento, 1916.
Commission on Land Colonization and Rural Credits. *Report.* Sacramento, 1916.
Industrial Accident Commission. *Report for 1913—June 30, 1914.* Sacramento, 1914.
———. *Report for July 1, 1917—June 30, 1918.* Sacramento, 1918.
Industrial Welfare Commission. *First Biennial Report, 1913-1914.* Sacramento, 1915.
———. *Second Biennial Report, 1915-1916.* Sacramento, 1917.
———. *Third Biennial Report, 1917-1918.* Sacramento, 1919.
*Journal of the Assembly,* for the years 1909, 1911, 1913, and 1915. Sacramento, 1909, 1911, 1913, 1915.

*Journal of the Senate,* for the years 1909, 1911, 1913, and 1915. Sacramento, 1909, 1911, 1913, 1915.
U.S. Congress. House of Representatives. Committee on Public Lands. *Hetch Hetchy Grant to San Francisco.* Report. 63d Cong., 1st sess.
U.S. *Congressional Record.* 83d Cong., 2d sess., Vol. C, 1954.

SECONDARY MATERIAL

ARTICLES

Armstrong, Barbara N. "Persons and Industrial Law," *California Law Review,* vol. 18 (March, 1930).
Bailey, Thomas A. "California, Japan, and the Alien Land Legislation of 1913," *Pacific Historical Review,* vol. 1 (March, 1932).
Barker, Charles A. "Henry George and the California Background of *Progress and Poverty,*" *California Historical Society Quarterly,* vol. 24 (June, 1945).
Barrows, David P. "Reorganization of State Administration in California," *California Law Review,* vol. 3 (Jan., 1915).
Barsness, Richard W. "Railroads and Los Angeles: The Quest for a Deep-Water Port," *Southern California Quarterly,* vol. 47 (Dec., 1965).
Bates, J. Leonard. "Fulfilling American Democracy: The Conservation Movement, 1907 to 1921," *Mississippi Valley Historical Review,* vol. 44 (June, 1957).
Bean, Walton E. "Boss Ruef, the Union Labor Party, and the Graft Prosecution in San Francisco, 1901–1911," *Pacific Historical Review,* vol. 17 (Nov., 1948).
Berthoff, Rowland. "The American Social Order: A Conservative Hypothesis," *American Historical Review,* vol. 65 (April, 1960).
Braeman, John. "Seven Progressives," *Business History Review,* vol. 35 (Winter, 1961).
Brewer, Helene Hooker. "A Man and Two Books," *Pacific Historical Review,* vol. 32 (Aug., 1963).
Burnight, Ralph F. "The Japanese in Rural Los Angeles County," *Studies in Sociology,* vol. 4 (June, 1920).
"California Clings to Her Parties," *Literary Digest,* Nov. 13, 1915.
Casstevens, Thomas W. "Reflections on the Initiative Process," in Eugene C. Lee, ed., *The California Governmental Process.* Boston and Toronto: Little, Brown, 1966.
Coletta, Paolo E. " 'The Most Thankless Task': Bryan and the California Alien Land Legislation," *Pacific Historical Review,* vol. 36 (May, 1967).
Connolly, C. P. "Big Business and the Bench," *Everybody's Magazine,* vol. 26 (March, 1912).
Croly, Herbert. "The Two Parties in 1916," *New Republic,* Oct., 21, 1916.
Crouch, Winston W. "The Initiative and Referendum in Cities," *American Political Science Review,* vol. 37 (June, 1943).
Daniels, Roger. "William Jennings Bryan and the Japanese," *Southern California Quarterly,* vol. 48 (Sept., 1966).

Daniels, Roger. "Westerners from the East: Oriental Immigrants Reappraised," *Pacific Historical Review*, vol. 35 (Nov., 1966).
Davenport, Frederick M. "Across the Continent with Hughes," *Outlook*, Sept., 13, 1916.
———. "The Case of Hiram Johnson—Not Guilty," *North American Review*, Feb., 1917.
———. "Did Hughes Snub Johnson?—An Inside Story. How and Why Charles Evans Hughes Lost California and the Presidency in 1916," *American Political Science Review*, vol. 43 (April, 1949).
Davis, Allen F. "The Social Workers and the Progressive Party, 1912–1916," *American Historical Review*, vol. 69 (April, 1964).
Dobrzensky, Milton W. "A Digest of Child Labor Laws and Regulations Applicable in California," *California Law Review*, vol. 8 (Sept., 1920).
Dodds, Gordon B. "The Historiography of American Conservation—Past and Prospects," *Pacific Northwest Quarterly*, vol. 56 (April, 1965).
Erdman, Henry E. "The Development and Significance of California Cooperatives, 1900–1915," *Agricultural History*, vol. 32 (July, 1958).
"Expenses of the State Government of California," *California Taxpayers' Journal*, vol. 2 (June, 1918).
Findley, James C. "Cross-Filing and the Progressive Movement in California Politics," *Western Political Quarterly*, vol. 12 (Sept., 1959).
Garraty, John A. "T. R. on the Telephone," *American Heritage*, vol. 9 (Dec., 1957).
Gass, Oscar. "The Literature of American Government," *Commentary*, vol. 41 (June, 1966).
Gates, Paul W. "The Homestead Law in an Incongruous Land System," *American Historical Review*, vol. 41 (July, 1936).
Gilmore, N. Ray, and Gladys W. Gilmore. "The Bracero in California," *Pacific Historical Review*, vol. 32 (Aug., 1963).
Grantham, Dewey W., Jr. "The Progressive Era and the Reform Tradition," *Mid-America*, vol. 46 (Oct., 1964).
Hays, Samuel P. "The Politics of Reform in Municipal Government in the Progressive Era," *Pacific Northwest Quarterly*, vol. 55 (Oct., 1964).
———. "The Social Analysis of American Political History, 1880–1920," *Political Science Quarterly*, vol. 80 (Sept., 1965).
Hennings, Robert E. "California Democratic Politics in the Period of Republican Ascendancy," *Pacific Historical Review*, vol. 31 (Aug., 1962).
———. "James D. Phelan and the Woodrow Wilson Anti-Oriental Statement of May 3, 1912," *California Historical Society Quarterly*, vol. 42 (Dec., 1963).
Herrin, William F. "Government Regulation of Railways," *California Law Review*, vol. 2 (Jan., 1914).
Hichborn, Franklin K. "The Party, the Machine, and the Vote—The Story of Cross-filing in California Politics," pts. 1 and 2, *California Historical Society Quarterly*, vol. 38 (Dec., 1959) and vol. 39 (March, 1960).
Holman, Alfred. "The Case of Hiram Johnson—Guilty," *North American Review*, Feb., 1917.

Bibliography 233

Howland, Harold. "The Conventions at Chicago," *The Independent*, June 19, 1916.
Hoyt, Franklin. "Influence of the Railroads in the Development of Los Angeles Harbor," *Historical Society Quarterly of Southern California*, vol. 35 (Sept., 1953).
Hundley, Norris C., Jr. "Katherine Philips Edson and the Fight for the California Minimum Wage, 1912-1913," *Pacific Historical Review*, vol. 30 (Aug., 1960).
Hutchinson, W. H. "Prologue to Reform: The California Anti-Railroad Republicans, 1899-1905," *Southern California Quarterly*, vol. 44 (Sept., 1962).
Huthmacher, J. Joseph. "Urban Liberalism and the Age of Reform," *Mississippi Valley Historical Review*, vol. 49 (Sept., 1962).
Ickes, Harold. "Who Killed the Progressive Party?" *American Historical Review*, vol. 46 (Jan., 1941).
"Income and Expenditures of Government in California, 1900-1942," *Tax Digest*, vol. 21 (Feb., 1943).
Iwata, Masakazu. "The Japanese Immigrants in California Agriculture," *Agricultural History*, vol. 36 (Jan., 1962).
Johnson, Alvin. "How California Was Lost," *New Republic*, Nov., 25, 1916.
Kelley, Robert. "Taming the Sacramento: Hamiltonianism in Action," *Pacific Historical Review*, vol. 34 (Feb., 1965).
Lapalombara, Joseph G., and Charles B. Hagan. "Direct Legislation: An Appraisal and a Suggestion," *American Political Science Review*, vol. 45 (June, 1951).
Larsen, Grace. "A Progressive in Agriculture: Harris Weinstock," *Agricultural History*, vol. 32 (July, 1958).
———, and Henry E. Erdman. "Aaron Sapiro: Genius of Farm Co-operative Promotion," *Mississippi Valley Historical Review*, vol. 49 (Sept., 1962).
Leuchtenberg, William E. "Progressivism and Imperialism: The Progressive Movement and American Foreign Policy, 1898-1916," *Mississippi Valley Historical Review*, vol. 39 (Dec., 1952).
Lincoln, A. "Theodore Roosevelt, Hiram Johnson, and the Vice-presidential Nomination of 1912," *Pacific Historical Review*, vol. 28 (Aug., 1959).
———. "My Dear Governor—Letters Exchanged by Theodore Roosevelt and Hiram Johnson," *California Historical Society Quarterly*, vol. 38 (Sept., 1959).
———. "My Dear Senator—Letters between Theodore Roosevelt and Hiram Johnson in 1917," *ibid.*, vol. 42 (Sept., 1963).
Lippmann, Walter. "The Case for Wilson," *New Republic*, Oct., 14, 1916.
Mann, Arthur. "The Progressive Tradition," in John Higham, ed., *The Reconstruction of American History*. New York: Harper and Bros., 1962.
Margulies, Herbert F. "Recent Opinion on the Decline of the Progressive Movement," *Mid-America*, vol. 45 (Oct., 1963).

Matthews, Fred H. "White Community and 'Yellow Peril,'" *Mississippi Valley Historical Review*, vol. 50 (March, 1964).
McConnell, Grant. "California Conundrum—Why It Votes G.O.P.," *Nation*, vol. 179 (Dec., 4, 1954).
McHenry, Dean. "Cross-Filing of Political Candidates in California," *Annals of the American Academy of Political and Social Science*, vol. 248 (Nov., 1946).
———. "The Pattern of California Politics," *Western Political Quarterly*, vol. 1 (March, 1948).
McKee, Irving. "The Background and Early Career of Hiram Warren Johnson, 1866–1910," *Pacific Historical Review*, vol. 19 (Feb., 1950).
Melendy, H. Brett. "California's Cross-Filing Nightmare: The 1918 Gubernatorial Election," *Pacific Historical Review*, vol. 33 (Aug., 1964).
Messing, John. "Public Lands, Politics, and Progressives: The Oregon Land Fraud Trials, 1903–1910," *Pacific Historical Review*, vol. 35 (Feb., 1966).
Mowry, George E. "The California Progressive and His Rationale: A Study in Middle Class Politics," *Mississippi Valley Historical Review*, vol. 36 (Sept., 1949).
Nash, Gerald D. "The Reformer Reformed: John H. Reagan and Railroad Regulation," *Business History Review*, vol. 29 (June, 1955).
———. "Bureaucracy and Economic Reform: The Experience of California, 1899–1911," *Western Political Quarterly*, vol. 13 (Sept., 1960).
———. "The California Railroad Commission, 1876–1911," *Southern California Quarterly*, vol. 44 (Dec., 1962).
———. "The Influence of Labor on State Policy, 1860–1920: The Experience of California," *California Historical Society Quarterly*, vol. 42 (Sept., 1963).
———. "The California State Land Office, 1858–1898," *Huntington Library Quarterly*, vol. 27 (Aug., 1964).
———. "The California State Board of Forestry, 1883–1960," *Southern California Quarterly*, vol. 47 (Sept., 1965).
Nash, Roderick. "The American Cult of the Primitive," *American Quarterly*, vol. 18 (Fall, 1966).
Noble, David W. "Herbert Croly and American Progressive Thought," *Western Political Quarterly*, vol. 7 (Dec., 1954).
Olin, Spencer C., Jr. "Hiram Johnson, the California Progressives, and the Hughes Campaign of 1916," *Pacific Historical Review*, vol. 31 (Nov., 1962).
———. "European Immigrant and Oriental Alien—Acceptance and Rejection by the California Legislature of 1913," *ibid.*, vol. 35 (Aug., 1966).
———. "Hiram Johnson, the Lincoln-Roosevelt League, and the Election of 1910," *California Historical Society Quarterly*, vol. 45 (Sept., 1966).
Penick, James Lal, Jr. "A Postscript to the Ballinger-Pinchot Controversy," *Pacific Northwest Quarterly*, vol. 55 (April, 1964).

Pillsbury, Arthur J. "Wright Law and Webb Bill Compared," *California Weekly*, March 4, 1910.
———. "An Adventure in State Insurance," *American Economic Review*, vol. 9 (Dec., 1919).
Pitchell, Robert J. "The Electoral System and Voting Behavior: The Case of California's Cross-Filing," *Western Political Quarterly*, vol. 12 (June, 1959).
"Political Miracles in California," *Outlook*, Oct. 25, 1916.
Putnam, Jackson K. "The Persistence of Progressivism in the 1920's: The Case of California," *Pacific Historical Review*, vol. 35 (Nov., 1966).
Rakestraw, Lawrence. "Sheep Grazing in the Cascade Range: John Minto vs. John Muir," *Pacific Historical Review*, vol. 27 (Nov., 1958).
Richardson, Elmo R. "Conservation as a Political Issue: The Western Progressives' Dilemma, 1909–1912," *Pacific Northwest Quarterly*, vol. 49 (April, 1958).
———. "The Struggle for the Valley: California's Hetch Hetchy Controversy, 1905–1913," *California Historical Society Quarterly*, vol. 38 (Sept., 1959).
Rowell, Chester H. "Chinese and Japanese in America," *Annals of the American Academy of Political and Social Science*, vol. 34 (Sept., 1909).
Saxton, Alexander. "San Francisco Labor and the Populist and Progressive Insurgencies," *Pacific Historical Review*, vol. 34 (Nov., 1965).
Scott, Andrew M. "The Progressive Era in Perspective," *Journal of Politics*, vol. 21 (Nov., 1959).
Sherman, Richard B. "The Status Revolution and Massachusetts Progressive Leadership," *Political Science Quarterly*, vol. 78 (March, 1963).
Smith, Geddes. "California Progressivism," *The Independent*, Aug., 30, 1915.
Solvick, Stanley D. "William Howard Taft and the Payne-Aldrich Tariff," *Mississippi Valley Historical Review*, vol. 50 (Dec., 1963).
Tager, Jack. "Progressives, Conservatives and the Theory of Status Revolution," *Mid-America*, vol. 48 (July, 1966).
"The Johnson Victory," *Literary Digest*, Sept., 23, 1916.
Thelen, Max. "The Public Utilities Act and Its Relation to the Public," in Eugene R. Hallet, ed., *Public Utility Act of California*. San Francisco, 1912.
Titus, Charles H. "Rural Voting in California, 1900–1926," *Southwestern Political and Social Science Quarterly*, vol. 8 (Sept., 1928).
———. "Voting in California, 1900–1926," *ibid.*, vol. 10 (June, 1929).
Vieg, John A. "A New Design for California Politics," *Western Political Quarterly*, vol. 13 (Sept., 1960).
Wheat, Carl I. "Practice and Procedure before the Railroad Commission of California," *California Law Review*, vol. 15 (Sept., 1927).
Wiebe, Robert H. "Business Disunity and the Progressive Movement, 1901–1914," *Mississippi Valley Historical Review*, vol. 44 (March, 1958).

THESES AND DISSERTATIONS (UNIVERSITY OF CALIFORNIA, BERKELEY, UNLESS OTHERWISE NOTED)

Batman, Richard Dale. "The Road to the Presidency: Hoover, Johnson, and the California Republican Party, 1920–1924." Unpublished Ph.D. dissertation, University of Southern California, 1965.

Beach, Frank L. "The Transformation of California, 1900–1920: The Effects of the Westward Movement on California's Growth and Development in the Progressive Period." Unpublished Ph.D. dissertation, 1963.

Bemis, George W. "Sectionalism and Representation in the California State Legislature, 1911–1931." Unpublished Ph.D. dissertation, 1935.

Bogart, Victor. "Chester H. Rowell and the Lincoln-Roosevelt League, 1907–1910." Unpublished M.A. thesis, 1962.

Clodius, Albert H. "The Quest for Good Government in Los Angeles, 1890–1910." Unpublished Ph.D. dissertation, Claremont Graduate School, 1953.

Crawford, James. "The Democratic Party of California and Political Reform, 1902–1910." Unpublished M.A. thesis, 1959.

Crockett, Earl C. "The History of California Labor Legislation, 1910–1930." Unpublished Ph.D. dissertation, 1931.

Dickson, Mildred E. "Third Party Technique, 1912–1916." Unpublished M.A. thesis, 1937.

Everett, Miles C. "Chester Harvey Rowell, Pragmatic Humanist and California Progressive." Unpublished Ph.D. dissertation, 1965.

Fuller, Levi Varden. "The Supply of Agricultural Labor as a Factor in the Evolution of Farm Organization in California.' Unpublished Ph.D. dissertation, 1939.

Hennings, Robert E. "James D. Phelan and the Wilson Progressives of California." Unpublished Ph.D. dissertation, 1961.

Jaques, Janice. "The Political Reform Movement in Los Angeles, 1900–1909." Unpublished M.A. thesis, Claremont Graduate School, 1948.

Knoche, Viola May. "The Gubernatorial Nomination of Hiram W. Johnson, 1910." Unpublished M.A. thesis, Stanford University, 1947.

Liljevist, Clifford B. "Senator Hiram Johnson: His Career in California and National Politics." Unpublished Ph.D. dissertation, University of Southern California, 1953.

Lopez, Espiridion B. "The History of the California State Federation of Labor." Unpublished M.A. thesis, 1932.

McAfee, Ward. "Local Interests and Railroad Regulation in Nineteenth Century California." Unpublished Ph.D. dissertation, Stanford University, 1965.

Milias, George Wallace. "Hiram Johnson's Campaign for the Governorship of California in 1910." Unpublished M.A. thesis, Stanford University, 1949.

Nash, Gerald D. "The Role of the State Government in the Economy of California, 1849–1911." Unpublished Ph.D. dissertation, 1957.

Nichols, E. Ray, Jr. "An Investigation of the Contribution of the Public

Speaking of Hiram Johnson to his Political Career." Unpublished M.A. thesis, University of Southern California, 1948.
Ohlson, Robert V. "The History of the San Francisco Labor Council, 1892–1939." Unpublished M.A. thesis, 1941.
Palmer, Hans C. "The Valley Road: The San Francisco and San Joaquin Valley Railway, 1895–1900." Unpublished M.A. thesis, 1959.
Pitchell, Robert J. "Twentieth Century California Voting Behavior." Unpublished Ph.D. dissertation, 1955.
Richardson, Elmo R. "The Politics of the Conservation Issue in the Far West, 1896–1913." Unpublished Ph.D. dissertation, University of California, Los Angeles, 1958.
Rose, Alice. "The Rise of California Insurgency." Unpublished Ph.D. dissertation, Stanford University, 1942.
Rowell, Edward Joseph. "The Union Labor Party of San Francisco, 1901–1911." Unpublished Ph.D. dissertation, 1938.
Staniford, Edward F. "Governor in the Middle: The Administration of George C. Pardee, Governor of California, 1903–1907." Unpublished Ph.D. dissertation, 1955.
Vest, William Anderson. "A Comparative Study of the Republican Factions in California, 1906–1912." Unpublished M.A. thesis, San Francisco State College, 1967.
Wood, Samuel E. "The California State Commission of Immigration and Housing: A Study of Administrative Organization and the Growth of Function." Unpublished Ph.D. dissertation, 1942.

BOOKS

Aaron, Daniel. *Men of Good Hope: A Story of American Progressives.* New York: Oxford University Press, 1951.
Abrams, Richard. *Conservatism in a Progressive Era: Massachusetts Politics, 1900–1912.* Cambridge: Harvard University Press, 1964.
Agresti, Olivia Rossetti. *David Lubin: A Study in Practical Idealism.* Berkeley and Los Angeles: University of California Press, 1941.
Bailey, Thomas A. *Theodore Roosevelt and the Japanese-American Crises.* Palo Alto: Stanford University Press, 1934.
Barker, Charles Albro. *Henry George.* New York: Oxford University Press, 1955.
Bates, J. Leonard. *The Origins of Teapot Dome: Progressives, Parties, and Petroleum, 1909–1921.* Urbana: University of Illinois Press, 1963.
Bean, Walton E. *Boss Ruef's San Francisco.* Berkeley and Los Angeles: University of California Press, 1952.
Bird, Frederick, and Francis Ryan. *The Recall of Public Officers.* New York: Macmillan, 1930.
Blum, John Morton. *The Republican Roosevelt.* New York: Atheneum Press, 1962.
Buchanan, William. *Legislative Partisanship: The Deviant Case of California.* Berkeley and Los Angeles: University of California Press, 1963.
Caughey, John Walton. *California.* Englewood Cliffs: Prentice-Hall, 1960.

Chambers, Clarke A. *California Farm Organizations.* Berkeley and Los Angeles: University of California Press, 1952.
Clar, C. Raymond. *California Government and Forestry.* Sacramento: California Department of Natural Resources, Division of Forestry, 1959.
Clark, Norman H. *The Dry Years—Prohibition and Social Change in Washington.* Seattle: University of Washington Press, 1965.
Cleland, Robert Glass. *California in Our Time: 1900–1940.* New York: Alfred A. Knopf, 1947.
Cresap, Dean R. *Party Politics in the Golden State.* Los Angeles: Haynes Foundation, 1954.
Croly, Herbert. *The Promise of American Life.* New York: Macmillan, 1909.
Cross, Ira B. *Financing an Empire: History of Banking in California.* Vol. II. Chicago, San Francisco, Los Angeles: S. J. Clarke, 1927.
Crouch, Winston W. *The Initiative and Referendum in California.* Los Angeles: Haynes Foundation, 1950.
———, Dean E. McHenry, John C. Bollens, and Stanley Scott. *California Government and Politics.* Englewood Cliffs: Prentice-Hall, 1964.
Daggett. Stuart. *Chapters in the History of the Southern Pacific.* New York: Ronald Press, 1922.
Daniels, Roger. *The Politics of Prejudice: The Anti-Japanese Movement in California and the Struggle for Japanese Exclusion.* Berkeley and Los Angeles: University of California Press, 1962.
Degler, Carl. *Out of Our Past: The Forces that Shaped Modern America.* New York: Harper Colophon, 1962.
Fite, Gilbert C. *The Farmers' Frontier, 1865–1900.* New York: Holt, Rinehart and Winston, 1966.
Forcey, Charles. *The Crossroads of Liberalism: Croly, Weyl, Lippmann and the Progressive Era, 1900–1925.* New York: Oxford University Press, 1961.
Garraty, John A. *Right-Hand Man: The Life of George W. Perkins.* New York: Harper and Bros., 1957.
Goldman, Eric F. *Rendezvous With Destiny: A History of Modern American Reform.* Rev. ed. New York: Vintage Books, 1959.
Gordon, Margaret. *Employment Expansion and Population Growth: The California Experience, 1900–1950.* Berkeley and Los Angeles: University of California Press, 1954.
Graham, Otis L., Jr. *An Encore for Reform: The Old Progressives and the New Deal.* New York: Oxford University Press, 1967.
Gusfield, Joseph R. *Symbolic Crusade: Status Politics and the American Temperance Movement.* Urbana: University of Illinois Press, 1963.
Haber, Samuel. *Efficiency and Uplift: Scientific Management in the Progressive Era, 1890–1920.* Chicago: University of Chicago Press, 1964.
Harbaugh, William Henry. *Power and Responsibility: The Life and Times of Theodore Roosevelt.* New York: Farrar, Straus, 1961.
Hays, Samuel P. *The Response to Industrialism, 1885–1914.* Chicago: University of Chicago Press, 1957.

———. *Conservation and the Gospel of Efficiency: The Progressive Conservation Movement, 1890–1920.* Cambridge: Harvard University Press, 1959.
Hichborn, Franklin K. *Story of the Session of the California Legislature.* Separate volumes for the years 1909, 1911, 1913, 1915, and 1917. San Francisco: James H. Barry, 1909, 1911, 1913, 1915, 1917.
Higham, John. *Strangers in the Land: Patterns of American Nativism, 1860–1925.* New Brunswick: Rutgers University Press, 1955.
Hofstadter, Richard. *The Age of Reform—From Bryan to FDR.* New York: Alfred A. Knopf, 1955.
———, ed. *The Progressive Movement, 1900–1915.* Englewood Cliffs: Prentice-Hall, 1963.
Hutchinson, W. H. *Oil, Land and Politics: The California Career of Thomas Robert Bard.* Norman: University of Oklahoma Press, 1965.
Iyenaga, T., and Kenoske Sato. *Japan and the California Problem.* New York: G. P. Putnam's Sons, 1921.
Johnson, Herbert B. *Discrimination against Japanese in California.* Berkeley: Courier Publishing Co., 1907.
Jones, Holway R. *John Muir and the Sierra Club: The Battle for Yosemite.* San Francisco: Sierra Club, 1965.
Knight, Robert E. L. *Industrial Relations in the San Francisco Bay Area, 1900–1918.* Berkeley and Los Angeles: University of California Press, 1960.
Kolko, Gabriel. *The Triumph of Conservatism: A Reinterpretation of American History, 1900–1916.* New York: Macmillan, 1963.
———. *Railroads and Regulation, 1877–1916.* Princeton: Princeton University Press, 1965.
Kraemer, Erich, and Henry E. Erdman. *History of Cooperation in the Marketing of California Fresh Deciduous Fruits.* Berkeley: Giannini Foundation of Agricultural Economics, 1933.
La Follette, Belle Case, and Fola La Follette. *Robert M. La Follette.* Vol. I. New York: Macmillan, 1953.
Lazarsfeld, Paul F., Bernard Berelson, and Hazel Gaudet. *The People's Choice: How the Voter Makes Up His Mind in a Presidential Campaign.* New York: Duell, Sloan and Pearce, 1944.
Leary, John L., Jr. *Talks with T.R.* Boston and New York: Houghton Mifflin, 1920.
Lee, Eugene C. *The Politics of Nonpartisanship—A Study of California City Elections.* Berkeley and Los Angeles: University of California Press, 1960.
Link, Arthur S. *Woodrow Wilson and the Progressive Era, 1910–1917.* New York: Harper and Bros., 1954.
———. *Wilson: The New Freedom.* Princeton: Princeton University Press, 1956.
———. *Wilson: Campaigns for Progressivism and Peace, 1916–1917.* Princeton: Princeton University Press, 1965.

Maxwell, Robert S. *La Follette and the Rise of the Progressives in Wisconsin.* State Historical Society of Wisconsin, 1956.
McConnell, Grant. *Private Power and American Democracy.* New York: Alfred A. Knopf, 1966.
McWilliams, Carey. *Factories in the Field.* Boston: Little, Brown, 1939.
——. *California: The Great Exception.* New York: Current Books, 1949.
Mead, Elwood. *How California Is Helping People Own Farms and Rural Homes.* University of California College of Agriculture, Agricultural Experiment Station. Circular no. 221. Berkeley, 1920.
Moos, Malcolm. *The Republicans.* New York: Random House, 1956.
Mowry, George E. *Theodore Roosevelt and the Progressive Movement.* Madison: University of Wisconsin Press, 1946.
——. *The California Progressives.* Berkeley and Los Angeles: University of California Press, 1951.
——. *The Era of Theodore Roosevelt, 1900–1912.* New York: Harper and Bros., 1958.
Nash, Gerald D. *State Government and Economic Development: A History of Administrative Policies in California, 1849–1933.* Berkeley: Institute of Governmental Studies, 1964.
Ostrander, Gilman. *The Prohibition Movement in California, 1848–1933.* Berkeley and Los Angeles: University of California Press, 1957.
Parker, Carleton H. *The Casual Laborer and Other Essays.* New York: Harcourt, Brace, and Howe, 1920.
Pegrum, D. F. *Rate Theories and the California Railroad Commission.* Berkeley: University of California Press, 1932.
Perry, Louis B., and Richard S. Perry. *A History of the Los Angeles Labor Movement, 1911–1941.* Berkeley and Los Angeles: University of California Press, 1963.
Pinchot, Amos R. E. *History of the Progressive Party, 1912–1916.* Washington Square: New York University Press, 1958.
Pomeroy, Earl. *The Pacific Slope—A History of California, Oregon, Washington, Idaho, Utah, and Nevada.* New York: Alfred A. Knopf, 1965.
Pusey, Merlo J. *Charles Evans Hughes.* Vol. I. New York: Macmillan, 1951.
Rappaport, Armin. *The British Press and Wilsonian Neutrality.* Palo Alto: Stanford University Press; London: Geoffrey Cumberlege Oxford University Press, 1951.
Richardson, Elmo R. *The Politics of Conservation: Crusades and Controversies, 1897–1913.* Berkeley and Los Angeles: University of California Press, 1962.
Robinson, Edgar Eugene. *The Presidential Vote, 1896–1932.* Palo Alto: Stanford University Press; London: Humphrey Milford Oxford University Press, 1934.
Robinson, W. W. *Land in California.* Berkeley and Los Angeles: University of California Press, 1948.
Rolle, Andrew. *California: A History.* New York: Thomas Y. Crowell, 1963.

Stimson, Grace Heilman. *Rise of the Labor Movement in Los Angeles.* Berkeley and Los Angeles: University of California Press, 1955.
Sullivan, Mark. *Our Times: The United States, 1900-1925.* Vol. V. New York: Charles Scribner's Sons, 1933.
Swanberg, W. A. *Citizen Hearst.* New York: Bantam Books, 1963.
Thelen, Max. *Report on Leading Railroad and Public Service Commissions.* Reprinted in Eugene R. Hallet, ed., *Public Utility Act of California.* San Francisco, 1912.
Thompson, Warren S. *Growth and Changes in California's Population.* Los Angeles: Haynes Foundation, 1955.
Timberlake, James H. *Prohibition and the Progressive Movement, 1900-1920.* Cambridge: Harvard University Press, 1963.
Villard, Oswald Garrison. *Fighting Years.* New York: Harcourt, Brace, 1948.
Waldo, Dwight. *The Administrative State—A Study of the Political Theory of American Public Administration.* New York: Ronald Press, 1948.
Warner, Hoyt Landon. *Progressivism in Ohio, 1897-1917.* Columbus: Ohio State University Press, 1964.
White, Gerald T. *Formative Years in the Far West: A History of Standard Oil Company in California and Predecessors Through 1919.* New York: Appleton-Century-Crofts, 1962.
Wickson, E. J. *Rural California.* New York: Macmillan, 1923.
Wiebe, Robert. *Businessmen and Reform: A Study of the Progressive Movement.* Cambridge: Harvard University Press, 1962.
———. *The Search for Order, 1877-1920.* New York: Hill and Wang, 1967.
Wilson, James Q. *The Amateur Democrat: Club Politics in Three Cities.* Chicago: University of Chicago Press, 1962.

# INDEX

# INDEX

Adamson Act, 161
Alien Land Act. *See* Anti-Oriental legislation
Anderson, Alden, 24
Anderson, John M., 154
Anti-injunction bill. *See* Labor legislation
Anti-Oriental legislation, 80-90, 177; Alien Land Act, 72, 87, 89-90; Chinese Exclusion Act, 81; Russo-Japanese War, 81; Chester Rowell and, 81, 84-85; Gentlemen's Agreement, 82; Asiatic Exclusion League, 82, 84, 87; Hiram Johnson's attitude and activities regarding, 84-90; Panama-Pacific International Exposition, 84-85, 88; intervention by Woodrow Wilson in, 86; William Jennings Bryan and, 87
Anti-Saloon League, 30; activities during Johnson administration, 54-55. *See also* Temperance movement
Asiatic Exclusion League. *See* Anti-Oriental legislation
Associated Oil Company, 15-16. *See also* Oil companies and production
Avery, Russ: and campaign against Southern Pacific, 7

Bailey, Thomas A.: on Wilson's intervention in California anti-Oriental legislation, 86
Ballinger, Richard A.: as secretary of interior, 51, 57; and Hetch Hetchy project, 52-53
Bancroft, Philip: reminiscing on aims of Lincoln-Roosevelt League, 178-179
Bard, Thomas R.: early career and opposition to Southern Pacific, 4, 16
Barnes, William, 62, 129
Barrows, David: and land colonization and rural credits, 105-107
Beach, Frank: on urbanization and political growth, 192 n. 14
Bean, Walton: on Ruef and California Republican party, 9
Bell, Theodore: as 1904 Democratic candidate for governor, 4; and 1910 gubernatorial election, 30-32
Benjamin, Raymond, 151
Beveridge, Albert: campaigns for Theodore Roosevelt in 1912, 61; keynote address at Progressive convention of 1912, 64
Big Four: organize Southern Pacific Railroad Company, 1
Blum, John Morton: on Theodore Roosevelt's break with Taft, 59; on Progressive party, 69
Board of Control, 41-43, 55, 173
Booth, Willis H., 124, 125, 126, 146, 151
Borah, William: on Hiram Johnson, 97
Brandeis, Louis D., 161
Brouilett, A. W.: on 1915 California labor legislation, 111
Bryan, William Jennings: sent to California by Woodrow Wilson, 87
Bureau of Corporations, 15, 16
Bureau of Labor Exchanges, 79-80, 111

245

## 246  Index

Bureau of Labor Statistics, 80, 94-95
Burke, Jere, 32
Burns, William J., 10

Calhoun, Patrick, 10, 32
California agriculture, 26-29, 76-80, 198 n. 32; Commission on Land Colonization and Rural Credits, 28; State Colonization and Rural Credits Commission, 80, 107, 177; land colonization and rural credits legislation, 105, 177; State Land Settlement Board, 107; statewide marketing distribution, 107-110, 177, 226 n. 15
California Consumer's League, 72
California Federation of Women's Clubs, 72
California Fruit Growers' Association, 108
California Fruit Growers' Exchange (Sunkist), 108, 110
California Fruit Union, 108
*California Outlook*, 70, 200 n. 3; favors Hiram Johnson for vice-president, 60; quoted, 104, 110-111, 112, 154, 194 n. 34
California Progressive party: founded in 1913, 93; disunity in 1914–1915, 94, 100, 103; strategy in 1916, 113-115, 124
California Supreme Court, 3, 39
*California Weekly*, 12
Caughey, John W.: on California railroad monopoly, 2
Chandler, Harry, 7
Child labor legislation. See Labor legislation
Chinese Exclusion Act. See Anti-Oriental legislation
Cleland, Robert Glass: on Hiram Johnson, 97
Colby, Bainbridge, 162
Cole, Cornelius, 141
Commission of Immigration and Housing, 72, 90, 91, 176, 209 n. 28; established by legislature, 79; activities in 1913–1915, 79-80
Commission of Land Colonization and Rural Credits, 28

Compulsory-arbitration bill. See Labor legislation
Conservation legislation, 55; recommended in Hiram Johnson's inaugural address, 35; legislation of 1911 and establishment of Conservation Commission, 49-53; appraised, 176
Crane, Murray, 121
Crocker, Charles, 1
Crocker, William: and 1916 campaign, 121-165 *passim*
Croly, Herbert: views on direct democracy, 43; and election of 1916, 161-162
Cross-filing, 44
Crouch, Winston: on "the people" vs. "the interests," 174
Curry, Charles F., 24, 29

Daniels, Roger: on anti-Oriental legislation, 88, 89, 212 n. 63
Davenport, Frederick M.: and campaign of 1916, 129-130, 132, 135-136; on Hughes's "snub" of Johnson, 136-143
Degler, Carl: on conservatism of progressive movement, 226 n. 19
Dickson, Edward, 22, 92-93, 96, 99, 220 n. 30; campaign against Southern Pacific, 7; and formation of Lincoln-Roosevelt League, 11; efforts to obtain vice-presidential nomination for Hiram Johnson, 60; on Hughes's "snub" of Johnson, 136-141
Direct democracy legislation, 225 n. 9; Direct Legislation League, 6; Herbert Croly's attitude toward, 43; California progressives' attitude toward, 43-44; 1911 legislative measures, 43-46; appraised, 173-175
Direct primary: adopted in 1909, 13; recommended in Hiram Johnson's inaugural address, 35; 1909 law amended in 1911, 44; appraised, 173-175
District advisory plan, 194 n. 31
Dunne, Peter Finley, 18

Index 247

Earl, Edwin T., 36, 99; publisher of Los Angeles *Express*, 11; launches vice-presidential drive for Hiram Johnson, 60; resentment toward Rowell, Lissner, Stimson, Avery, 96
Edgerton, Edwin: railroad commissioner, 39
Edson, Katherine Philips, 90, 149; early career and campaign for minimum-wage legislation, 72-73; member of Industrial Welfare Commission, 73-74; letter from Rowell, 97; letter from Hiram Johnson, 122-123; on Hughes's "snub" of Johnson, 137; on California supporters of Wilson, 223 n. 19
Eight-hour law for women. See Labor legislation
Ellery, Nathan, 24
Erdman, Henry, 109; on farmers' refusal to support cooperatives, 108
Ernst, Hugo, 135
Eshleman, John, 169; railroad commissioner, 38-39; candidate for lieutenant governor in 1914, 100-101
Everett, Miles: on Johnson's support of alien land bill, 211 n. 61

Farnham, Charles, 135; and Hughes's "snub" of Johnson, 138-143
Finn, Tom, 133
Flint, Thomas, 5
Forcey, Charles: on *New Republic* editors and 1916 election, 161
French, Will J., 75

Gage, Henry T., 4; 1898 Republican gubernatorial candidate, 3
Gandier, Daniel M.: legislative superintendent of Anti-Saloon League, 30; and local-option measure, 54-55
Garfield, James R., 123; as secretary of interior, 52
Gates, Lee C., 7; initiative, referendum, and recall, 44-45
Gentlemen's Agreement, 82

Gibson, Mrs. Frank, 80
Gillett, James N.: 1906 Republican gubernatorial candidate, 9
Glavis, Louis R., 51
Gordon, Alexander: railroad commissioner, 38-39
Gordon, Margaret, 190 n. 4
Grenner, Gustav, 94
Griffen, Thomas F., 48

Haber, Samuel: on scientific management in government, 172
Hale, Matthew, 162
Harbaugh, William Henry: on Progressive party, 63-64
Harriman, Edward, 2
Haynes, John Randolph, 7; organizes Direct Legislation League, 6
Hays, Samuel P.: on conservation, 49-50, 53; appraises Progressive movement, 180-181; on municipal reform, 192 n. 17
Heney, Francis J., 95, 170; and Ruef prosecution, 9-11; as potential gubernatorial candidate, 20-21; charter member of National Progressive Republican League, 58; at Republican convention of 1912, 62; senatorial primary victory in 1914, 99-100; 1914 defeat by Phelan for United States Senate, 101-103; supports Wilson in 1916, 162; praises Hiram Johnson to E. W. Scripps, 199 n. 44
Hennings, Robert: on progressive Democrats, 30-31; on 1914 election, 102
Hepburn Act, 15
Herrin, William F.: as chief consel and political boss for Southern Pacific, 9, 191 n. 8; involvement in San Francisco graft prosecution, 10; and election of 1910, 32; quoted in 1913, 171
Herriot, Paul, 137
Hetch Hetchy dispute, 52-53
Hichborn, Franklin: on legislature of 1909, 12, 193 n. 30; on direct legislation, 45-46; and prohibitionists, 54, 205 n. 49

## 248  Index

Hofstadter, Richard: on Progressive movement, 172, 179-180
Hughes, Charles Evans, 115; and 1916 Republican convention, 117-120; visited by Hiram Johnson, 121; campaign of 1916, 121-168 *passim;* "snubs" Johnson, 136-143
Huntington, Collis P., 1, 2, 5

Ickes, Harold, 142
Independent Oil Producers' Agency, 17, 23. *See also* Oil companies and production
Industrial Accident Board, 47, 74
Industrial Accident Commission, 70, 72, 75, 90, 176
Industrial Welfare Commission, 72, 73-74, 90, 175-176
Initiative, referendum, and recall, 55; in Los Angeles, 6-7; discussed in Hiram Johnson's inaugural address, 35; legislation of 1911, 45-46; appraised, 173-175
Interstate Commerce Commission, 15

Johnson, Grove, 22, 114, 196 n. 10
Johnson, Hiram, 1, 11, 36-37, 227 n. 7; joins graft prosecution, 10; as candidate for governor and early career, 21-23; campaign and election of 1910, 24-33; inaugural address of, 34-35; urges adoption of railroad bill, 37; signs Public Utilities Act, 39; attitude toward corporations, 41; campaigns for direct-legislation measures, 46; and conservation and Hetch Hetchy dispute, 50-53; and temperance and local option, 54; achieves national prominence, 56; charter member of National Progressive Republican League, 58; and Theodore Roosevelt, 59, 60-61; at Republican convention of 1912, 62-63; receives vice-presidential nomination at 1912 Progressive convention, 64; writes Lissner, 65; campaign of 1912, 66-69; opening address of 1913, 71; supports minimum-wage legislation, 73; praised for support of Workmen's Compensation Act, 75; discusses immigrant problem with Simon Lubin, 77-78; attitude toward Commission of Immigration and Housing, 80; and anti-Oriental legislation, 84-90; wants to organize new party in California, 92-93; concerned about unemployment, 94-95; and party disunity, 95-96; personality and character of, 96-99; discusses Senate race with Heney, 99-100; wins 1914 gubernatorial race, 100-103; inaugural address of 1915, 104; and land colonization and rural credits, 105-107; and statewide marketing distribution, 107-110; prolabor reputation in 1915, 111; and nonpartisan election law, 111-112; political strategy in 1916, 113-116; and Progressive convention of 1916, 119-121; politics and campaign of 1916, 122-168 *passim;* Hughes's "snub" of, 136-143; distrusts William Stephens, 169-170; administration appraised, 171-182

Johnson, Hiram, Jr., 197 n. 18
Johnson, Leroy, 136-37
Johnson, Mrs. Hiram, 21, 22
Johnson, Robert Underwood, 53
Johnson, Walter: on effects of a Hughes victory, 59
Jordan, Frank, 150

Kansas City *Journal,* on reaction against Progressivism, 112
Kearney, Denis, 190 n. 3
Keesling, Francis V.: elected vice-president of Republican State Central Committee, 94, 144; campaign of 1916, 124-125, 132-153 *passim,* 224 n. 27; and Hughes's "snub" of Johnson, 136-143; 219 n. 17, 220 n. 37; letters to, from local Republicans, 185-186
Kelley, Florence, 73
Kent, William, 95; congressional candidate in 1910, 50; and anti-Oriental legislation, 86
Knight, George A., 32
Knox, Philander, 84

## Index    249

Kolko, Gabriel: on railroad regulation and progressivism, 225 n. 5
Kraemer, Erich, 109; on farmers' refusal to support cooperatives, 108

Labor Camp Act, 80
*Labor Clarion:* on 1915 state legislative session, 111
Labor legislation: recommended in Hiram Johnson's inaugural address, 35; enacted in 1911, 46-49; workmen's compensation, 46-47, 55, 74-76, 111, 175; eight-hour law for women, 47-48, 55, 103, 175, 203 n. 31; anti-injunction bill, 49; compulsory-arbitration bill, 49; restricting child labor, 49, 175; minimum-wage, 72-74, 103, 207 n. 9, 208 n. 12; of 1915 session praised, 111; appraisal of progressive, 175-176
La Follette, Robert M., 33, 61; letter from Meyer Lissner, 18; and La Follette League and National Progressive Republican League, 58; "physical breakdown" of, and withdrawal of candidacy, 59-60
Land colonization legislation. See California agriculture
Lane, Franklin K.: 1902 Democratic gubernatorial candidate, 3-4; member of Interstate Commerce Commission, 15
Larsen, Grace, 109; on rural credits legislation, 106
Law and Order Committee, 134
Lewis, Austin, 79
Lincoln-Roosevelt League, 7, 170; early activities of, 11-13; and 1910 campaign, 23, 25, 31
Link, Arthur S.: on Wilson and fight for anti-Oriental legislation, 86; on reasons for Wilson victory in 1916, 160, 162
Lippmann, Walter, 161-162; on election of 1916, 155
Lissner, Meyer, 59, 65, 92-93, 96, 181; campaign against Southern Pacific, 7; quoted, 18-19, 21; letter from Hiram Johnson on Alien Land Act, 89; political strategy in 1916, 113-115, 151; views on Progressive legacy, 179
Lodge, Henry Cabot, 118
Los Angeles *Express*, 7, 11, 96
Los Angeles *Times*, 7, 167; quoted, 146, 158; building, dynamiting of, 200 n. 44
Los Angeles Voters' League, 7
Loveland, H. D.: railroad commissioner, 38-39
Lubin, David, 77, 106, 208 n. 21
Lubin, Simon, 90, 110, 177, 181; early career and Commission of Immigration and Housing, 76-80
Luce, Edgar A.: letter to George Mowry, 98; letter to John Francis Neylan, 153

McCabe, Al, 25, 26, 113
McClatchy, C. K., 5, 36, 54, 78, 99
McClatchy, V. S., 5, 211 n. 46
McConaughey, Charles, 75
McConnell, Grant: on progressives' use of nonpartisan devices, 174
McCormick, Medill, 60, 159
McLaughlin, John P., 94-95
McPherson, H. E., 108
Madsen, Martin, 213 n. 22
Maguire, James G.: 1898 Democratic candidate for governor, 3
*Manchester Guardian*, 159
Mann, Arthur: on entrepreneurial aspects of progressive reform, 181
Martin, Irving, 36, 116
Mead, Elwood: and State Colonization and Rural Credits Commission, 107
Metcalf, Victor H., 82
Miller and Lux, Inc., 15
Mines, W. W., 136, 141, 186
Minimum-wage legislation. See Labor legislation
Moos, Malcolm: on Hughes's anticipation of defeat, 222 n. 1
Mowry, George, 3, 126; on reformers, 6; on Railroad Commission, 14; on railroad legislation, 18; on Theodore Roosevelt's break with Taft, 59; on California Republican party in 1912, 66; on Roosevelt's support in West, 68; on Hiram Johnson, 96-97; letter

250  *Index*

Mowry, George (*continued*)
from Edgar Luce, 98; on 1914 election, 102; on California Progressives' foreign-policy views, 113; on "regular" Republicans, 124; on Hughes's campaign and defeat, 136, 147-148, 159, 163, 166; on Hughes's "snub" of Johnson, 143; on Johnson's labor record, 175; appraises Progressive movement, 180
Muir, John: and Hetch Hetchy dispute, 52-53
Munsey, Frank, 63, 92
Murdock, Victor, 162
Mussel Slough incident, 5

Nash, Gerald D.: on Railroad Commission, 14; on Southern Pacific's political control, 190 n. 2
National Progressive Republican League, 58
Naturalization Act of 1906, 211 n. 54
*New Republic*, 161-162
New York *Evening Post*, 157
New York *Times*, 156, 157
Neylan, John Francis, 170, 173, 202 n. 18; chairman of Board of Control, 42; on 1916 campaign, 153-154
Nolan, John I., 49
Nonpartisan election laws, 44, 55, 110, 166
Norris, Frank: quotation from *The Octopus*, 1

Odgers, Harriet, 25
Ohlson, Robert V.: on Hughes and labor vote, 219 n. 25
Oil companies and production, 15-17, 195 n. 44, 201 n. 14
Older, Fremont, 36, 95, 99; opposition to Ruef machine, 9; attitude toward trusts, 68; letter from Hiram Johnson, 116
Ostrander, Gilman: on temperance, 55; quoted, 196 n. 13, 199 n. 36
Otis, Harrison Gray, 7; conservative opposition to Southern Pacific, 5; and campaign of 1916, 136, 141

*Pacific Outlook*, 200 n. 3
Panama-Pacific International Exposition. *See* Anti-Oriental legislation
Pardee, George C., 99, 204 n. 42; Republican candidate for governor in 1902, 4; chairman of Conservation Commission, 51
Parker, Carleton H., 208 n. 19
Parker, John M., 162
Parker, Walter, 32
Pegrum, D. F.: on California railroad regulation, 14
Penrose, Boies, 62, 121
Perkins, George, 63, 116, 118, 125, 216 n. 3
Petroleum Development Corporation, 16
Phelan, James D., 210 n. 35; mayor of San Francisco, 8; support for graft prosecution, 9; on Orientals, 81; letter from Woodrow Wilson, 86; defeats Heney for U.S. Senate in 1914, 101; letter to Henry Morgenthau, 199 n. 43
Philadelphia *North American*, 158
Pillsbury, Arthur J., 75; cautions reform forces, 70-71
Pinchot, Gifford, 57, 60, 121, 176; speaks on behalf of Hiram Johnson in 1910, 50; and Hetch Hetchy project, 52-53; campaigns for Theodore Roosevelt in 1910, 61
Porter, Warren, 13
Porterfield, W. H., 32
Progressive National Committee, 113, 159
Progressive party: formation of, 63; convention of 1912, 64, 206 n. 26; decline of, 92; convention of 1916, 117-120
Public utilities, 55, 172; included within Railroad Commission jurisdiction, 38-39; Public Utilities Act, 39-40
Pusey, Merlo J.: quoted, 122, 126, 127, 128, 132, 142

Railroad legislation, 171-172; early history of Railroad Commission, 13-15; Stetson bill, 17-18, 36, 37,

Index 251

38, 55; recommended in Hiram Johnson's inaugural address, 35; Railroad Commission strengthened and reorganized by 1911 legislature, 37-41; and "long-and-short haul" principle, 201 n. 4
Raker, John A., 53
Rea, James W., 191 n. 8
"Regular" (conservative) Republicans, 4; in 1912, 65-66, 69; in 1913-1914, 94; in 1915, 112; gain control of Republican delegation in 1916, 115; politics and campaign of 1916, 124-168 *passim*
Republican National Committee, 62, 94, 129
Republican party: convention of 1912, 61-62; convention of 1916, 117-120
Republican State Central Committee, 94, 132, 136, 143, 149-151; in 1910, 33; in 1912, 65; disbands in 1913, 93; and Hughes campaign of 1916, 152-166 *passim*
Richardson, Elmo R.: on conservation, 50; on Louis Glavis, 51
Robins, Raymond, 119
Roosevelt, Theodore, 9, 33; considers 1912 presidential candidacy, 58-59; consults Hiram Johnson, 59; wins California's first presidential primary, 61; attends Republican convention of 1912, 62-63; nominated by Progressive convention of 1912, 64; and campaign of 1912, 66-69; and Gentlemen's Agreement, 82; blocks anti-Oriental legislation, 84; letter from Hiram Johnson, 95-96; on U.S. foreign policy, 112-113; and Republican and Progressive conventions of 1916, 116-120; and election of 1916, 158; apologia for, 183-184; distrusts Hughes, 216 n. 4
Root, Elihu, 117
Rowell, Chester H., 36, 59, 71, 116, 170; editor of Fresno *Republican*, 5; and formation of Lincoln-Roosevelt League, 11-13; quoted, 21, 21-22, 23, 24, 25-26, 58; and prohibitionists, 54; on Orientals, 81, 84-85, 210 n. 36; wants to organize new party in California, 92-93; on Hiram Johnson, 97; defeated by Heney in 1914 senatorial primary, 100; letters to Hiram Johnson, 102, 115; and land colonization and rural credits, 105-107; politics and campaign of 1916, 120-168 *passim;* criticized by Martin Madsen, 213 n. 22
Ruef, Abraham, 40, 95; boss of Union Labor party, 8; receives bribes, 9; controls political machine, 9-10
Rural credits legislation. *See* California agriculture

Sacramento *Bee,* 5, 78; on Johnson's control of 1915 legislature, 105
Sacramento *Star:* quoted, 122, 150
San Francisco *Bulletin,* 5, 9, 135
San Francisco *Call,* 5
San Francisco Chamber of Commerce, 134
San Francisco *Chronicle,* 5; on 1910 Republican platform, 31
San Francisco *Examiner,* 5
San Francisco *Globe,* 32
San Francisco Labor Council, 72, 75, 111
Santa Fe Railroad Company, 16; challenges Southern Pacific, 4; forced to reduce rates, 40; suit filed against, 41
Sapiro, Aaron: and statewide marketing distribution, 109-110, 181, 215 n. 16
Saxton, Alexander: on 1914 labor vote for Johnson, 203 n. 34
Scharrenberg, Paul, 75
Schmitz, Eugene E.: mayor of San Francisco, 8; receives bribes, 9; conviction reversed, 10
Scientific management, viii, 35, 90, 172-173, 212 n. 64
Shover, John L.: on labor support for Hiram Johnson, 226
Smoot, Reed, 121
Southern Pacific Railroad Company, 171; early years of, 1-2;

Southern Pacific (*continued*) opposition to political influence of, 2-8; links with oil companies, 15; attitude of reformers toward, 36; forced to reduce rates, 40
Spreckels, Rudolph, 9, 11; letter from John D. Works, 93-94
Standard Oil Company, 3, 15, 17
Stanton, Philip, 24, 94
State Colonization and Rural Credits Commission, 80, 107
State Compensation Insurance Fund, 75-76
State Federation of Labor, 75; endorses Employer's Liability Act, 47; endorses eight-hour law for women, 48
State Land Settlement Board, 107
State Market Bureau, 109
Statewide marketing distribution. *See* California agriculture
Steffens, Lincoln, 33
Stephens, William, 141, 169-170, 215 n. 29
Stetson bill. *See* Railroad legislation
Stimson, Marshall: and campaign against Southern Pacific, 7, 22, 92-93, 141, 151; views on Progressive legacy, 179; on opposition to Heney, 195 n. 3
Stockton *Record*, 16
Sullivan, Mark, on Hughes's "snub" of Johnson, 138
Sullivan, Matt I., 11, 60

Taft, William Howard: and Hetch Hetchy dispute, 52; California progressives dissatisfied with, 57-58; loses California presidential primary, 61; nominated by Republican convention of 1912, 63
Temperance movement, 30, 177; and 1911 local-option legislation, 54-55
Thelen, Max: legal counsel for Railroad Commission, 38; member of reorganized Railroad Commission, 39
*The People's Choice*, 163-164

Union Labor party, 8
Union Oil Company, 4, 16, 17
"United Republicans," 114-115, 166

Vanna, W. A., 48
Van Valkenburg, E. A., 158
Vest, William A.: compares Republican factions, 227 n. 22

Wallace, Albert J.: Hiram Johnson's running mate in 1910, 23, 30; criticizes lack of progressive support, 197 n. 20
Washington *Times:* promotes Johnson for vice-presidency, 61
Weinstock, Harris, 90, 177, 181, 215 n. 16; possible gubernatorial candidate, 21-22; member of Industrial Accident Commission, 75; and land colonization and rural credits, 105-107; and statewide marketing distribution, 107-110
Western Pacific Railroad Company: challenges Southern Pacific, 4; suit filed against, 41
Weyl, Walter, 161
Wheatland hop fields riot, 76, 79, 176, 208 n. 19
Wheeler, Charles S., 11
White, Gerald T.: on antirailroad feeling in California, 16
White, William Allen: quoted, 119, 144, 158, 216 n. 6
Wiebe, Robert: on progressivism and middle class, 200 n. 1
Willard, Charles Dwight, 5; attitude toward trusts, 68
Willcox, William R.: and Hughes campaign of 1916, 121, 124-144 *passim*
Wilson, Woodrow: 1912 Democratic presidential nominee, 64; criticized by Theodore Roosevelt in 1912, 67; wins election of 1912, 68-69; and California anti-Oriental legislation, 86-87; and election of 1916, 157, 160-164; summons Hiram Johnson to Washington, D.C., 169
Woman suffrage, 44, 55
Wood, Samuel E.: on Simon Lubin

and Commission of Immigration and Housing, 76-77
Workingmen's party, 190 n. 3
Workmen's compensation legislation. *See* Labor legislation
Works, John D., 134, 218 n. 33; U.S. senatorial candidate in 1910, 23-24; named U.S. senator, 36; attitude toward trusts, 68; objects to formation of California Progressive party, 93-94; letter to Charles Evans Hughes, 151-152; criticizes lack of progressive support, 197 n. 20
Wright railroad bill, 17-18

Yoell, A. E., 84
Young, C. C., 105

www.ingramcontent.com/pod-product-compliance
Lightning Source LLC
Chambersburg PA
CBHW021700230426
43668CB00008B/676